The Presidential
Pardon Power

The Presidential Pardon Power

Jeffrey Crouch

University Press of Kansas

Published by the University

Press of Kansas (Lawrence,

Kansas 66045), which was

organized by the Kansas

Board of Regents and is

operated and funded by

Emporia State University,

Fort Hays State University,

Kansas State University,

Pittsburg State University, the

University of Kansas, and

Wichita State University

Library of Congress Cataloging-in-Publication Data

Crouch, Jeffrey P.
  The presidential pardon power / Jeffrey Crouch.
    p. cm.
  Includes bibliographical references and index.
  ISBN 978-0-7006-1646-6 (cloth : alk. paper)
  1. Pardon—United States. 2. Executive power—United States.
I. Title.
  KF9695.C76 2009
  342.73′062—dc22   2009000848

British Library Cataloguing-in-Publication Data is available.

Printed in the United States of America

10 9 8 7 6 5 4 3 2 1

The paper used in this publication is recycled and contains 30
percent postconsumer waste. It is acid free and meets the minimum requirements of the American National Standard for Per-
manence of Paper for Printed Library Materials Z39.48-1992.

CONTENTS

ACKNOWLEDGMENTS

I would like to acknowledge and offer my appreciation to a number of people who were integral to this book. Thanks to Mike Briggs and the wonderful staff at the University Press of Kansas for the opportunity to work with them. Two widely respected scholars, Mike Genovese and Bob Spitzer, offered many helpful comments and encouragement in their reviews of an early version of the manuscript for the Press. Their enthusiasm for this project was critical to making the book a reality. Thanks also to Phil Cooper and David Gray Adler for reading that draft and endorsing the finished product.

I owe a large debt to John Kenneth White, Phil Henderson, Mark Rozell, and Lou Fisher. Their comments and queries helped me develop this subject into a workable research project. Special thanks to John Kenneth White for the years of teaching and mentoring that culminated in this project. While writing, I received a generous travel grant from the Gerald Ford Fellowship Program to visit the Gerald R. Ford Library in Ann Arbor, Michigan. Documents and videotapes located by archivist Stacy Davis contributed significantly to the breadth and depth of my research on the Nixon pardon. Special thanks to Mark Rozell for suggesting the Ford Library visit and sharing other invaluable research tips.

At the book stage, Mark Rozell and Lou Fisher provided invaluable guidance and feedback. Mark encouraged me to write and present a conference paper on the pardon power and has been an exceptional mentor. In his role as the public law section editor of *Presidential Studies Quarterly*, Lou encouraged me to contribute a scholarly piece, "Presidential Misuse of the Pardon Power," to the journal's December 2008 issue. I am honored to have received this opportunity from the leading scholar of our time on separation of powers, and I hope that a touch of Lou's legendary attention to detail has rubbed off on the book. Given the neglect of the clemency power by most political scientists, I am particularly fortunate to have had these top clemency scholars involved in this endeavor. The final version of the book owes much to their careful reading of multiple versions of the manuscript.

Other prominent clemency experts with whom I have been in close contact include P. S. Ruckman Jr. (who allowed me to use his excellent graphics), Margaret Love, and George Lardner Jr. I have also received excellent advice from Andrew Blum, an attorney, who gave the legal chapter a close look, and Matt

Green, a congressional scholar who read the entire manuscript and made a number of helpful points. Very special thanks to Mistique Cano for multiple manuscript readings and feedback and, more important, for patiently sharing me with the clemency power.

I appreciate the collegial work environment fostered by my terrific colleagues at American University. I am particularly grateful to Rick Semiatin and Diane Lowenthal for their wise counsel and to Dean David Brown for his backing over the last several years. Finally, I want to thank my parents, Paul and Christine Crouch, for enthusiastically supporting my decision to spend the best years of my life in college, law school, and graduate school. This book is dedicated to them.

Introduction

At 11:05 A.M. on a Sunday morning, September 8, 1974, a grim President Gerald Ford faced a single video camera and thirteen members of the White House Press Corps. From the Oval Office, he read the following statement:

> Now, therefore, I, Gerald R. Ford, President of the United States, pursuant to the pardon power conferred upon me by Article II, Section 2, of the Constitution, have granted and by these presents do grant a full, free, and absolute pardon unto Richard Nixon for all offenses against the United States which he, Richard Nixon, has committed or may have committed or taken part in during the period from July [sic—January] 20, 1969 through August 9, 1974.[1]

President Ford then signed Proclamation 4311 granting a full pardon to former president Richard Nixon for any federal offenses he may have committed as president of the United States.[2] A month earlier, Nixon had resigned from the presidency in disgrace to avoid being impeached for his role in the Watergate scandal. The tape of the Nixon pardon—which was not carried live[3]—was broadcast to the nation later that day.[4]

After signing the pardon, President Ford walked out of the White House without answering questions from reporters, climbed into a limousine, and rode to Burning Tree Country Club for an afternoon of golf. Upon Ford's departure, reporters on hand were given copies of four documents: Ford's pardon proclamation, his statement, an opinion from Attorney General William Saxbe that reaffirmed Nixon's ownership of his presidential materials, and the "Nixon-Sampson Agreement" spelling out the logistics of access to the former president's records.[5]

Pardoning Nixon was President Ford's first act of presidential clemency, and it was unique. No American president had ever been pardoned. In contrast to most presidential pardons, Nixon's was issued before he had been convicted of, or even charged with, a crime, and his offenses were not specified in the language of the pardon.[6] Also, President Ford chose not to follow the Department of Justice's regulations regarding pardon applications, an unusual decision in a clemency case.

The Nixon pardon effectively ended the Watergate investigation, but the scandal's collateral effects were felt for years. Watergate was largely (if not solely) to blame for Republicans losing in droves during the 1974 midterm elections, and the scandal frustrated Ford's campaign to win election to the presidency in 1976.[7] One of Watergate's key consequences, the independent counsel statute,[8] provided presidents with political cover to make the other most controversial pardons since the Civil War: George H. W. Bush's pardon of former defense secretary Caspar Weinberger and other Iran-Contra figures, and Bill Clinton's conditional clemency offer to members of the FALN, a Puerto Rican Nationalist group, as well as his "last-minute" pardons of fugitive financier Marc Rich and others. President George W. Bush's decision to commute the prison sentence of Vice President Richard Cheney's former chief of staff, I. Lewis "Scooter" Libby, has joined this exclusive list. By the end of Bush's term in office, there may be others, but none of his post-Libby clemency decisions as of this writing in November 2008 have earned anywhere near the attention of the Libby commutation.

Two Pardon Paradoxes

Today, presidential pardons are granted almost exclusively in innocuous cases, where the merciful president will not suffer any political damage from his choice of clemency recipients. In most cases, recent presidents have tried very hard to avoid hidden dangers in their clemency decisions. For example, other than Scooter Libby, President George W. Bush has granted clemency almost exclusively to well-vetted offenders who have waited years for a decision, committed nonviolent offenses, or both.

Even more important is the tendency of recent presidents to avoid risk by simply pardoning less. Declining clemency rates over the past several decades are at odds with the all but unlimited clemency power in the Constitution. Thus, the first "pardon paradox"[9] is that this nearly limitless constitutional power has been used less and less over time. This paradox—that such a powerful prerogative would wither on the vine from underuse—is particularly perplexing considering how much modern presidents have expanded their powers in some other arenas, such as war-making and budgeting, to name just two.[10]

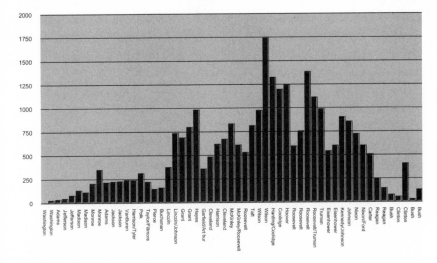

Presidential pardons by administration, 1789–2008: Individual acts of clemency.
Source: P. S. Ruckman Jr., *Pardon Me, Mr. President* (forthcoming), used by permission.

A second "pardon paradox" is that, despite presidents' usual concern for political safety, each of our last three chief executives has made at least one very controversial clemency decision involving his political party's executive branch officials or supporters. President George H. W. Bush's pardons of Caspar Weinberger and other Iran-Contra figures; President Bill Clinton's conditional clemency offer to members of the FALN, along with his "last-minute" pardons of Marc Rich and others; and President George W. Bush's commutation of Scooter Libby's prison sentence were all big stories that earned considerable media attention and general public condemnation.

The public's harsh response to these clemency decisions can be explained by three common characteristics: First, few of these clemency recipients had stood trial for their offenses. The presidential pardon power was meant to be a check on the judiciary, but in most cases it is not appropriate for presidents to use it to avoid the judiciary altogether. Second, these presidents waited until late in their presidencies, when they were safe from direct electoral penalty, to grant politically risky pardons. Third—and most important—each president granted clemency for self-interested reasons. George H. W. Bush and George W. Bush each pardoned executive branch officials whose trials or testimony may have dragged the president into court, whereas Bill Clinton used the clemency power to curry favor with Puerto Rican voters in New York for his wife Hillary's Senate campaign and for Vice President Al Gore's presidential bid. He freed Marc Rich after Rich's ex-wife had donated half a million dollars to Clinton's presidential library.

The Theory

A main argument of this book is that the clemency power is being abused by these modern presidents, who have used it to protect themselves or their subordinates or to reward supporters. In doing so, they may have been hiding criminal offenses or illegally paying off supporters—in other words, committing potentially impeachable offenses. In the chapters to come, I will examine the historical and legal background of the clemency power, with a particular focus on the framers' intent. Then, based on this framework, I will argue that a president who uses the clemency power to pursue his own personal interest is acting contrary to what the framers of the Constitution had in mind. I suggest that this type of behavior is becoming more common.

Since Watergate, presidents have been more willing to use clemency not merely as an "act of grace," or "for the public welfare," as the framers intended, but also as a political weapon to close investigations of their allies or to reward political contributors. This was not always the case: In past investigations into the executive branch conducted by outside prosecutors, presidents rarely used the presidential pardon power to interfere in the justice system.

The post-Watergate world is different from what preceded it. One of the Watergate era's legacies, the independent counsel statute, has provided recent presidents with a politically convenient pretext for protecting fellow partisans. The pardon power became a political weapon for the president to use to thumb his nose at the political opposition. Although the independent counsel statute expired in 1999 and was not renewed, its legacy is still alive and well. Even three decades after Watergate, judicial investigations remain colored by political influences, and presidents are only too happy to take advantage of the ambiguity.

I am not suggesting that the framers never anticipated that a president would abuse the pardon power for political or personal gain—quite the contrary. As legal scholar Daniel Kobil explained, "The framers were aware that [pardoning] was a political action. What's different now is that although it's a political power, we're seeing that public officials are so frightened or politically opportunistic that they are unwilling to wield it at all. They don't want to issue anything that could smack of controversy and come back to haunt them."[11] At the same time, I suggest, our three most recent presidents have abused the pardon power for legal or financial gain, but only when they were immune to political consequences.

Political scientists have not spilled much ink exploring presidential attitudes toward pardoning. I suggest, however, that the idea that granting fewer pardons protects political capital fits well with established principles about presidential power. According to *The American Presidency* by Clinton Rossiter and *Presidential Power* by Richard Neustadt, a president acting as "chief executive" and "party leader" sometimes best protects his power when he chooses *not* to do something. Pardons rarely provide any political benefit to presidents, and they always involve some risk to their political capital. The stakes are even higher in a mass media environment where a president is more apt to "go public"[12] to raise support for his programs and is expected by the press to provide the American people with rhetorical justifications for controversial decisions.[13]

The current political environment rewards—or at least does not punish—a president who is sparing with the pardon power. This observation is supported by a look at the nearly straight-line decline in the percentage of approved clemency petitions granted by recent presidents. Thus, the president does not pardon much, and when he does, few notice. In the cases where *everyone* will notice, two of our most recent three presidents were less reluctant to "get back" at investigators than their predecessors had been. These outside investigators are now painted by partisans as politically motivated or, at minimum, overzealous, which provides political cover for presidents to use the pardon power for self-interested reasons. This book will explain how the tendency of recent presidents to take advantage of the post-Watergate political environment has affected presidential pardoning practices and will examine the consequences of this phenomenon for the modern presidency.

Plan for the Book

In this work I investigate the significant historical, legal, and political aspects of the modern presidential pardon power. Chapter 1 provides an overview of the pardon power and the Constitution. Here, I explore the historical context for the American pardon power as it developed from ancient times through English and early American history. Turning to the Constitution, I discuss the various powers and responsibilities assigned to the president and explain how the pardon power fits into the mix. I also discuss the various forms that clemency can assume, from a full pardon down the line to a temporary reprieve. Then, I track the development of the pardon attorney bureaucracy and describe how one may apply for presidential clemency. I address several "big picture" questions about clemency, including whether the president has a duty to pardon, to whom the president must answer for clemency decisions, and the framers' goal for the pardon power.

Chapter 2 considers key legal precedents for presidential and legislative clemency powers. In the first half of this chapter, I examine case law explaining the legal parameters of the presidential pardon power: its nature, extent, effect, and limits. In the second half, I consider the arguments for a congressional clemency power by reviewing the struggles between the president and Congress during several key Civil War and Reconstruction cases. I look closely at two cases that may provide some support for a congressional clemency power, and then discuss whether the president and Congress each have a clemency power.

Chapter 3 examines some of the most controversial clemency grants handed out before Watergate. First, I point out that most clemency actions go all but unnoticed by the general public, unless celebrity status or unusual circumstances raise the profile of the clemency recipient. This has always been the case. I also show that today, fewer clemency applicants are successful in their efforts to secure presidential mercy. I discuss several factors that may have contributed to recent presidential stinginess regarding clemency. Next, I look more closely at a few of the most controversial pre-Watergate clemency acts: pardons for the Whiskey rebels, for example, and commutations for Eugene Debs, Marcus Garvey, Oscar Collazo, and James Hoffa. Even these highly controversial decisions are justifiable, I argue, for various reasons. Then, I explore the lasting impact of Watergate, the press, and public opinion on presidential pardons. In the last pages of the chapter, I suggest that, for reasons explored in the remainder of the book, the scandal and the Nixon pardon have made a lasting impression on President Ford's successors.

Chapter 4 is devoted to an analysis of a key consequence of Watergate: the infamous pardon of Richard Nixon. Here, I examine a number of clemency-related issues that received their first modern consideration in this case, including the public's three most pressing questions: whether

Ford and Nixon had made a "deal"—the presidency for a pardon; the legality of the pardon; and the timing of the pardon. I also analyze the political fallout from the pardon and weigh the impact of the mass media, the opinions of political elites, and public opinion polls.

Chapter 5 lays out case studies of four important pre-Watergate outside investigations into executive branch misbehavior: These were dubbed the Whiskey Ring, the Oregon Land Frauds, Teapot Dome, and the Income Tax Scandal. I suggest that three of the four investigated presidents—Theodore Roosevelt, Calvin Coolidge, and Harry Truman—behaved properly and allowed the independent investigators to conduct thorough, unencumbered investigations. The fourth, Ulysses Grant, did not. Unlike these earlier examples, Watergate shook the confidence of the public, so much so that it led to the passage of the independent counsel statute. I note how the statute changed over time and discuss the most famous Supreme Court case on topic, *Morrison v. Olson.* I contend that unlike their predecessors, post-Watergate presidents have been willing to argue that unfair treatment by an independent counsel justifies a grant of presidential clemency for their supporters.

Chapter 6 offers an analysis of how our most recent three presidents—George H. W. Bush, Bill Clinton, and George W. Bush—have abused the clemency power for personal reasons. I look at the circumstances leading up to each clemency grant, the grant itself, and the reaction of political and media elites as well as the general public to each grant. As I point out, the Scooter Libby commutation, which followed the independent counsel statute era, suggests that outside investigations into executive branch misbehavior are now assumed to be politically motivated. As a result, presidents are no longer afraid to use clemency to protect executive branch officials from prosecution.

Finally, in the Conclusion, I explore the political environment created by Watergate and review President Ford's options for handling the predicament created by his predecessor. Despite conflicting evidence, I conclude that he made the difficult decision to pardon Richard Nixon for the right reason: the good of the country. Next, I turn to the highly controversial clemency actions of George H. W. Bush, Bill Clinton, and George W. Bush, arguing that they acted for personal reasons in making highly controversial clemency grants to executive branch officials or donors. Each of these clemency decisions was made by a president protected from electoral consequences. This phenomenon comes close to realizing one of the framers' greatest fears: that presidents might use clemency to shield their executive branch officials. In light of the apparent shortcomings of the clemency power, I consider alternatives for changing it. Ultimately, I suggest that the pardon power does not require constitutional amendment; however, I believe that the public should be more vigilant about holding presidents accountable for their clemency decisions. Unless average Americans sound a warning siren for Congress, future presidents will continue to feel safe to use clemency to cover up for their aides and supporters. Only by holding the current president accountable will future presidents think twice about abusing the presidential pardon power.

1 The Pardon Power and the Constitution

A main argument of this book is that the clemency power is being abused by modern presidents to protect themselves or their subordinates or to reward supporters. Before one can judge their clemency decisions, however, one must understand how the clemency power works. The most logical starting point for this inquiry is the pardon clause of the Constitution. Article II, Section 2, Clause 1, gives the president the power to "grant reprieves and pardons for offenses against the United States."[1] The chief executive may use the clemency power to check decisions of the federal judiciary. However, his power to do so is itself checked in three ways. First, in order to qualify for a presidential pardon, a crime must have been committed.[2] Second, it must be a crime "against the United States" (a federal crime).[3] Finally, a pardon cannot be granted "in cases of impeachment."[4] The plain language of Article II, Section 2, specifically excludes impeachment from the pardon power because impeachment is the ultimate check on the presidency available to the other branches of government. Other than these three restraints, the presidential pardon power is—on its face—unlimited.

Perhaps because of the apparent simplicity of its constitutional grounding, the general public does not quite grasp the complexities of the clemency power. On some level, it is intuitive that to "pardon" someone is to excuse or lessen the consequences of a crime. This is only scratching the surface, however. Presidents have a number of pardoning options at their disposal, and even scholars are hard-pressed to predict (or explain) what they may do. Anyone wishing to fully understand the clemency framework and to form educated opinions about specific clemency decisions, however, would do well to learn more about both the philosophy behind the clemency power and the mechanics by which it works. This chapter will address these two areas of inquiry: First, we will look at the historical roots of clemency and the intent of the framers of the Constitution for the pardon clause, and then we will look at how the clause has been interpreted and applied over time.

To develop a more complete understanding of the clemency power, it is not enough to look at the text of the constitutional clause by itself—we must also consider the context in which the clemency power has developed. The elements of that context include, first, the foundation of the American pardon power. The framers drew upon several cultures in concocting their own version of clemency power. Second, the pardon power's context can be partially derived from how the clemency language in Article II has been interpreted by the courts. There is a world of difference between, for example, a full "pardon" and a temporary "reprieve." Third, the process for obtaining clemency usually requires an applicant to work with the Office of the Pardon Attorney and comply with rules established by federal regulations. These procedures also form part of the context of the pardon power. Finally, we need to ask the "big picture" questions about clemency: Does the president *have* to use it? To whom is the president responsible for clemency decisions? What is the goal of the pardon power? These are also important considerations that will be explored in detail in this chapter.

Clemency in Historical Perspective: From Ancient Times to America's Founding

To begin, I will provide a short historical sketch of how the presidential pardon power found its way into the Constitution. A brief examination of a few key moments in pardoning history will help to illuminate how the pardon power has evolved over the years. American pardoning practices have their roots in ancient societies. In fact, the American understanding of clemency stretches back through time to the most ancient legal code known to man, the Code of Hammurabi, which was used by the Babylonians in about the eighteenth century B.C.[5] Though a detailed analysis of the various legal codes of the past several thousand years and their incarnations of pardon is beyond the scope of this study,[6] a brief consideration of clemency in ancient Greece and Rome is certainly worthwhile, for it can illuminate a few of the ways that clemency powers have been used in the past and still influence clemency practices today.

Unlike in the United States, not every society has entrusted clemency powers to a single executive. For example, the people of ancient Athens decided democratically who would receive mercy.[7] Because an applicant for pardon needed the signatures of 6,000 Greek citizens, only those with celebrity status had a realistic chance of obtaining clemency.[8] In the United

States, by contrast, only the president is responsible for pardon decisions, and ultimately only his support truly matters.

Perhaps the most famous Roman pardon was Pontius Pilate's release of Barabbas instead of Jesus Christ. The Romans and the Jews pardoned on special occasions, such as holidays and coronation days, and Pilate freed Barabbas as the crowds demanded as part of a Passover tradition. The Romans demonstrated an understanding of the political value of pardon via their practice of "decimation," through which only one out of every ten soldiers in a mutinous company was killed. Here, the state enforced discipline and punished wrongdoing while simultaneously demonstrating mercy and frugality by not unnecessarily wasting soldiers' lives. Jump forward to the American Civil War, and we see a similar use of mercy when President Abraham Lincoln used the pardon power strategically to welcome back to the Union an ever-increasing number of Confederates, a practice continued by Andrew Johnson following Lincoln's assassination.[9]

The examples from ancient times illustrate the emphasis placed on "considerations of expediency rather than justice" in the Greek and Roman cultures. These cultures used the power of a ruler to pardon offenders and opponents to forge practical solutions to politically difficult situations. They were not preoccupied, as the framers would be, with using clemency as a "fail-safe" for their respective justice systems, because they believed that law and justice were one and the same. As one clemency scholar explained, "The law itself was thought by many early cultures to originate in infallible sources such as God or the people, and thus to embody principles of justice adequately. If the law was itself synonymous with justice, there would have rarely been need to create exceptions to the law to further justice."[10] In other words, the law was—by definition—just. If an exception to the law was granted, it was for reasons unrelated to ensuring that justice was done.

This rationale prevailed worldwide in the decades before the American founding. Indeed, the king of England and other seventeenth- and eighteenth-century European monarchs granted pardons for a variety of "practical" reasons, including "to reward their friends and undermine their enemies, to populate their colonies, to man their navies, to raise money and to quell rebellions." These practices raised nary an eyebrow among their subjects because, as one pardon scholar has noted, "the pardoning power . . . was analogous in theory and practice to divine grace. Like grace . . . a royal pardon was thought of as a personal gift. Therefore, it required no justification and was not subject to criticism."[11] The practice of pardoning for reasons other than to do justice was eventually codified in English law.[12]

Constitutional scholar William Duker pointed out that "prior to the seventeenth century, the English monarch's power to pardon was absolute," and that power continued virtually undiminished until what Duker calls "the greatest constitutional crisis involving the executive power to pardon," a 1678 struggle between King Charles II and Parliament regarding the latter's attempt to impeach Thomas Osborne, the earl of Danby and lord high treasurer of England.[13]

The king had enraged the legislature by pardoning Osborne before Parliament could conclude his impeachment, setting the stage for a confrontation over the extent of the king's clemency powers. Parliament reacted by questioning whether the king had acted legally and debated whether to limit the king's pardoning power. Eventually, the two sides compromised: Osborne was not impeached, but he did spend five years incarcerated in the Tower of London. More importantly, Parliament used the crisis as a springboard to pass legislation to rein in the king's clemency powers.[14] The resulting acts passed by Parliament were the Habeas Corpus Act of 1679, the 1689 Bill of Rights, and the 1700 Act of Settlement.[15] The particular issue raised by the Osborne incident—whether a pardon may bar impeachment—was resolved in the Act of Settlement, which mandated that "no pardon under the great seal of England [shall] be pleadable to an impeachment by the commons in parliament."[16] Parliament itself was able to issue pardons via legislative act by 1721.[17]

The Osborne incident and its fallout remain important today because its findings, according to a clemency scholar, "gave form to the pardoning power for almost three centuries." The English colonial governing authorities in the "New World" had been granted a broad pardon power by the king.[18] As the American equivalents to the English Crown and Parliament, the president and Congress would have their own heated confrontations over the clemency powers much later, during the Civil War and Watergate. First, though, the framers of the Constitution had to determine whether to establish a national clemency power in the first place, and if so, how it would work.

Scholars know that the American framers drew upon their English heritage and writings by great political thinkers such as John Locke and Baron de Montesquieu for the general principles they used to construct the new

American government. What is less known is that these monumental minds weighed in on the pardon power. In his *Second Treatise of Government*, Locke wrote that one element of an executive's "prerogative" power would be "a power, in many cases, to mitigate the severity of the law, and pardon some offenders."[19] Montesquieu found in *The Spirit of the Laws* that monarchs may actually benefit from using clemency. He was less enthusiastic about the need for a clemency power in a republic, however, finding it "not so necessary."[20]

Whereas Montesquieu doubted the utility of a pardon power in a republic, the great English jurist William Blackstone argued that a pardon power simply could not function in a democracy. He wrote that clemency was an important advantage in a monarchy, which features "a magistrate who has it in his power to extend mercy, wherever he thinks it is deserved: holding a court of equity in his own breast, to soften the rigour of the general law, in such criminal cases as merit an exemption from punishment." Used wisely, he contended, clemency can endear a monarch to his subjects by making him appear merciful. However, Blackstone warned that pardoning in a democracy "can never subsist" because "it would be impolitic for the power of judging and of pardoning to centre in one and the same person." The result would be that the magistrate administrating the laws would "very often . . . contradict himself," and the people would have a warped sense of right and wrong since they "would find it difficult to tell whether a prisoner were discharged by his innocence, or obtained a pardon through favour."[21]

Blackstone's observation about the inappropriateness of granting pardons in a democracy where one magistrate could both judge and pardon did not go unnoticed in the American states. American scholars disagreed with Blackstone's analysis and fired back with both barrels. In 1791, James Wilson defended the vesting of the pardon power via the Constitution in the president, noting that despite Blackstone's warning, there was no such danger in the United States, where "we have discovered, that the law is higher than the magistrate, who administers it; that the constitution is higher than both; and that the supreme power, remaining with the people, is higher than all the three."[22] Joseph Story articulated a defense for the American scheme in 1833. Classifying Blackstone's rationale as "extremely forced and artificial," Story argued that these concerns were simply irrelevant in a government such as the one formed in the United States, "where there is a separation of the general departments of government, legislative, judicial, and executive, and the powers of each administered by distinct persons."[23]

The Constitution's assignment of the powers to judge and pardon to the judiciary and the executive, respectively, is but one example of the framers' careful plan to separate powers among the branches of the federal government and create a system whereby each branch would have the ability to "check and balance" the others. Taking a page out of Montesquieu's book, the framers divided the constitutional powers among the executive, judicial, and legislative branches. As pointed out generations later by Justice Robert Jackson in his concurring opinion in *Youngstown Sheet & Tube Co. v. Sawyer* (1952), the president's powers are at their highest point when he acts according to the express or implied authority of Congress.[24] However, the framers understood that each of the three branches would often have its own priorities.

Not comfortable trusting human nature, James Madison warned in Federalist No. 51 that "ambition must be made to counteract ambition." The checks and balances, he said, were necessary because "if men were angels, no government would be necessary. If angels were to govern men, neither external nor internal controls on government would be necessary."[25] The framers knew that disputes would be settled by constant battle between the executive and legislative branches.[26]

The pardon power is an important constitutional "check and balance" power for the president. While the president may pardon, one observer has noted, "Congress defines crimes and their punishments and the judiciary interprets and applies those laws and punishments."[27] Based on their own discussions, the framers believed that the presidency was the best place to lodge the power to excuse federal crimes. A closer look at their deliberations reveals that this was far from a universally accepted arrangement, at least at first.

As any casual student of American history knows, the framers harbored a deep suspicion of a strong executive following the American Revolution. In the era leading up to the drafting of the Constitution, the states had significantly curbed their governors' clemency powers. A majority of state governments featured a clemency power shared between the governor and the legislature, or vested in the legislature alone. The governors of New York, Delaware, Maryland, North Carolina, and South Carolina were the only ones with all of the pardoning authority.[28] Under the Articles of Confederation, there was no national clemency power (or true national executive, for that matter).

This was the state of affairs when the framers met at the Constitutional Convention in Philadelphia in 1787. The pardon power was not one of the more popular items on the agenda. In fact, no pardoning provisions existed in the main plans of government formally considered at the beginning of the convention.[29] Notably, the text of Edmund Randolph's Virginia Plan and William Paterson's New Jersey Plan did not mention clemency.[30] However, John Rutledge added to the margin of the Virginia Plan language for a pardon clause resembling that of the Act of Settlement of 1700, and this language was adopted by the Committee on Detail and then added to Article X of an early draft of the Constitution.[31] August 6 marked the first formal appearance of the pardoning power at the convention.[32] The resulting clause read that the federal executive "shall have power to grant reprieves and pardons; but his pardon shall not be pleadable in bar of an impeachment."[33]

Adopting a pardon power would fit into the Federalists' view that a strong executive should have this kingly power; Anti-Federalists expressed deeply held reservations, particularly about whether to include the Senate in pardon decisions, or whether a president might excuse his executive officials from treason. The pardoning clause was not discussed by the convention until August 25, when Roger Sherman, delegate from Connecticut, made a motion to drop the phrase "power to grant reprieves & pardon" and replace it with the phrase "to grant reprieves until the ensuing session of the Senate, and pardons with consent of the Senate." Sherman's home state voted aye, but the other eight states all opposed—and defeated—Sherman's motion. Also on that day, the delegates unanimously agreed to insert the phrase "except in cases of impeachment" after "pardons." The delegates voted 6–4 to drop the phrase "but his pardon shall not be pleadable in bar" from the pardon clause.[34]

Perhaps the most historically significant exchange regarding the pardon power occurred two days later, on August 27, when Maryland delegate Luther Martin and Pennsylvania delegate James Wilson debated whether the words "after conviction" should be added after the phrase "reprieves and pardons" to limit the chief executive's pardon power by allowing only post-conviction pardons:

> Mr. L. Martin moved to insert the words "after conviction" after the words "reprieves and pardons"

Mr. Wilson objected that pardon before conviction might be necessary in order to obtain the testimony of accomplices. He stated the case of forgeries in which this might particularly happen.—Mr L. Martin withdrew his motion.[35]

On September 10, Edmund Randolph listed a number of objections he had against the Constitution as it was currently constituted. Relevant here is Randolph's objection to "the unqualified power of the President to pardon treasons." The delegates agreed unanimously with his request to refer to committee a motion regarding pardons made in cases of treason.[36]

Five days later, Randolph engaged fellow delegates George Mason, James Wilson, Rufus King, Gouverneur Morris, and James Madison in debate over whether cases of treason should be excluded from the pardoning power. Randolph argued to exclude treason from the scope of the president's pardon power for fear of a president involved in treasonous activities:

Art: II. sect. 2. "he shall have power to grant reprieves and pardons for offences against the U. S. &c"

Mr Randolph moved to "except cases of treason." The prerogative of pardon in these cases was too great a trust. The President may himself be guilty. The Traytors may be his own instruments.

Col. Mason supported the motion.

Mr Govr Morris had rather there should be no pardon for treason, than let the power devolve on the Legislature.

Mr Wilson. Pardon is necessary for cases of treason, and is best placed in the hands of the Executive. If he be himself a party to the guilt he can be impeached and prosecuted.

Mr. King thought it would be inconsistent with the Constitutional separation of the Executive & Legislative powers to let the prerogative be exercised by the latter—A Legislative body is utterly unfit for the purpose. They are governed too much by the passions of the moment. In Massachusetts, one assembly would have hung all the insurgents in that State: the next was equally disposed to pardon them all. He suggested the expedient of requiring the concurrence of the Senate in Acts of Pardon.

Mr. Madison admitted the force of objections to the Legislature, but the pardon of treasons was so peculiarly improper for the President that he should acquiesce in the transfer of it to the former, rather than leave it altogether in the hands of the latter. He would prefer to either an association of the Senate as a Council of advice, with the President.

Mr Randolph could not admit the Senate into a share of the Power. [T]he great danger to liberty lay in a combination between the President & that body—

Col. Mason. The Senate has already too much power—There can be no danger of too much lenity in legislative pardons, as the Senate must con [sic] concur, & the President moreover can require 2/3 of both Houses.[37]

Essentially, the framers were arguing here about which branch should have the power to pardon treason: the executive or the legislative. Randolph and Mason hesitated to give the president the power to pardon for treason in case the president himself was a traitor and used his clemency power to pardon his accomplices. Wilson responded that it was important to allow the president the flexibility to pardon for treason, and that if a president were implicated, he could be impeached and removed from office. Madison suggested that responsibility for awarding clemency in cases of treason could be transferred to Congress, or that at least the Senate could advise the president, and Randolph reminded the others of the danger presented by combining the executive and legislative powers. Mason agreed with Randolph, arguing that "the Senate already has too much power." Alexander Hamilton revisited this issue in Federalist No. 69. Ultimately, Randolph's motion failed.[38]

The foregoing discussion was the last conversation on the pardon power that occurred during the convention.[39] However, it highlighted one of the most contentious areas of disagreement regarding the clemency power, both during and after the convention, as well as during the Civil War. As suggested in later chapters, the Anti-Federalists' question regarding whether to trust the president to act responsibly toward his own executive branch officials was prescient, and it remains an important issue today.[40]

Once the Constitution was signed, the framers set out to explain their work. The pardon power's role in cases of treason received a fair amount of attention from the Constitution's proponents. On November 29, 1787, Luther Martin spoke on the debate over the pardon power in his Genuine Information, a report on the convention to the Maryland State Legislature. Martin reported that the framers found the pardon power to be "extremely dangerous," and he explained the debate over treason, including the decision that the president should have the power to pardon even in cases of treason.[41] As pointed out by several legal scholars, little debate over the pardon power occurred at the state ratifying conventions,[42] although on July 28, 1788, James Iredell made a fairly lengthy statement at the North Carolina Ratifying Convention about the pardon debate.[43]

Perhaps the most famous defense of the pardon power was made by Alexander Hamilton. In Federalist No. 69, attempting to quell Anti-Federalist concerns, he argued that the Constitution provided adequate protection against abuse because it allowed the president to pardon in virtually any circumstances "except in cases of impeachment." Despite the wide reach of the clemency power, he said, the protections were adequate because the president would always be subject to impeachment if he acted improperly, even if he pardoned treasonous executive branch allies.[44]

Hamilton went into greater detail in Federalist No. 74. Here, he indirectly made a case for the principles of "decision, activity, secrecy and dispatch" that were called for in Federalist No. 70 by pointing out the need for a broad clemency power—vested in one person—to ease the harsh consequences of cold statutory language, where appropriate:[45]

> Humanity and good policy conspire to dictate that the benign prerogative of pardoning should be as little as possible fettered or embarrassed. The criminal code of every country partakes so much of necessary severity that without an easy access to exceptions in favor of unfortunate guilt, justice would wear a countenance too sanguinary and cruel. As the sense of responsibility is always strongest in proportion as it is undivided, it may be inferred that a single man would be most ready to attend to the force of those motives which might plead for a mitigation of the rigor of the law, and least apt to yield to considerations which were calculated to shelter a fit object of its vengeance. . . . One man appears to be a more eligible dispenser of the mercy of the government than a body of men.[46]

With the clemency power vested in one responsible individual—the president—Hamilton argued, crucial decisions could be made in a much more timely manner than if that power were shared with the legislative branch. This advantage was particularly important when the nation faced the gravest of circumstances:

> The principal argument for reposing the power of pardoning in this case in the Chief Magistrate is this: in seasons of insurrection or rebellion, there are often critical moments when a well-timed offer of pardon to the insurgents or rebels may restore the tranquility of the commonwealth; and which, if suffered to pass unimproved, it may never be possible afterwards to recall. The dilatory process of convening the legislature, or one of its branches, for the purpose of obtaining its sanction to the measure, would frequently be the occasion of letting slip the golden opportunity.[47]

In vesting the pardoning power solely in a president, the framers adopted the English view of the clemency power.[48] American pardon practices have taken their own path, however, as the Supreme Court has given the American pardon power a broader scope than that enjoyed by the British king.[49]

Features of the Pardon Power: Scope and Implementation

What does the clemency power in the Constitution allow the president to do? Although the framers were sensitive to the danger of unleashing an American monarch, they nonetheless entrusted the president with this unique, kingly power. Unlike other presidential prerogatives, the pardon power does not depend upon the Senate's approval.[50] In contrast to the virtually unlimited pardon power, treaties require a two-thirds majority Senate concurrence,[51] and appointments to federal offices do not occur without the support of the Senate.[52]

Other Article II powers that do not rely on the Senate (or Congress as a whole) are unclear from the plain text of the Constitution. The president is charged to "take care"[53] that the laws be executed. He holds the "executive power,"[54] a hazy grant that today encompasses executive orders, executive privilege, and executive agreements.[55] Equally important is the president's power as "commander in chief,"[56] a clause that presidents routinely cite today when deploying military forces even without congressional approval.

Perhaps the most important presidential power is the right to veto proposed legislation,[57] but this power is found in Article I, not Article II. The president holds a few other duties: providing Congress with information on the state of the union, adjourning or convening Congress, and receiving ambassadors and commissioning officers.[58] But at least in the eyes of the pardoned individual, none of these can measure up to the power to forgive an offender for a federal crime.

Forms of Federal Executive Clemency

Does the phrase "reprieves and pardons" in the Constitution limit the president to only those two forms of clemency? Despite the general public's tendency to refer to any manifestation of clemency as a "pardon," a full pardon is only one of a number of options available to the president. There are in fact five main forms that clemency can assume, with a "full pardon" being the broadest in scope. A full pardon gives its recipient "the most sweeping remission of the consequences that normally attend violation of the law." Just how "sweeping" a pardon can be—and the difference between an absolute pardon and a conditional pardon—is discussed in the next chapter. Second, in a "commutation," the offender is given a lesser sentence than that originally designated by the court. A commutation is different from a pardon in that the legal stigma remains for the commuted offender.[59] These are the two most common forms of executive clemency still granted today. Third, the president has the power "to remit fines and forfeitures."[60] Fourth, the president can grant a reprieve, which is "the most limited form of clemency . . . nothing more than the temporary postponement of punishment."[61]

A final and unique form of clemency is amnesty. "Amnesty," which comes from the Greek *amnestia*, or "forgiveness," is typically granted to a group rather than an individual, is often given pre-conviction, and usually rests on the judgment that the public welfare is better served by ignoring a particular crime than by punishing for it. Unlike a pardon, an amnesty does not excuse the crime; however, in the eyes of the law, amnesty and pardon are treated about the same.[62] An amnesty is often announced following the conclusion of a war, and—as will be discussed in the next chapter—the Civil War set the stage for a monumental struggle between Congress and the president over the clemency power.

The Office of the Pardon Attorney

The Office of the Pardon Attorney in the Department of Justice assists the president with clemency decisions. Increased demand for clemency has led to the development of this bureaucracy devoted solely to handling clemency applications. Generally speaking, applications for executive clemency are first screened by the pardon attorney, and petitioners must follow a number of federal regulations in order for their cases to be reviewed. Except in high-profile cases, presidents usually grant clemency to applicants they have never met. One commentator, noting the layers of bureaucracy between clemency applicants and the president, described the relationship as "like that of the princess to the pea."[63] The attorney general is responsible for the Department of Justice and its agencies, including the Office of the Pardon Attorney, to which the department delegates the authority to process petitions for executive clemency.[64]

The evolution of the Pardon Attorney's Office illustrates how the executive branch has adapted over time to meet the demands of changing circumstances.[65] Much like other executive branch bureaucracies, the office developed gradually. Before 1850, preparatory and advisory functions regarding clemency requests were performed by the attorney general and the secretary of state. Around 1850, the attorney general took over these duties and performed them exclusively. The Department of State continued to issue pardons on the president's behalf until June 16, 1893, when an executive order issued by President Grover Cleveland transferred this last remaining State Department responsibility to the attorney general.[66]

On March 3, 1865, the Office of Pardon Clerk was created within the Office of the Attorney General.[67] Another law, passed on March 3, 1891, replaced the pardon clerk with a pardon attorney.[68] The Office of the Pardon Attorney predated the Department of Justice, which was not created until 1870.[69] The role of assistant pardon attorney was added on June 10, 1918.[70] The pardon attorney provides information and advice on the overwhelming majority of pardon applications but is not required to process an application or recommend clemency before the president may unilaterally decide to grant clemency. The pardon attorney's role is purely advisory, meaning that the president reserves the right to accept or reject his advice.

Nearly all clemency applications are first routed through the Pardon Attorney's Office. Indeed, a president who grants clemency outside the pardon attorney bureaucracy often creates a reason for media attention simply by deviating from the norm. The FALN pardons were notable for how

President Clinton ignored the pardon attorney and the advice of law enforcement, while the Nixon pardon, the Iran-Contra pardons, the Marc Rich pardon (at least until the very end), and the Scooter Libby commutation were all handled outside the "normal" process. Still, it is no surprise that these volatile decisions were considered outside routine application procedures. The presidents considering clemency in these cases most likely wished to avoid giving the media any advance notice that these controversial decisions were coming. Preserving secrecy would have proved difficult if the applications of those figures were added to the rest of the pool. Another reason these decisions were kept under wraps is that the Pardon Attorney's Office is not designed to handle political matters. As former pardon attorney Reed Cozart suggested, clemency applications under his watch (spanning three presidents) "have always been considered on their merits, without any political or other type of pressure." Even if a president was facing political pressure, Cozart contended, a controversial applicant would be treated the same way as anyone else, or even penalized, but not advantaged.[71] In any case, the pardon attorney apparatus is not designed to judge whether a pardon would be a wise move under the prevailing political circumstances.[72] The pardon attorney's role is to do the president's bidding, and then allow the chief executive to make the final call.

Once the pardon attorney has reached a decision on a clemency petition, the Pardon Attorney's Office sends a recommendation to the associate attorney general, who then determines what, if any, recommendation the Department of Justice will make to the president.[73] In an interview, Pardon Attorney Roger Adams declined to answer a question about how often the president actually follows Department of Justice recommendations on clemency matters. Moreover, the White House Counsel's Office does not record how often it agrees or disagrees with the pardon attorney, and this probably helps to ensure that the president receives uninhibited advice.[74]

Secrecy is sacrosanct when it comes to clemency applications. The clemency application process aims to preserve the privacy of applicants. Unless the attorney general decides that "their disclosure is required by law or the ends of justice," materials supporting a petition for clemency are viewed only by the officials processing the petition.[75] Though these internal deliberations, and, since 1932, a president's reasons for granting clemency, remain long-standing secrets, clemency decisions are not as secret as they once were. While the *Annual Report* of the attorney general published from 1894 through 1932 once provided many specifics on individual cases, the Roosevelt administration discontinued the practice of publishing data on individual clemency decisions in favor of providing aggregate information, and Roosevelt's successors followed the practice. Still, since early 2001, researchers have had access to information on who has been pardoned, what their offenses were, and when their pardons were issued.[76] Some clemency data are available online, and the Pardon Attorney's Office has released a set of CDs containing scans of older clemency warrants, thereby opening new avenues for research.

Applying for Federal Executive Clemency

Updated procedures for petitioning the president for executive clemency can be found in the Federal Register, 28 CFR 1.1–1.11. They may also be accessed via the Pardon Attorney's Office Web site (found at http://www.usdoj.gov/pardon/clemency.htm). These rules require that anyone seeking a "pardon, reprieve, commutation of sentence, or remission of fine shall execute a formal petition" (although, of course, the president may consider clemency requests from applicants outside this formal process), address it to the president of the United States, and—if seeking clemency for a nonmilitary offense—submit it to the pardon attorney.[77] As noted earlier, only offenses committed against the United States qualify for clemency.[78]

The application's strict requirements and waiting period keep the potential applicant pool relatively small. According to the regulations, "no petition for pardon should be filed until the expiration of a waiting period of at least five years after the date of the release of the petitioner from confinement" or—assuming the offender was not sentenced to prison—a minimum of five years following the date of conviction for the offense.[79] Those offenders on probation, parole, or supervised release "generally" are advised to wait before submitting petitions for clemency.[80] A petitioner should demonstrate "exceptional circumstances" before filing a petition for commutation of a sentence—including remission of a fine—if "other forms of judicial or administrative relief" are available.[81]

The attorney general has the discretion to investigate a petition "as he or she may deem necessary and appropriate," relying on the Federal Bureau of Investigation (FBI), among other governmental entities. If the petitioner committed an offense with a victim and the attorney general determines that the victim should be contacted, "reasonable effort" is required to notify the victim(s) of all of the following: (1) that the offender has petitioned for executive clemency; (2) that the victim may comment on the appropriateness of granting clemency in the case; and (3) whether the president awards or declines clemency. The attorney general must review every petition and accompanying information and make a recommendation to the president as to whether clemency would be appropriate.[82] Most cases do not receive a positive recommendation.

The President's Duty to Pardon

Does a president actually have a duty to use the clemency power? I suggest that a president should pardon regularly and vigorously. Despite the risk of a clemency decision backfiring, a president should not put off or avoid clemency decisions. Inactivity can be just as politically risky as granting a questionable pardon, for several reasons. First, if a president does not use the pardon power often enough, the public does not develop confidence in his pardon decisions. The consequence of fewer pardons is, of course, that observers become more suspicious and skeptical of those lucky few who are pardoned. Not using the pardon power at all, or hardly at all, can be seen as just as detrimental as using it too much.[83]

Second, presidents who regularly grant clemency to applicants who go through the "normal" pardon process can always blame the screening mechanism when a pardon goes awry. When a president relies on an administrative process that helps filter applications and sends only the most meritorious ones to his desk, the president can treat pardons as routine and impersonal, which can in turn help insulate him from criticism if a controversial pardon is given.[84] Presidents should try to convey the impression that pardon decision-making is an impartial process. As a former pardon attorney has pointed out, "where the decision-making process is perceived as having independent integrity, whatever decision results is likely to be accepted without too close a look at its merits."[85] The converse is also true.

Finally, the public sees the pardon power as one of the president's responsibilities. As with developing a budget, managing a war, or anything else in which the president takes the lead, the president is expected to take reasonable clemency risks and then make himself available for the public's approval or disapproval.[86] On occasion, the risk may not pan out. President William Howard Taft recalled that sometimes pardon recipients act in predictable ways, but other times they do not:

There has been a custom in the Presidential office of pardoning men who are supposed to be near their death to enable them to go home and die with their families. The difficulty in such cases is in being certain that death is near. I had two notable cases in which I was assured by the prison authorities that death was imminent, and that if they were to be released at all, to die, they ought to be released at once. I instituted as thorough an investigation as I could through the army and navy surgeons in the employ of the government and reached the conclusion from the evidence submitted that death was certain. I pardoned them both. One man died and kept his contract. The other recovered at once, and seems to be as healthy and active as any one I know.[87]

Mistakes, though unfortunate, are part of the job of serving as president of the United States. Only by making decisions that involve some risk to his popularity can a president get things done, meet public expectations, and either use up or replenish his political capital.

Accountability Issues

The pardon power is essentially unlimited in the Constitution, so one natural concern is the president's accountability for clemency grants. To whom does the president answer for controversial clemency decisions? The answer: Congress and the courts. Chapter 2 explains how case-law precedents usually prevent Congress from directly checking the president's pardon power. However, the Constitution does not leave the other two branches defenseless.[88] The legislature has two key weapons it may use against the executive's clemency power. Both are draconian measures: First, Congress may amend the Constitution according to Article V;[89] and second, Congress may impeach the president under Article II, Section 4.[90]

Draconian measures aside, however, Congress is still not completely powerless. One way the legislative branch may affect pardon decisions is to informally request documents, hold hearings, and channel or even create public disapproval of certain pardons. These tactics were used in the Nixon pardon, in the Iran-Contra case, in Clinton's FALN and "last-minute" clemency decisions, and in the Scooter Libby commutation.[91] Congress may even decide to issue subpoenas and hold executive officials in contempt.[92] The president, of course, has always argued that Congress may not exercise oversight regarding pardon decisions.[93] However, President Ford willingly appeared before the Hungate subcommittee (named after the subcommittee chairman, Missouri Congressman William Hungate) to discuss the Nixon pardon. Congress and the courts were unusually involved in looking into President Clinton's controversial clemency decisions: Congress passed an unprecedented resolution of disapproval rebuking Clinton for the FALN situation,[94] the House Government Reform Committee conducted hearings on the Marc Rich pardon, and a grand jury looked into the circumstances surrounding several of the "last-minute" pardons.[95] Congress also held a hearing after the Scooter Libby commutation.[96]

Congress does enjoy a number of indirect (political) checks on the president's pardon decisions. If the public felt strongly enough, it could compel Congress to exercise its constitutional pressure points, via funding cuts, legislative stalemate, and—if necessary—impeachment, to both punish the pardon decision and force the president to think twice before making another controversial clemency decision.[97] In this sense, as constitutional scholar Edward Corwin famously observed about control over foreign affairs, the brief pardon clause in the Constitution can be viewed as another "invitation to struggle" to the executive and legislative branches over constitutional roles and powers.[98]

While the president and Congress fight for supremacy, another tense dynamic is at play between the president—who typically seems to enjoy the constitutional power to grant clemency without interference from the other two branches of government—and the judiciary, which is charged with ensuring the constitutionality of the president's actions.[99] The courts do not normally pay much attention to individual presidential pardons and have usually assumed a "hands-off" posture when asked to settle disputes involving the presidential pardon power. Still, this stance has developed over time because of several courtroom clashes between the executive and legislative branches. I will consider the key legal cases that determined the parameters of the clemency power more carefully in the next chapter.

The Goals of the Pardon Power

The framers' aim in establishing the pardon power was that a virtually unlimited prerogative, coupled with constant political accountability, would be sufficient to force presidents to use clemency in the nation's best interests. As one pardon scholar has pointed out, "The judgment of history is whether the President acted in the broader national interest and not whether he protected his immediate public and political standing."[100]

The public has a right to expect a president to do what he believes is right regardless of personal consequences. As will be shown in later chapters, presidents do not always fulfill this expectation.

Conclusion

The clemency power is one of the few remnants of kingly power vested in the president by the Constitution. Despite serious misgivings about trusting such a far-reaching prerogative in a monarch-like figure, the framers debated and ultimately decided that someone had to be trusted to make such decisions and then be held accountable for them. Considered alongside other Article II powers, the clemency clause is unique in its stark, powerful mandate to the president. With that power comes the discretion to use the clemency power to completely excuse an offense, to merely postpone full punishment, or to select from a range of other options.

The screening mechanism provided by the Pardon Attorney's Office can help a president find political safety. There are always risks to making clemency decisions, but the Pardon Attorney's Office can help by weeding out risks and sometimes taking the blame for a bad decision. Despite the risks, a president should regularly and generously use his clemency power. Establishing a record helps to build public confidence in the president's decisions. Whatever help the pardon attorney provides, the Constitution makes the pardon power the president's responsibility. It makes sense for a president to use political capital on pardons, for it is usually only by using political capital that a president can earn more of it. The framers' goal was for the president to use the pardon power in pursuit of the larger national good.

In the clemency realm, Congress is not without its own levers of influence against the president. Generally speaking, the courts have limited Congress's interference with the pardon power in most cases. Next, I will pursue a case law analysis to show that the chief executive enjoys a broad, virtually unlimited clemency power, but that the clemency power may not belong to the president alone.

2 Executive and Legislative Clemency Power

The focus of this chapter is the legal framework that has made it possible for current presidents to abuse the clemency power to protect themselves or executive branch officials or to reward supporters. Evidence exists in case law for a presidential and possibly a legislative clemency power. In a few landmark cases, the courts have defined key characteristics of presidential pardons and have more or less protected the president from congressional interference. Thus sheltered, presidents have worried little about legal consequences for their clemency grants.

Although the courts have not spoken on congressional clemency in great detail, they have at least acknowledged the possibility that Congress has clemency powers of its own. This is an important issue, as the Constitution—on its face—seems to commit all clemency powers to the president. Any clemency decision made by Congress would seem to interfere with the president's decision to grant or withhold clemency.

Most cases discussing the pardon power focus only on the president, and these cases have created a fairly well-developed understanding of the president's pardon power. Presidents have generally enjoyed free rein—legally, if not always politically—to pardon whomever they wish, for whatever reason they wish. The general role that the judiciary has carved out for itself is "bifurcated," in that a president's reasons for pardoning are generally accepted, but courts will still review cases for unacceptable effects of pardons.[1] Indeed, courts will not invalidate even an "irrationally, misguidedly, or corruptly" granted pardon, but they will review the "constitutionality of the grant, typically whether due process and separation of powers have been honored."[2]

The characteristics of the presidential pardon power that I will explore in this chapter are its nature, extent, effect, and limits. The presidential clemency power—somewhat perplexingly—has two equally valid rationales explaining its nature: the idea that a pardon is an "act of grace" shown by the president to the offender, and the diametrically opposed view that clemency should be granted "as part of the Constitutional scheme"—that is, for the good of the public rather than for the benefit of the individual offender. The extent of the pardon power is broad: A president may pardon at any time following the commission of a crime. However, a pardon does not make an offender "a new man." What effect can a pardon have? In one case, where common law held that a potential witness who had been convicted of larceny could not testify because his testimony would be unreliable, a pardon restored his competency to take the stand. A pardon can restore an offender's competency to vote, but it is not absolute, in that a state may still take into account a pardoned federal offense when sentencing an offender for a subsequent state offense. Nonetheless, a pardon can restore federal and state civil rights. A president may pardon criminal, but not civil, contempt. A president has broad authority regarding conditions added to pardons, but the pardon power also has real limits. Once I have examined these characteristics of the presidential pardon power in more detail, I will look at the evidence for a congressional clemency power.

Executive Clemency Power

The plenary power[3] of federal executive clemency is intended to help bring the United States as close as possible to "equal justice under law." A presidential pardon power is necessary because a perfect justice system is impossible to create—no legislator can pass laws that will lead to a fair result in every possible circumstance.[4] The clemency power, simply put, is intended to provide for a solution in cases where—for whatever reason—normal legal procedures have produced an outcome that seems unjust.

Scholars disagree over who should benefit from the clemency power: the individual offender, or society as a whole.[5] One view is "that the President has a duty to pardon, not so much to do justice in particular cases, but to be merciful as a more general obligation of office."[6] Another outlook is that the clemency power should be used to serve the public welfare, in that the president should ask himself: "Will the public welfare be better served by exercising the power of clemency for this particular case?"[7] Two unanimous Supreme Court decisions have reached these diametrically opposed conclusions, yet both remain valid law.

The earlier rationale, that the president by "act of grace" grants clemency to the lucky chosen few, was first explained in *United States v. Wilson*, an 1833 decision which was also the first Supreme Court case to look at clemency issues. The key legacy of this case is the majority opinion, in which Chief Justice John Marshall, writing for a unanimous Court, explained his view of the nature of the presidential pardon power.

Marshall, connecting British pardon principles and practices to the American understanding of the pardon, suggested that English history would be a useful guide for understanding American federal executive clemency.[8] He then provided the most oft-quoted passage of the Court's opinion:

> A pardon is an act of grace, proceeding from the power intrusted [sic] with the execution of the laws, which exempts the individual, on whom it is bestowed, from the punishment the law inflicts for a crime he has committed. It is the private, though official, act of the executive magistrate, delivered to the individual for whose benefit it is intended, and not communicated officially to the court.[9]

He suggested that, as with the British kings, the American chief executive's pardon power stemmed from the mercy and private discretion of the president himself.[10] The chief justice argued that the intended recipient of a presidential pardon had the power to either accept or reject the president's mercy:

> A pardon is a deed, to the validity of which, delivery is essential, and delivery is not complete, without acceptance. It may then be rejected by the person to whom it is tendered; and if it be rejected, we have discovered no power in a court to force it on him.[11]

In other words, if the true nature of the pardon was that it was an "act of grace," a recipient retained the power to decide whether to accept it or not, much as a recipient of a parcel of land had the power to accept the land or not. For the land transaction to be completed, the deed had to be both delivered to the recipient and accepted by the recipient. So, too, with clemency: No acceptance equals no transaction. In *Wilson*, the key point was the fact that George Wilson had refused to produce a pardon for the Court's notice. Thus, the justices did not consider the pardon in his case.[12]

The opinion of the unanimous *Wilson* Court was apparently contradicted, however, by another unanimous Court opinion. In a "watershed"[13] 1927 case called *Biddle v. Perovich*, the court reviewed Vuco Perovich's conviction for first-degree murder and his death sentence.[14] President William Howard Taft had commuted Perovich's death sentence to life imprisonment, but Perovich refused to accept the commutation.[15] Writing for himself and the other justices (Chief Justice Taft recused himself to avoid a conflict of interest), Justice Oliver Wendell Holmes declined to extend the "act of grace" reasoning of *Wilson* to *Biddle*. In the unanimous decision, Justice Holmes provided a different rationale for the pardon power. Passing on the opportunity to review British pardon principles as Marshall had, he wrote:

> A pardon in our days is not a private act of grace from an individual happening to possess power. It is a part of the Constitutional scheme. When granted it is the determination of the ultimate authority that the public welfare will be better served by inflicting less than what the judgment fixed. [citation omitted] Just as the original punishment would be imposed without regard to the prisoner's consent and in the teeth of his will, whether he liked it or not, the public welfare, not his consent determines what shall be done.[16]

Legal scholars disagree over the effect of the latter decision on the "act of grace" rationale. Did the Court in *Biddle* abandon the "act of grace" rationale? Are both approaches still valid today? One sign that the more recent rationale had been accepted was offered by President Taft himself, who noted that the duty to exercise the pardon power "is a most difficult one to perform. . . . The only rule he can follow is that he shall not exercise it against the public interest."[17] And yet, the original rationale has not gone away. In a recent article, former pardon attorney Roger Adams referred to pardon decision-making as "all a matter of grace."[18] *Wilson* was never overruled, and both rationales are apparently in play today. Still, just because these rationales are widely accepted does not mean they are scrupulously followed by presidents. The presidential pardon power has been invoked by our last three presidents not only in circumstances involving these traditional reasons for exercising executive clemency—showing mercy or ensuring justice—but also in circumstances where the president has enjoyed a personal benefit from the pardon decision.

These presidents have been able to abuse the clemency power in part because of its broad extent. In other words, the courts allow significant latitude to the president regarding his use of the pardon power. The constitutional language granting the pardon power is sparse, and the boundaries of the pardon power have been worked out over time through clashes between the president and Congress. As the majority in *Hoffa v. Saxbe* (1974) noted, "from the very first the Court recognized the inherently broad scope of the pardoning power."[19] Indeed, *Ex parte Garland* (1866) described an extremely flexible clemency power.[20] Here, the majority opinion by Justice Stephen Field noted that the pardon power granted by the Constitution

> thus conferred is unlimited, with the [impeachment] exception stated. It extends to every offence known to the law, and may be exercised at any time after its commission, either before legal proceedings are taken, or during their pendency, or after conviction and judgment. This power of the President is not subject to legislative control. Congress can neither limit the effect of his pardon, nor exclude from its exercise any class of offenders. The benign prerogative of mercy reposed in him cannot be fettered by any legislative restrictions.[21]

According to *Garland*, the pardon power may be used at any time after a crime is committed, whether before, during, or after legal proceedings, conviction, and judgment. The timing of a presidential pardon mentioned in *Garland* has been reaffirmed in subsequent cases.[22]

Though the president has a variety of options for using the pardon power, its effect remains unclear. Another, more controversial passage from *Ex parte Garland* suggests an extraordinarily wide-ranging effect:

> A pardon reaches both the punishment prescribed for the offence and the guilt of the offender; and when the pardon is full, it releases the punishment and *blots out of existence the guilt*, so that in the eye of the law *the offender is as innocent as if he had never committed the offence*. If granted before conviction, it prevents any of the penalties and disabilities consequent upon conviction from attaching; if granted after conviction, it removes the penalties and disabilities, and restores him to all his civil rights; it makes him, as it were, *a new man*, and gives him a new credit and capacity. There is only this limitation to its operation: it does not restore offices forfeited, or property or interests vested in others in consequence of the conviction and judgment.[23]

In a few recent cases, attorneys have argued that this overly broad language suggests that a pardon makes its recipient "a new man," putting him in exactly the same position as an innocent person. The better rule is that a pardon falls short of complete restoration.

Why the confusion over the effect of the clemency power? Ex parte Garland owes key parts of its somewhat confusing rationale to the early English understanding of clemency's effect. Professor Samuel Williston has marked the date of the first observations of English pardon law at the mid–thirteenth century. Quoting the English jurist Henry de Bracton, he articulated the early English understanding of the effect of a pardon: "A person justly and duly outlawed is not restored to anything except to the king's peace, that he may go and return and have protection, but he cannot be restored to his rights of action and other things, for he is like a new-born infant and a man as it were lately born." Bracton's choice of the phrase "new-born infant" has led to uncertainty. As Williston pointed out, it "seems to be the basis of any subsequent assumption that a pardoned offender is to be regarded as an innocent man. The extract, however, shows clearly enough that the writer's idea was not that the offence was regarded by the law as not having been committed, or even as no longer existing, but that the offender, so far as concerned the future, acquired the legal capacity of an innocent man."[24] The language employed here by Bracton is a key source of the ambiguity over the effect of clemency in America.

Williston also cited the English legal decision Cuddington v. Wilkins (1615) as "probably . . . the main foundation of the impression that after a pardon the law could not thereafter see the convict's guilt."[25] Similarly important was another misinterpreted English case, Searle v. Williams (1619), on which Williston commented:

> But that the court meant that the legal infamy of the conviction was removed, not that the offender was "as innocent as if he had never committed the offence" is evident from the following sentence in the report: "It was said, that he could no more call him thief, in the present tense, than to say a man hath the pox, or is a villain after he be cured or manumised, but that he had been a thief or villain he might say."[26]

These misunderstandings of the true effect of the pardon power have influenced the American comprehension of federal executive clemency.

Several American cases have reexamined just how far the "new man" principle—that is, the power of a pardon to restore certain rights to an offender—should be extended. In an 1892 case, *Boyd v. United States*, the Court found that despite a common law rule that a potential witness convicted of federal larceny charges was therefore incompetent to testify, Martin Byrd could testify because a presidential pardon had restored his competency as a witness.[27]

In a 1914 case, *Carlesi v. New York*, the Supreme Court recognized that the effect of a pardon was not really to "blot out of existence the guilt, so that in the eye of the law the offender is as innocent as if he had never committed the offence." Although *Carlesi* recognized a broad view of the effect of a pardon, the majority held that a presidential pardon did not make the offender "a new man," and that a pardon was something less than the complete erasing of an offense, in that an earlier, pardoned federal offense could still be considered by a state when that state was punishing the offender for a state offense.[28]

Does a pardon make an offender a "new man" sufficiently to reclaim state civil rights? In the 1975 case *Bjerkan v. United States*, the Court of Appeals determined the effect of a federal pardon on the "collateral consequences" of an offender's conviction, in this case, its recipient's state civil rights.[29] Although a pardon does not take away the stigma associated with conviction, or the fact that the conviction occurred, the court determined that it could remove some of the bad effects. The court adopted Williston's view[30] and drew the distinction as follows: Later court proceedings could consider the fact that someone committed a crime, but they could not consider the conviction itself, after a pardon was given. In other words, a pardon could erase the results of a *conviction*, but any effects of *committing* the crime continued on. Here, the court ruled that a presidential pardon brought back James Bjerkan's state and federal civil rights.[31]

Ex parte Grossman stands for the proposition that the president can pardon for criminal contempt of court, but not for civil contempt of court.[32] In *Grossman*, the majority decided that unlike civil contempt cases, "criminal contempts were within the understood scope of the pardoning power of the executive."[33] The two offenses serve different purposes: Whereas a civil contempt is "coercive" and is imposed to pressure someone to follow the court's instructions, a criminal contempt is "strictly punitive" and typically requires "a determinate sentence of imprisonment or a fine." While a criminal contempt is clearly a pardonable offense after *Grossman*, "civil contempts of court are not." Indeed, the president's pardon power is limited to "offenses against the United States," and civil litigants in a suit between private parties are not eligible because the United States does not have an interest in the proceedings.[34]

Perhaps a more important finding for our purposes was that *Grossman*, according to constitutional scholar William Duker, "arms the President with a power that enables him to shield his subordinates against judicial interference."[35] In other words, as another scholar suggested, it "effectively enabled the president to shield subordinate executive branch personnel from both judicial inquiry and congressional investigation."[36] Although *Grossman* clarified that presidents have the legal power to excuse their executive branch officials from criminal contempt of court, it is only recently that they have had the political cover to do so.

Aside from impeaching or refusing to reelect a president who abuses the pardon power, the courts have identified roughly four constitutional limits on the pardoning power. The first limit is that "a pardon cannot interfere with the vested property rights of third parties in violation of the Takings Clause." The second is that "a pardon cannot require the payment of funds from the Treasury in violation of the Spending Clause." These two limits are spelled out in the Civil War cases discussed later. The third limit, from *Hoffa v. Saxbe*, is that "a pardon cannot require a prisoner to forfeit his constitutional rights unreasonably." Fourth, the Court recognizes that "the procedures by which a pardon is granted must comply with the Fifth Amendment's Due Process Clause," as discussed in the context of Justice Sandra Day O'Connor's concurrence in *Ohio Adult Parole Authority v. Woodard* (1998), where she suggests that "some minimal procedural safeguards" may be required.[37] We will examine *Woodard*'s relevance more closely at the end of this chapter.

Although recent pardon cases have not expanded the reach of the clemency power, a few have tested its boundaries and helped establish clear limits. A few pardon recipients have argued that a pardon should not only forgive the offense but also erase any sign of the conviction, including court records. One such case was *United States v. Noonan* in 1990, in which an amnestied draft evader suggested that one effect of President Jimmy Carter's 1977 amnesty proclamation was to grant violators of the Military Selective Service Act who had been excused by the proclamation the right to have records relating to their draft offenses expunged. The majority framed the issue as follows: "whether restoring 'full political, civil and other rights' may entitle the pardoned person to expunction of a criminal record on other grounds." The court concluded that Noonan's pardon did not erase the record of his conviction.[38]

One of George H. W. Bush's most controversial pardon recipients, former CIA deputy director for operations Clair George, was indicted and found guilty of making a false statement and committing perjury in his congressional testimony regarding the Iran-Contra investigation. Before his conviction could be entered, however, he was pardoned. George then requested that the court reimburse him for more than $1 million in attorneys' fees. The statute under which George claimed reimbursement allowed the court to award attorneys' fees to persons who—like George— were "subjects" of an independent counsel investigation, but only if that "subject" was not indicted. George was indicted, but he argued that his pardon restored his eligibility to qualify for reimbursement.[39]

The court noted that Clair George's request asked it to violate Article I, Section 9, Clause 7, of the Constitution, which requires any payment of money from the U.S. Treasury to be appropriated by law. Moreover, George's request did not fit under the statutory language that allowed reimbursement only to unindicted claimants. The court found that "the pardon does not remove his disability." It noted that the wide-ranging dictum from *Garland* had been narrowed over time and did not extend far enough into the past of George's offense to save his claim. The majority wrote that "because a pardon does not blot out guilt or expunge a judgment of *conviction*, one can conclude that a pardon does not blot out probable cause of guilt or expunge an *indictment*. George's disability remains."[40]

In a D.C. Court of Appeals case,[41] another Iran-Contra figure, former assistant secretary of state for inter-American affairs Elliott Abrams, challenged the Board on Professional Responsibility's decision to suspend him from practicing law in Washington, D.C., for one year. The board reached this decision after finding that Abrams's false (although unsworn) congressional testimony regarding the U.S. government's role in the Iran-Contra affair constituted "dishonesty, deceit or misrepresentation." After Abrams pleaded guilty to criminal charges, President George H. W. Bush granted him a full and unconditional pardon. Abrams's argument on appeal was not that his pardon prevented disciplinary proceedings from being brought against him. Instead, he argued that his pardon, which unquestionably blotted out his *convictions*, also blotted out *the underlying con-*

duct that led to the convictions. As a result, Abrams argued that the board's charges against him must be dismissed.[42]

The court agreed with Abrams to the extent that his pardon set aside his convictions and the legal consequences of those convictions, but the agreement ended there. The court said that Abrams's pardon "could not and did not require the court to close its eyes to the fact that Abrams did what he did." It could not restore the moral character necessary for him to continue to practice law, and the "court's authority to impose professional discipline was not nullified by the presidential pardon."[43]

May a president grant a conditional pardon? And if so, how much flexibility does a president have when attaching conditions to a pardon? Can the president request that a clemency recipient agree to give up additional rights? In 1833's *United States v. Wilson*, the Court suggested that "a pardon may be conditional. . . . It may be absolute or conditional."[44] It was not until 1855 that the Court directly confronted the question of whether the president may grant a pardon that requires the recipient to do or not do something in order for the clemency grant to take effect.

William Wells was convicted of murder and sentenced to hang. Wells accepted a conditional pardon from President Millard Fillmore.[45] The pardon commuted Wells's death sentence to life in prison. Wells accepted the pardon, then later argued that the condition was "illegal," in that the president was violating the separation of powers by essentially legislating a new penalty for him. He also contended that a president could not grant a conditional pardon because the Constitution did not specifically grant that power.[46]

The Court found that the power to grant a conditional pardon was one manifestation of the constitutional pardon power. Moreover, it found that the decision to substitute punishments was made by Wells himself, not the president.[47] In other words, the president was not legislating a new punishment for Wells; he simply offered Wells a choice of punishments. After *Wells*, the president could condition a grant of clemency on the intended recipient's agreement to, as noted by one pardon scholar, "virtually any terms."[48]

The president's power to grant a conditional pardon was challenged again in a 1974 case, *Schick v. Reed*. In 1960, President Dwight Eisenhower commuted Maurice Schick's 1954 death sentence to life in prison with the express understanding that Schick would never be eligible for parole.

Schick agreed, then served twenty years from the date of his death sentence before challenging the condition.[49] The statutory punishments in effect at the time of Schick's offense for murder (Schick's crime) were either the death penalty or life imprisonment with possible parole.[50] Controversy swirled around the condition in Schick's pardon waiving his right to parole, a requirement that was imposed by Eisenhower and not contemplated by the statute under which Schick was convicted.

Without the condition in the pardon waiving his right to parole, Schick argued, he could have been eligible for parole consideration in 1969.[51] The Court found that the pardon power included the power to commute sentences, as long as the penalty did not violate the Constitution.[52] The president thus had the power under Article II, Section 2, to craft individual sentences for particular defendants, provided he did "not aggravate punishment[s]" imposed by statute.[53] Congress could not interfere with the president's pardon power.[54] Rather, since the pardon power was a specific, constitutionally granted prerogative, any limitations on the power could only be located in the Constitution itself.[55]

The *Schick* decision reignited the debate on the scope of the president's pardon power vis-à-vis Congress. Some legal scholars expressed reservations regarding this decision because the Court arguably rubber-stamped a condition that may have unconstitutionally *increased* Schick's punishment. "By definition," one scholar argued, "the exercise of the pardoning power contemplates a *lessening* of the judicially imposed penalty." In other words, by merely *changing* and not actually cutting the penalty, the executive would be trespassing on the legislature's turf. The legislature's ability to dictate punishment functions as a limit on the executive's pardon power, not merely as a form of protection for the individual up for clemency.[56] Other legal scholars concurred.[57]

Not all legal scholars had qualms or reservations about this decision, though. According to another line of thought, the Court correctly decided that the clemency power could win out over congressional action. Though acknowledging the argument that Article II, Section 2, Clause 1, forbids a president from increasing an offender's penalty, another scholar suggested that conditional pardons were different: As long as the convict agreed, he or she should in essence be allowed to trade away constitutional rights. Nonetheless, he recognized that on occasion—specifically, when waiving rights would "threaten critical social values . . . or . . . 'shock the conscience' . . . or impose new punishment"—courts should step in anyway.[58]

Given the courts' preference for a sweeping clemency power, the latter line of argument appears most persuasive.

The *Schick* decision posed a perplexing question: Under what circumstances would a conditional pardon *not* be accepted? In another 1974 case, *Hoffa v. Saxbe*, the D.C. District Court suggested an answer. On December 23, 1971, President Richard Nixon granted a sentence commutation to Teamsters president James Hoffa that reduced his sentence to only six and a half years in prison, provided he would agree not to be involved in any labor organization management until March 6, 1980. The D.C. District Court heard Hoffa's suit to have the condition in his pardon warrant held invalid.[59]

The court tackled the main question in the case: Did limiting Hoffa's union management activities until 1980 offend the Constitution? To decide, the court established a new constitutional standard for evaluating the appropriateness of a conditional pardon.[60] The *Hoffa* majority articulated a two-pronged test that, according to one scholar, "remains the most explicit statement by a federal court of the limitations that may constrain the exercise of the executive clemency power."[61] Those conditions are, "first, that the condition be directly related to the public interest; and second, that the condition not unreasonably infringe on the individual commutee's constitutional freedoms."[62] Applying this new test, the court upheld the condition in Hoffa's pardon warrant.[63] Under the more confining limits of this new test, the president was still allowed to award a pardon for any reason he wished, but he could not issue a conditional pardon that violated either "prong" of this test.[64] Hoffa disappeared while this case was pending, and it ended soon thereafter.[65]

The nature, extent, effect, and limits of the presidential pardon power seem relatively clear, but those parameters were developed over years of court challenges that continue still today. The evidence for a legislative pardon power is less compelling. Nevertheless, a closer look at the precedents for a congressional clemency power will show that there are good reasons why pardoning has generally been left to presidents.

Congressional Clemency Power

The Constitution assigns the power to "grant reprieves and pardons" to the president, and this grant has been found to include other uses of the clemency powers, including the ability to grant amnesty. However, according to some scholars, Article II, Section II, Clause 1, is not an *exclusive* grant of clemency power to the president. The Constitution does not explicitly state that only the president may exercise clemency powers (although Congress does not enjoy a similar constitutional clause), and a court has never held that the president's pardon power forbids Congress from passing general amnesties. What is more, if Congress is allowed to grant amnesties, it is only logical that it should also be allowed to pardon individuals.[66] Congress could, for example, give pardons where the president refused to act.[67] One can support a congressional pardon power even if it is not practical for Congress to use it.[68]

The question as to whether Congress has its own pardoning authority has never been directly confronted by the courts.[69] Still, Congress has not been shy about attempting to claim clemency powers for itself. The legislature's most aggressive attacks on the presidential pardon power occurred during several Civil War and Reconstruction cases. The political atmosphere—supercharged by the historic battle between the North and the South—heightened the stakes for a struggle over which branch had the power to grant amnesty to former Confederates, a situation that, according to one scholar, led to "the most significant congressional efforts to constrain and regulate the President's pardoning power."[70]

The Supreme Court had ruled that the president had the power to grant a general amnesty in 1872, but it refused to weigh in again until a serious struggle between Congress and the president made intervention necessary.[71] Congress made a power grab for a share of the pardoning power by adding a controversial clause to one of a series of Confiscation Acts. The Confiscation Acts were created by the legislature to provide a mechanism for handling the disposition of Confederate property. Article II, Section 2, Clause 1, notwithstanding, this Confiscation Acts clause[72] purported to grant the president the power to "pardon and amnesty" rebels.[73] President Abraham Lincoln issued two "pardon and amnesties,"[74] and President Andrew Johnson issued four,[75] as they pursued their goal of "lessening the man power of the Confederacy."[76] The president, of course, had the power to "grant reprieves and pardons" under the Constitution, but did he have the power to issue amnesties as well? Did Congress have amnesty powers of its own? The Court decided the first question in the affirmative in 1872, but the second issue has still not been definitively settled.

In the cases analyzed below, I revisit the struggle between pro-amnesty presidents Abraham Lincoln and Andrew Johnson and anti-amnesty Radical Republicans in Congress. In refereeing these cases, the Court's approach nearly every time was to allow the president a wide scope of authority, although it allowed or disallowed the pardons granted in the particular circumstances of the cases. Even so, at least two cases, *The Laura* (1885) and *Brown v. Walker* (1896), represent some support for the idea that perhaps Congress has its own clemency power.

One of the most sensitive questions faced by the United States government during the Civil War was how to entice Confederates to rejoin the Union. A related question was how to treat them: Should they be punished? If so, how severely? The Supreme Court tackled one manifestation of these questions in *Ex parte Garland*. On July 2, 1862, Congress passed a law requiring all federal officers except the president to swear an oath that they had never aided or served in the Confederate government.[77] This law was broadened on January 24, 1865, when Congress required attorneys who wished to practice in the federal courts to also take the oath.[78] A. H. Garland, a former U.S., then Confederate, officeholder from Arkansas, had taken an oath in 1860 before he was admitted to the American bar, but he had since participated in the rebellion and was unable to take the new oath. Nonetheless, he received a full pardon from the president in July 1865, and then petitioned to practice law without having sworn the oath, contending that the January 24, 1865, act of Congress was unconstitutional, or that if it was constitutional, his pardon should relieve the need to take another oath.[79]

The Supreme Court agreed with Garland, finding that Congress's new oath requirement was void as a bill of attainder and ex post facto law. While the Court acknowledged that Congress generally enjoyed the right to establish "qualifications" for attorneys, in Garland's situation, it said, Congress had wielded this power not merely to establish "qualifications," but to punish Garland for his disloyalty. Perhaps more important than Garland's fate was Justice Stephen Field's oft-cited dicta (or discussion unrelated to the central holding of the case) on the scope and effect of the presidential pardon power discussed earlier.[80] Even today, attorneys on either side of a pardon controversy reliably cite this passage when a pre-indictment pardon is at issue. In this and subsequent cases (notably Ford's pardon of Nixon), the Court has consistently upheld the president's right to grant a pre-indictment pardon.

Another point explored earlier was Justice Field's wide-sweeping pronouncement of the pardon power's reach. The *Garland* Court's apparent misinterpretation of English precedents initially led to the understanding that the American pardon power was virtually unlimited in its reach.[81] Although the sweeping dicta of the second passage would gradually be reined in by later cases, the more relevant point here is that once again, the Court sided with the president's view of the pardon power and against Congress.

Another Civil War–era case, *Armstrong's Foundry*, addressed the sensitive question regarding ownership of property belonging to Confederate sympathizers that had been confiscated by and forfeited to the U.S. government. John Armstrong owned Armstrong's Foundry in New Orleans, Louisiana, which was seized by the U.S. government as forfeited property because it was used in the rebellion. During the condemnation process, Armstrong produced a full "pardon and amnesty" granted to him personally by the president. He argued that the pardon forgave his offense and required the U.S. government to return the foundry to him.[82]

In court, the attorney general argued that the penalty provided by the applicable statute—the Confiscation Act of August 6, 1861[83]—was meant to suppress *property* from being used in the rebellion, not to punish individual offenders. Thus, he contended that the pardon could only relieve Armstrong *himself* from a penalty, not his property. The Supreme Court majority disagreed with the attorney general.[84]

Other cases considered in this chapter proceeded under the Confiscation Act of August 6, 1861 (like *Armstrong's Foundry*), the Confiscation Act of July 17, 1862, or under the Captured and Abandoned Property Act of March 12, 1863. Claimants would not always recover from the government, but the president's pardon power was nearly always upheld by the Court, as will be shown.

In *United States v. Padelford*, as in *Garland*, another clash between a presidential amnesty and congressional legislation intended to defeat the president's amnesty proclamation resulted in a presidential victory. Edward Padelford, a Savannah, Georgia, bank director, bowed to intense Confederate pressure in April 1861 and committed $5,000 of his personal funds and $100,000 of his bank's funds to a $15 million loan to the Confederates. Sometime before October 1863, Padelford "voluntarily executed" as surety three bonds for personal friends that allowed them to assume Confederate offices and avoid dangerous military service.[85]

President Lincoln announced his first amnesty proclamation on December 8, 1863.[86] Padelford was included among the amnestied class and complied with the proclamation's relevant provisions. The Union recaptured

Savannah on December 21, 1864, and Padelford proclaimed his allegiance to the Union under this amnesty proclamation on January 18, 1865.[87] Even so, *after* Padelford had sworn his allegiance to the Union, the government seized and sold cotton belonging to Padelford and another man, Randolph Mott, and deposited the proceeds in the U.S. Treasury.[88] Padelford and Mott filed a petition in the Court of Claims under the Captured and Abandoned Property Act for the proceeds of the sale of their cotton.[89] Their claims were heard separately; Padelford won in the lower court, the government appealed, and the Supreme Court agreed to hear the case.[90] Before the Supreme Court could hear the case, though, Congress passed a law requiring claimants in Padelford's position to "prove affirmatively" their constant loyalty during the rebellion.[91]

Citing *Garland* and *Armstrong's Foundry*, the Court found that the amnesty proclamation excused Padelford from any disloyalty, and—despite the new law requiring affirmative proof of loyalty—ruled that Padelford was entitled to the proceeds of his cotton.[92] Once again, the Court sided with the president. However, not all claimants were able to successfully claim their proceeds as easily as Padelford was. As will be shown later, the statute under which a claimant pursued his or her proceeds apparently made a difference to the Court.

In *United States v. Klein*, V. F. Wilson had voluntarily become surety for Confederate officers, but later swore his loyalty to the Union under President Lincoln's December 8, 1863, amnesty proclamation.[93] Upon Wilson's death in 1865, John Klein, Wilson's administrator, filed a petition with the Court of Claims to recover the proceeds of the sale of Wilson's cotton, which had been abandoned to the government and sold, with the proceeds deposited in the U.S. Treasury, according to the Captured and Abandoned Property Act.[94] The Court of Claims decided on May 26, 1869, that Wilson was entitled to the proceeds of his cotton, but the government appealed later that same year. On April 30, 1870, the Court announced its decision in *Padelford*, a case with similar facts to *Klein* that allowed Padelford, the claimant, to recover his proceeds.[95]

However, two congressional actions complicated Klein's case. First, on January 21, 1867, Congress repealed section 13 of the Confiscation Act of July 17, 1862, which had purported to give the president the power to proclaim "pardon and amnesty."[96] Second, shortly after the *Padelford* decision, Congress passed a proviso attached to an appropriations bill that the Court later found—to Congress's chagrin—had as its "great and controlling purpose . . . to deny to pardons granted by the President the effect which this court had adjudged them to have."[97]

The Court disposed of the first question presented by this case, that is, whether the president continued to have the power of "pardon and amnesty" even after the repeal of section 13 of the Confiscation Act, with a resounding yes. The president continued to have the power to declare an amnesty even though the Constitution on its face seemed to only grant the president the power to "grant reprieves and pardons." Sound policy reasons supported this interpretation in this particular case. The Court understood that Congress intended in its Captured and Abandoned Property Act not to divest the title to proceeds from original owners, whether rebel or not, but rather to use the Treasury as a trustee until the original property owners had an opportunity to proclaim their loyalty to the Union and recover their property. The Court noted that the repeal of the statute occurred after the end of the Civil War, and that even though it was repealed, the nation's obligation to restore the rights of property or its proceeds to those receiving pardons continued on, as did the effect of the president's pardon offer itself.[98]

Congress fared no better with its second legislative attempt to frustrate the president's pardons. The Court looked back to the nation's founding for the principle that "each of the great co-ordinate departments of the government—the Legislative, the Executive, and the Judicial—shall be, in its sphere, independent of the others." Reiterating the pardon clause in Article II, Section 2, the Court noted that "to the executive alone is intrusted the power of pardon; and it is granted without limit." Although the power to grant "amnesty" is not specifically awarded to the president in the Constitution, the Court reached the same conclusion as another contemporary case, *Armstrong v. United States*, that "pardon includes amnesty."[99]

The Court's decision in this case ended the controversy over whether "pardon and amnesty" language included in congressional legislation could give Congress some control over the president: It could not. The Court had decided that for sound policy reasons, and—more importantly, via constitutional interpretation—that the pardon power gave the president the ability to grant amnesties free from congressional interference. Whether Congress had its own powers of amnesty, however, remained unclear. The Court disapproved Congress's attempt to use legislation to force the Court to check the president by denying to his pardons their proper effect.[100] The Court ruled that through this proviso, "Congress has inadvertently passed the limit which separates the legislative from the judicial power," and held the legislation to be void.[101] The Court then affirmed the Court of Claims judgment in favor of Klein. Another battle between the president and Congress refereed by the Supreme Court, another victory for the president.

Not all rebels were U.S. citizens. In one case, a question arose as to whether non–U.S. citizens who had joined the rebellion should benefit from the president's amnesty proclamation and be able to recover their property. In *Carlisle v. United States* (1872), the claimants were English citizens living in the United States before the rebellion. They had petitioned in the Court of Claims under the Captured and Abandoned Property Act for the value of cotton that was stored in Alabama before it was seized and sold, with the proceeds deposited into the U.S. Treasury. The Court of Claims, however, ruled that because the claimants had knowingly sold saltpeter (to be used for manufacturing gunpowder) to the Confederates, they were not entitled to recover the proceeds. The Supreme Court agreed with the Court of Claims that these actions by the claimants constituted providing aid and comfort to the rebellion, but found that they were still entitled to recover the proceeds of their cotton as long as they met the requirements of President Johnson's December 25, 1868, amnesty proclamation, and provided their status as aliens did not foreclose recovery.[102]

Setting their alien status aside for a moment, the Court found that prior decisions (*Padelford, Klein, Armstrong,* and an additional case not considered here, *Pargoud v. United States*[103]) suggested that the claimants would otherwise qualify for reimbursement.[104] As with "native" rebels, the aliens were subject to American law for treason and aiding the enemy and were eligible to be punished for its violations. Similarly, they should benefit from the president's amnesty proclamation.[105] The Court ruled that the president's December 25, 1868, amnesty proclamation was meant to include aliens in the claimants' position, and allowed the claimants to recover their proceeds. The president's amnesty proclamation was thus broadened to include noncitizens as well as citizens.

Perhaps the most important contribution of the next case to understanding the presidential pardon power was that the Court explicitly spelled out that "the constitutional grant to the President of the power to pardon offences must be held to carry with it, as an incident, the power to release penalties and forfeitures which accrue from the offences."[106]

The facts of *Osborn v. United States* (1876) are somewhat confusing, but

lead to a clear result. During the rebellion, a man named Brown had mortgaged some real estate he owned in Kansas and used the proceeds to
secure bonds that—once he was found to be a Confederate sympathizer—
were then forfeited to the U.S. government under the Confiscation Act of
1862.[107] In June 1863, the month after the forfeiture, the Kansas District
Court ordered debtors on the bonds to pay them off, or else the mortgaged
properties would be sold. Most debtors failed to pay, and the sale of some
properties brought in over $20,000, which was "indiscriminately mixed"
with proceeds from other confiscation cases. The money was not deposited into the U.S. Treasury, but added to a fund used by court officers to
pay those who assisted with the condemnation proceedings and sales.[108]

In April 1866, Brown petitioned the court to recover the proceeds of his
property. He pursued only the proceeds because he could not recover the
bonds or the property, since title to each had since vested in a third party.
Earlier, in September 1865, Brown had received a full "pardon and
amnesty," which contained a condition that he "should not by virtue of the
pardon claim any property, or the proceeds of any property, which had
been sold by the order, judgment or decree of a court under the confiscation laws of the United States."[109]

As noted by the majority in a later case, *Knote v. United States* (1877), the
Circuit Court in *Osborn* opined that Brown should be allowed to recover the
proceeds because he had been pardoned, the proceeds were still under the
court's control, and there was no other impediment preventing their
restoration to him.[110] The Supreme Court majority in *Osborn* agreed,[111] finding that the pardon forgave the offense (treason) that led to the forfeiture,
and that since no third-party rights in the property had vested, Brown was
entitled to the proceeds. The Court noted that Brown's conditional pardon
did not prevent his recovery under the circumstances.[112]

The fact situation in *Osborn* is included above to illustrate how the result
of these Civil War cases can turn on two factors: the statute under which
the property at issue was taken, and whether or not the proceeds of that
property had been deposited in the U.S. Treasury. Contrast the result in *Osborn* with that of *Knote v. United States*.

Knote owned property in West Virginia that—in accordance with the
1862 Confiscation Act—was condemned, forfeited to the U.S. government,
and then sold, with its $11,000 in sale proceeds deposited into the U.S.
Treasury. Knote tried unsuccessfully to claim the proceeds of the sale from

the government under President Johnson's December 25, 1868, unconditional full "amnesty and pardon."[113]

Justice Field gave the opinion of the Court.[114] Citing *Klein*, the Court reaffirmed that it recognized no legal difference between the terms "pardon" and "amnesty": "All the benefits which can result to the claimant from both pardon and amnesty would equally have accrued to him if the term 'pardon' alone had been used in the proclamation of the President. In Klein's case, this court said that pardon included amnesty."[115]

The Court seemed to regard the fact that the proceeds had been paid into the Treasury as a crucial difference from cases such as *Osborn*, where the Treasury had not yet entered the picture. In *Knote*, the Court seemed to place great emphasis on the fact that rights to the property had vested elsewhere, and that the new owner should be protected even over the pardoned original owner.[116] Applying this logic to the U.S. Treasury as if it were a third-party purchaser, the Court declared that "if the proceeds have been paid into the treasury, the right to them has so far become vested in the United States that they can only be secured to the former owner of the property through an act of Congress. Moneys once in the treasury can only be withdrawn by an appropriation by law."[117] If, however, as in Brown's case, the proceeds had not yet been paid into the Treasury, the Court suggested, Knote's pardon may have allowed him a chance to recover.[118] However, "The proceeds have . . . passed when paid over to the individual entitled to them, in the one case, or are covered into the treasury, in the other."[119] Thus, because Knote's property had been seized by the government and the proceeds vested in the Treasury, the Court ruled against him and prevented him from recovering the proceeds, absent an act of Congress.

The Court found that claimants in Knote's situation are simply out of luck, pardoned or not, because a pardon cannot force the U.S. Treasury to pay anyone unless Congress orders it to do so.[120] As a result, the Court ruled in *Knote* that the appropriations power of Congress can limit the reach of the pardon power. This case does not, however, support the idea that Congress could influence the president's power to issue a pardon by using appropriations limitations. Any direct congressional action in any form—whether via statute or restriction on appropriations—would unconstitutionally interfere with Article II. Although this decision prevents a pardon from affecting the title to property seized by the government before a pardon and sold to a third person, it would not have prevented Knote from recovering the proceeds if the government had remained in control of the property.[121]

As noted above, in *Knote*, the Court seized upon the fact that the proceeds from the claimant's land were deposited in the U.S. Treasury as a key to denying the claimant's recovery. This is confusing, since claimants in other cases (*Padelford, Klein,* and *Carlisle*) had been allowed to recover their proceeds even from the U.S. Treasury. However, claimants Padelford, Klein, and Carlisle proceeded under the 1863 Captured and Abandoned Property Act for their recoveries. Of the cases considered here, only Brown, like Knote, proceeded under the 1862 Confiscation Act. The crucial difference between claimants Brown and Knote was apparently the fact that Brown's proceeds had not yet been deposited in the U.S. Treasury at the time of his claim and Knote's had. The limit on the president's pardon power imposed by this case is one of the few instances where the Court favored Congress's view. The next case is another.

On March 3, 1861, Simeon Hart, an El Paso, Texas, resident, was an active Confederate sympathizer; by April, he had joined the Confederates and was supplying the rebellion with supplies, money, and transportation to aid their campaign into New Mexico. On November 3, 1865, he received a full pardon for his participation in the rebellion. Hart claimed that the United States owed him money for supplies he had delivered to the U.S. government.[122]

In the Court of Claims, the majority applied Joint Resolution No. 46, approved March 2, 1867, in which Congress essentially forbade the U.S. government from paying any outstanding account existing before April 13, 1861, that was owed to a Confederate.[123] Although the resolution stated that "no pardon heretofore granted, or hereafter to be granted, shall authorize the payment of such account, claim or demand," the court noted that its final decision did not rely on this provision. Despite Hart's contentions, the court held that his presidential pardon would not lead to payment.[124] The Supreme Court agreed.[125]

To his dismay, Hart was unable to recover for any pre–April 13, 1861, expenses, and the Supreme Court also agreed with the Court of Claims' ruling that the government did not owe Hart for his post–April 13, 1861, expenses either.[126] Thus, in a slightly different factual scenario from *Knote*, the Supreme Court reaffirmed its earlier ruling that even a presidential pardon could not force Congress to pay a debt out of a general appropriation unless Congress had authorized it.

Despite the courts' preference in these Civil War cases for allowing the president a virtually unchecked clemency power, two other cases seemed to suggest that the pardon power was not exclusively the president's, and that Congress might indeed have its own pardon power. The first case to provide some evidence for a congressional clemency power was The Laura (1885).

At the time of The Laura, federal statutes regulating steam vessels on U.S. waters limited the number of passengers that could be on board at one time. The libellant in this case sued to enforce a lien for payment of a penalty of $5,611 for violations of what were essentially "maximum occupancy" statutes. Before a trial could be held in the district court, the owner of the steamship produced a warrant issued by the secretary of the treasury giving him "all the right, claim and demand of the United States . . . to said forfeiture . . . on payment of costs." As a result, once the costs were paid, the libel case was dismissed. The libellant argued that the case should not have been dismissed; he believed that the statute allowing the secretary of the treasury to issue the warrant of remission conflicted with—and encroached upon—the "exclusive" pardon power of the president, who enjoyed the sole right to remit fines, penalties, and forfeitures imposed by the United States.[127]

Instead of following the more likely course of action here—that is, quickly agreeing that the power to remit forfeitures or penalties resulting from breaking federal laws was exclusively vested in the president via Article II, Section 2, Clause 1, the Court hesitated,[128] then reached the somewhat surprising conclusion that the federal statute that gave the secretary of the treasury the power to remit fines, penalties, and forfeitures imposed on steamship owners for occupancy violations was, indeed, constitutional. The presidential pardon power, according to the Court, was not "exclusive," in that it had been exercised by the secretary of the treasury and other officers since the late eighteenth century under similar circumstances. In an earlier case cited in the majority opinion, the Court had "arguably acceded to the practice," according to one scholar.[129] As a result, The Laura provides some support for the idea that the pardon power is not exclusively vested in the president. Another scholar, however, disagreed that this case did much to advance that notion, characterizing The Laura as "slim authority for the proposition that Congress may itself grant pardons or amnesty."[130] Another case, Brown v. Walker, did more to suggest that Congress might have pardoning powers of its own.

In *Brown v. Walker* (1896), petitioner Theodore Brown had responded to a subpoena and was answering questions as a witness in front of a grand jury regarding a violation of the Interstate Commerce Act when he decided to exercise his Fifth Amendment right to remain silent. A federal immunity statute that applied to witnesses testifying under subpoena from the Interstate Commerce Commission (ICC) provided these witnesses (such as Brown) with "transaction immunity" from being charged with any crimes as a result of their testimony.[131]

The *Brown* majority seems to have supported—implicitly, if not explicitly—"the right of the federal government, by statute or by pardon, to thrust immunity involuntarily upon a recalcitrant witness." The Court found that the protections offered by the federal statute were—according to one scholar—just as broad as the Fifth Amendment and, in any case, sufficient to protect Brown.[132] The Court, comparing the statute's effect to a general amnesty, acknowledged that the presidential pardon power had "never been held to take from Congress the power to pass acts of general amnesty" and that "the distinction between amnesty and pardon" was "of no practical importance."[133] What is more, the Court found that—similar to a pardon—the immunity provided by the federal statute that covered Brown prevented him from asserting his Fifth Amendment privilege to refuse to answer the grand jury's questions.[134] This is because once a witness has received the immunity provided by the federal statute, he cannot claim that his answers will incriminate and penalize him—he already "stands with respect to such offense as if it had never been committed." The dissent contended that the federal statute in question essentially allowed Congress to grant a pardon, which was solely the prerogative of the president.[135]

What does the *Brown* decision mean today? One scholar has argued that, according to *Brown*, "the power to grant clemency has been held to be vested concurrently in the Congress."[136] Other scholars are more skeptical. One factor mitigating against a congressional pardon power is the possibility that the president's pardon preferences may be affected by Congress's decision to pardon—or not pardon—an offender. Another problem with allowing Congress to grant clemency would be the likelihood that pardon decisions would be subject to the same "log-rolling, deal-making," and other means of passing legislation that would "be inconsistent with the Pardon clause" and "bad policy as well." Then there is the dearth of examples since the founding: Congress has only exclusively granted one general amnesty in the past (under the Fourteenth Amendment, following the Civil War). Thus, despite "some statutory examples of legislative amnesty, there is no clear past practice that would influence the interpretation of congressional amnesty power."[137]

Despite what these two odd cases seem to suggest, the latter appears to be the better line of reasoning, especially given the framers' intent to keep at least the Senate out of the pardoning business. As noted in Chapter 1, George Mason and Edmund Randolph were cautious about combining the Senate and the president's powers in pardoning decisions, finding that, in Mason's words, "the Senate already has too much power."[138]

Conclusion

This chapter establishes that the presidential pardon power, which exists in a brief passage in Article II, Section 2, Clause 1, has over time been explored and explained by court decisions. The courts have interpreted the various characteristics of the presidential pardon power, including its nature, the extent of the power, its effects, its limits, and the difference between an absolute and a conditional pardon.

Although lacking a constitutional pardon clause of its own, Congress aggressively involved itself in clemency decisions by passing legislation to interfere with the president's pardons or amnesties of the Civil War and Reconstruction era. We looked at two cases that suggest that Congress may have clemency powers of its own. The better line of argument seems to be for a president-dominated clemency power, based on prior practice as well as the fact that any clemency decision made by Congress would seem to interfere with the president's decision to grant (or withhold) clemency.

The courts' approach to clemency cases over the years has been propresident, and they have generally protected the clemency power from congressional interference. In a concurring opinion in *Public Citizen v. U.S. Dept. of Justice* (1989), the Court used the pardon power as an example of a presidential power that is free from legislative meddling.[139]

The courts have in most cases upheld a broad clemency power and assumed a "hands-off" attitude when reviewing clemency cases. In a case involving a state clemency decision, *Ohio Adult Parole Authority v. Woodard* (1998), the Court reaffirmed that "pardon and commutation decisions . . . are rarely, if ever, appropriate subjects for judicial review."[140] In her *Woodard* concurring opinion, Justice Sandra Day O'Connor "left the door open" for Court review to ensure nonarbitrary state pardon processes.[141] Though

O'Connor carefully limited her comments to state pardon cases, another pardon scholar has astutely observed that the same logic could apply to presidential pardons. He argued that "the Court has not indicated that it will turn a blind eye to any and all [pardoning] procedures," but admitted that it is difficult to imagine a likely scenario where the Court *would* intervene in a presidential pardoning decision.[142] The Supreme Court remains ready to step in when clemency challenges occur.

The Court's preference for the president does not mean that Congress is powerless, however. Congress has always been able to express its displeasure with particular pardons by holding hearings, cutting off funding for presidential programs, creating legislative stalemate, holding up executive appointments, or, in extreme cases, impeaching the president or even amending the Constitution. It has rarely taken any of these steps. In fact, relatively few pardons have received much attention from either Congress or the general public. Those acts of clemency that have received an unusual amount of attention, the reasons for this disparate treatment, and the consequences for the modern presidency are the focus of the remaining chapters of this book.

3 Clemency before Watergate

Over the course of American history, clemency cases have run the gamut in terms of how much publicity they have received. Whereas most cases have been all but anonymous, a few have made front-page headlines. In the typical clemency case, qualifying for presidential mercy requires an applicant to appeal to the pardon attorney. A successful clemency application is extremely rare—and an applicant is very lucky if his case, among thousands, has been selected for mercy. Still, few take notice, under normal circumstances—the average successful applicant remains relatively anonymous. Aside from a press release issued by the Justice Department, most of these situations slip completely under the public radar.

Before the explosion of interest accompanying Watergate and the Nixon pardon, presidents nevertheless did make a number of clemency grants that stood out in the minds of the American public. In these high-profile cases, press coverage generally tracked the development of a criminal case against a suspect, his or her conviction and sentence, and then, sometimes years later, the clemency award. Although difficult (if not impossible) to quantify, the level of attention paid to these cases by the public and the press distinguishes these pardons from the more typical clemency decisions, which received very little attention, if any at all.

The purpose of this chapter is to convey a rough sense of how presidents used the pardon power in both small-scale and highly visible clemency cases before Watergate, and how often they used it. After describing a few characteristics of the "average" clemency recipient, I show that modern presidents are using the clemency power less and facing more of a case backlog. I briefly discuss some of the factors influencing this situation.

Then, in light of a precedent set by President George Washington (and echoed in the Supreme Court decisions in United States v. Wilson and Biddle v. Perovich), I argue that presidents should use clemency either as an "act of mercy" for the individuals involved, or "in the public interest," but not for personal gain—that is, to protect themselves or their associates from the justice system or to advantage powerful supporters or donors. I analyze several of the more notable high-profile clemency cases in American history to show that, although many of the most famous clemency grants were awarded for political reasons, even the most volatile grants made by presidents before Watergate tracked one or both of these justifiable rationales.

The case studies discussed in this chapter share some characteristics that distinguish them from the volatile post-Watergate clemency actions discussed later. In these cases, clemency was awarded posttrial and pre-election. That is, the clemency recipient had stood trial, and the granting president was still eligible for reelection—and therefore accountable to the electorate—at the time of the clemency grant. The clemency recipients here did not receive full pardons (commutations were preferred) and had at a minimum gone through the justice system and spent some time in prison. Most importantly, these decisions did not involve presidential abuse of the pardon power.

The Average Applicant's Uphill Climb

Who is the "average" clemency applicant, and why does he need clemency? The typical applicant is in many ways a typical American. He may need a pardon to qualify for a particular job, or he may wish to have his civil rights restored so that he may vote, sit on a jury, or even run for public office. An average applicant who actually receives clemency has a long road to travel before a signed pardon warrant leaves the president's desk, and he faces long odds that his case will ever be acted upon. Average clemency applicants of the past century have faced particularly long odds. Since 1900, presidents have granted pardons or commutations to fewer and fewer offenders despite having a virtually unlimited legal power to grant them. This is perplexing. As former pardon attorney Margaret Love has noted, "Most pardons are not controversial."[1] Pardoning practices vary from one president to the next, of course. Still, there is no mistaking that presidents in general have become less and less likely to grant pardons and commutations over the past 100 years.

There are a number of reasons why presidents issue fewer pardons now than in the past. Since Watergate, the impact of public opinion and an ever-watchful media have encouraged presidents to tread carefully. Other reasons not directly related to the president's preferences have contributed as well. Society has become less tolerant of criminals, and this attitude comes through in the executive branch's pardon apparatus, the Office of the Par-

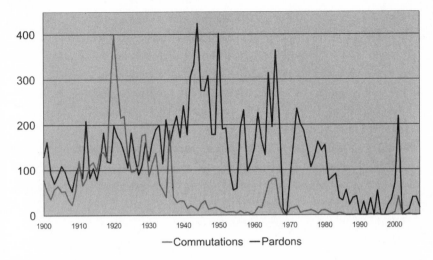

Pardons versus commutations, 1900–2007. Source: Office of the Pardon Attorney. Chart by P. S. Ruckman Jr., used by permission.

don Attorney. The screening process has become less generous, with less sympathetic officials considering applications, and waiting periods increasing. Several other factors are involved: The criminal justice system has evolved, opening avenues of relief other than presidential clemency; the crimes eligible for clemency have changed; and presidents have faced many more applications for relief as prison populations have climbed.

Clemency before Watergate

The first nationally recognized pardons (although technically not his first overall) were granted by President George Washington on July 10, 1795, when he gave amnesty to participants in the Whiskey Rebellion in Pennsylvania.[2] President Washington defused the rebellion by excusing those participants who agreed to swear their allegiance to the United States. Of the fewer than 100 rebels brought to justice, only about 20 actually stood trial. Two defendants, John Mitchell and Philip Vigol, were found guilty of treason against the government and sentenced to hang.[3] However, Washington decided to pardon the two, citing in their November 2, 1795, pardon warrant the facts that the rebellion had been extinguished and that "the principal and end of human punishment [is] the reformation of others."[4]

Washington further explained his rationale for the clemency decisions to Congress in his Seventh Annual Address on December 8, 1795. Because "the misled have abandoned their errors," Washington said, he felt it appropriate "to pardon generally the offenders here referred to, and to extend forgiveness to those who had been adjudged to capital punishment." What is more, Washington noted that the pardons were motivated both by mercy and by concerns about the public interest: "I shall always think it a sacred duty to exercise with firmness and energy the constitutional powers with which I am vested, yet it appears to me no less consistent with the public good than it is with my personal feelings to mingle in the operations of Government every degree of moderation and tenderness which the national justice, dignity, and safety may permit."[5]

Washington's successor, John Adams, pardoned participants in Fries's rebellion, and Adams's successor, Thomas Jefferson, pardoned everyone prosecuted under Adams's Alien and Sedition Acts. Later, in 1815, President James Madison pardoned the "Barataria Pirates." Decades later, the Civil War marked the first time the presidential pardon power attracted serious attention or criticism, for reasons explored earlier. Presidents have also issued amnesties following numerous other wars.[6]

Throughout most of American history, presidents have implicitly—if not always explicitly—adopted some variation of the dual rationales mentioned by Washington. The specific public reasons motivating a clemency decision may vary widely, as pardon scholar P. S. Ruckman Jr. noted in a 1997 study.[7] Still, even in high-profile cases involving sensitive political matters, presidents have usually awarded clemency as an "act of grace" or "for the public interest," the "public interest" in many of these situations being consistent with Alexander Hamilton's argument in Federalist No. 74 to pardon to "restore the tranquility of the commonwealth" or to quell a potential uprising early on. These rationales were apparently in the minds of a few twentieth-century presidents who granted clemency to politically relevant offenders. In looking at a few key cases, we shall proceed chronologically. Warren Harding is thus the first twentieth-century president considered here who used the clemency power to defuse a potentially volatile situation.

Eugene Debs

President Warren Harding commuted five-time Socialist Party of America presidential candidate Eugene Debs's sentence to time served. Debs had attracted headlines on a number of occasions, but in this case he had been convicted of violating the Espionage Act for criticizing the U.S. government's role in World War I as well as certain provisions of the Selective Service Act. He was sentenced to serve ten years in federal prison.[8] Once the Supreme Court refused to review his case, Debs was left with only federal clemency as a way out.[9] While in prison, Debs received the Socialist Party presidential nomination and won about 1 million votes.[10]

That the case was a political hot potato for President Harding was recognized by the New York Times, which reported that, "if Debs is released, it is believed that it will be based on grounds of political expediency."[11] The Times reported several months later that Harding intended to give Debs special attention, as "the President has let it be known that he considers the fact that Debs was his opponent [in the 1920 presidential race] puts his case in a class by itself."[12]

In a report to the president, Attorney General Harry Daugherty noted that although a full pardon was not appropriate, a commutation would ensure that "the ends of justice would be served" by the president's "gracious act of mercy." Alluding to the potential political consequences of keeping Debs behind bars, Daugherty noted the possibility that Debs's "prolonged confinement" could "have an injurious effect on a large number of people who will undoubtedly regard his imprisonment unjustifiable. . . . If this thought affected only a few, it would be immaterial, but undoubtedly a large number of persons will entertain this same view." Given this fact, along with Debs's age and physical weakness—and the fact that he had the "personal charm" to be "a very dangerous man, calculated to mislead the unthinking and afford an excuse for those with criminal intent," the attorney general advised the president to commute Debs's sentence.[13] On December 23, 1921, Harding commuted the sentences of twenty-four "political prisoners," including Eugene Debs.[14]

Marcus Garvey

President Calvin Coolidge dealt similarly with nationalist movement leader and Jamaican "Back to Africa" activist Marcus Garvey, a man who regularly inspired such strong feelings in his supporters and opponents that his "colorful" gatherings frequently required police supervision.[15] As a journalist and lecturer in the United States, Garvey formed the Universal Negro Improvement Association (UNIA) in 1914 and promoted the idea of an African nation for blacks. To facilitate the movement, he formed two companies, the Black Star Steamship Line and the Black Star Steamship

Company, which he intended to be solely staffed by blacks, and sold stock in the companies to individual African American investors. The plan was unsuccessful, and Garvey faced charges for misappropriating the funds he had raised.[16]

On June 18, 1923, Garvey was found guilty of mail fraud for using the U.S. mail in a plan to sell stock to investors in the bankrupt Black Star Steamship Line.[17] He was sentenced to serve five years in prison and to pay a $1,000 fine.[18] Two weeks later, 2,000 African Americans gathered to express their disagreement with the prosecution of Garvey and to sign a petition urging his release.[19] The protests continued for weeks. Black citizens appealed to the mass media for reconsideration of Garvey's case via a flood of telegrams.[20] On November 23, 1927, President Coolidge commuted Garvey's sentence, and Garvey was deported as an "undesirable alien" to his homeland.[21]

Oscar Collazo

Garvey presented a particularly touchy quandary because slavery and civil rights are sensitive issues in the United States. America's role in the status of Puerto Rico has aroused strong feelings in activists as well. The desire of radical Puerto Rican nationalists to free their country from American control during the Truman administration led to two particularly notorious attacks on U.S. governmental institutions in the 1950s, the first of which centered on Puerto Rican nationalists and would-be assassins Griselio Torresola and Oscar Collazo.

On the afternoon of November 1, 1950, Torresola and Collazo stormed Blair House in Washington, D.C., the temporary residence of the Truman family while repairs were under way at the White House. The two exchanged fire with White House guards in a failed bid to assassinate President Harry Truman, who had been napping in an upstairs bedroom.[22] Torresola was killed, and Collazo was seriously wounded; Private Leslie Coffelt, a White House guard, was also killed, and two other White House guards were wounded.[23] The attempted assassination occurred two days after another Nationalist Party attack on the Puerto Rican capital and was intended to drum up support for Puerto Rican independence.[24] Collazo survived his injuries, stood trial, and was convicted on four counts, including premeditated murder. Two of Collazo's convictions carried a mandatory death penalty.[25] He was sentenced to be electrocuted, but President Truman commuted his death sentence to life imprisonment.[26]

Although the White House made the clemency announcement without warning or explanation, according to the *New York Times*, Truman, who took pride in himself "as one who has done more for Puerto Rico than any other President," had apparently been motivated by "compassion and the desire to make a gesture of friendship to the people of Puerto Rico at a time when they were implementing the new constitution recently authorized by Congress." Truman commuted Collazo's sentence on July 24, 1952, the day before the new constitution was to take effect. Noting that Puerto Rico had never had a death penalty—a stance that would continue under the new constitution—the *Times* reported that Truman had "acted chiefly on his own judgment, weighing the fact of the killing of one of his guards and the wounding of two others against the significance that would be attached to his gesture in the island." Perhaps not a small consideration was the fact that Collazo, who had not asked for clemency on his own, had been the subject of "some petitions in his behalf" from "Puerto Ricans in New York's Upper East Side," Collazo's old neighborhood. Coincidentally or not, Truman did not grant clemency to Collazo until after he had already announced that he would not seek a second full term as president.[27]

James Hoffa

Before he became the subject of the most notorious pardon in U.S. history, President Richard Nixon made a key clemency grant to labor leader James "Jimmy" Hoffa. Hoffa, the former president of the International Brotherhood of Teamsters, was sentenced to serve thirteen years in prison for jury tampering (eight years) and pension fund fraud (five years). Two days before Christmas in 1971, President Nixon commuted Hoffa's prison term to time served, with the condition that Hoffa give up all of his labor-management activities until the last day of his original sentence.[28]

Hoffa was one of hundreds granted clemency by President Nixon, but the *New York Times* zeroed in on the political implications of the Hoffa commutation, noting that Hoffa remained "enormously popular" with "rank-and-file" Teamsters, and that mercy had been urged by William Loeb, *The Manchester Union Leader* publisher and "the single most powerful Republican in the Presidential primary state of New Hampshire," an important consideration for reelection candidate Richard Nixon.[29] Gallup polls did not reveal any significant impact on Nixon's job-approval ratings: He was at 50 percent approval from December 10 to 13, and he remained at 49 percent approval from January 7 to 10, 1972.[30] Hoffa did not enjoy his new freedom for long: On July 30, 1975, he was apparently kidnapped outside Detroit and was never heard from again.[31]

Impact of Pre-Watergate Clemency

The commutations discussed above were unquestionably given in controversial circumstances. Labor issues, questions about race, and Puerto Rican independence were divisive issues, and yet each of these situations was treated less harshly by the press and the public than the explosions that accompanied the Nixon pardon, the Iran-Contra pardons, Clinton's pardon of the FALN and his "last-minute" pardons of Marc Rich and others, and George W. Bush's Libby commutation discussed in the next several chapters.

One reason for the difference is that the American public does not like pretrial pardons, postelection pardons, or both occurring together. These crucial dissimilarities help distinguish the clemency actions analyzed here from the later, more controversial ones: The Richard Nixon pardon was pretrial; the Iran-Contra pardon of Caspar Weinberger and the Marc Rich pardon were both pretrial and postelection; and the FALN and Scooter Libby commutations were posttrial, postelection. As noted above, labor leaders Debs and Hoffa and movement figures Garvey and Collazo had all stood trial before having their sentences commuted. They were not given full pardons.

Second, and most important, these older, inherently political clemency actions did not involve presidential abuse of the pardon power. Presidents in these pre-Watergate cases used the pardon power either as an "act of mercy" for the individuals involved or "in the public interest," not for legal or financial gain. None of these presidents was attempting to stop an investigation into executive branch wrongdoing or acting in order to reward supporters.

Watergate, the Press, and Public Opinion

The firestorm of criticism following President Gerald Ford's pardon of Richard Nixon may be one reason why everyday clemency applicants have an arduous, uncertain road ahead of them. In most cases, the president does not want to unnecessarily enrage the public with a clemency decision. Public opinion has a powerful influence on presidential pardoning practices. As pointed out by Acting Pardon Attorney David Stephenson in a 1982 *New York Times* interview, Presidents John Kennedy and Lyndon Johnson were two of the more generous presidents when it came to clemency until harsh criticism of Johnson's practices spurred him to end nearly all pardons.[32] After being criticized by newspapers and a senator about commuting the sentence of an alleged mobster, he apparently became gun-shy, granting just five commutations over the next year and a half.[33] Stephenson also noted a post-Watergate tendency for pardons to be tougher to obtain: "Going back to Watergate, there's much greater reluctance to grant pardons so readily. Standards are much stricter these days."[34]

Watergate is the first factor I will discuss here that has made post-Watergate pardons different from earlier clemency decisions. The scandal firmly established the political power of extra-constitutional factors such as the mass media and public opinion polls. The impact of these forces may seem low at first glance—especially if they are compared to constitutional checks—but underestimating their power could be a crucial mistake for a modern president contemplating a controversial pardon. As has always been the case, the press determines when a pardon deserves more than just cursory analysis from the public. Though the media cannot directly penalize a president for a pardon decision, they can raise the profile of a questionable pardon and persuade other political actors to put pressure on the president about his decision.

The modern president understands the power of the press. In order to protect his power, the president generally prefers to make clemency decisions that will not bring about much scrutiny. The result is the possibility that "at least one person, but probably many more, who deserve clemency will be passed up because his or her case may be too controversial and likely to make the headlines."[35] As scholars have pointed out, presidents have come to rely upon the press both as a means to broadcast their messages if the strategy is "going public" and as a way to inform citizens of the president's motives for controversial actions.[36] Therefore, any presidential aspirant must take careful notice of the fates of former presidential candidate Governor Howard "I Have a Scream" Dean and ex-senator George "Macaca" Allen and recognize that the Internet, blogs, cable television, and Web sites such as YouTube, Facebook, and MySpace can give "legs" to even a seemingly minor story, nourishing a "feeding frenzy" in the mass media "echo chamber" that contributes to real-life political damage.[37] Thus, when intense attention is focused on a president's pardoning decisions, the stakes increase accordingly.[38] As the media have become more prevalent and important in American life, the public's uneasy feelings about the pardon power have also increased.[39]

Indeed, public opinion holds greater potential for influence over presidential decision-making than ever before. As famously argued by political scientist Richard Neustadt, presidents are very concerned with maintaining their public popularity and adding to their political capital.[40] Tracking polls have become invaluable tools for measuring a president's public standing, especially in election season, and today public opinion can be measured more quickly and more accurately than in the past. Since the 22 percent job-approval-rating dive (from 71 percent to 49 percent) suffered by President Ford after the Nixon pardon, his successors have been painfully aware that an unpopular pardon decision can drain a president's political capital in a hurry. As technology continues to improve a president's capacity for measuring his public standing, even routine decisions take on added importance. Thus, the fear of bad press and low public opinion ratings have given post-Watergate presidents strong disincentives to pardon.

A second factor that may help explain why presidents are pardoning less is the fact that society has grown less tolerant of criminals. Different scholars identify one or another modern presidential administration as the breaking point, but generally all agree that something has changed in the past twenty to thirty years or so.

This attitude change is apparent in several ways, including popular support for stricter sentencing requirements. But another area that reflects changing attitudes about crime is the more restricted process used by the executive branch to consider pardon applications.

During the Carter administration, the attorney general started passing his responsibilities to lower-ranking officials whose primary concern was to ensure law enforcement rather than to review convictions evenhandedly.[41] In 1979, Deputy Pardon Attorney Raymond Theim said, "The feeling is that we should do as little as possible to grant relief. . . . It's a dangerous trend for the executive to override the function of the courts and the parole system too much, both from the point of view of balance of power and of possible corruption."[42] By the time Bill Clinton took over as president, the Justice Department was basically rubber-stamping convictions rather than reconsidering them.[43] Margaret Love, addressing this situation again in 2007, said: "There was an almost perfect storm of changes in the department that allowed the prosecutors to take charge, basically, and kind of strangle the pardon power in the department. My department didn't care. They trivialized the pardon power. It was not a high priority. It was no priority."[44]

Not only are less sympathetic officials handling pardon applications, but changes in the application process have generally forced pardon applicants to wait longer periods of time before they may apply for clemency. Regulations adopted under President John Kennedy that remained in place until 1983 required applicants to wait for a minimum of three years after release from confinement before petitioning for a pardon, and for five years for "serious" crimes involving, for example, violence or narcotics. In 1983, new provisions promulgated under President Ronald Reagan extended the waiting periods to five and seven years, respectively.[45] Overall, since 1980 more stringent internal requirements and a stingier review process have resulted in fewer pardon cases referred to the White House with a positive recommendation.[46]

Also, although beyond the scope of this study, it is worth noting that some structural changes in the criminal justice system may help account for the declining number of pardons. Pardons were sometimes used early in America's history to encourage witnesses to testify on behalf of the prosecution, but this use has largely been replaced by immunity statutes.[47] Parole and probation statutes enacted in 1910 and 1925 eased much of the pardon power's burden.[48] What is more, before 1907 those convicted of federal felonies did not enjoy a statutory right to appeal. Federal executive clemency was the main mechanism for fixing federal court errors in criminal cases up to that point.[49]

The overall value of the clemency power's "safety valve" function has decreased as the criminal justice system has improved over time. Today, criminal defendants have a number of post-conviction options: They may file posttrial motions for acquittal under Federal Rules of Criminal Procedure 29 or ask for a new trial by invoking Federal Rules of Criminal Procedure 33. Also, they may protest their convictions in appeals to the Circuit Court of Appeals or to the Supreme Court. They may also file collateral relief motions requesting reversal of their sentences under 28 U.S.C. 2255 for defects in either the conviction or sentence.[50]

The crimes eligible to be pardoned by the president have also evolved. Since the ratification of the Twenty-First Amendment on December 5, 1933, which repealed the Eighteenth Amendment's establishment of Prohibition, alcohol-related crimes have not been as common as they once were. As federal crime rates increased in the Prohibition era, pardons became more difficult to obtain; conditional pardons have been increasingly displaced by parole and probation.[51]

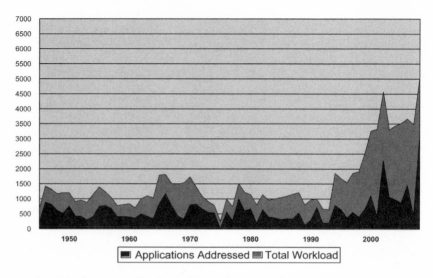

Total workload versus applications addressed, 1945–2008. Chart by P. S. Ruckman Jr., PardonPower.com, used by permission.

Perhaps most importantly, a combination of harsher federal drug legislation and tighter sentencing requirements has led to a significant bump in the number of federal inmates over the past twenty years: in 1990, there were 65,526 federal prisoners, but by 2000, there were 145,416.[52] By July 2008, the federal prison population surpassed 200,000.[53] At the same time, clemency applications are way up: Bill Clinton received more clemency petitions than Jimmy Carter, Ronald Reagan, and George H. W. Bush combined. Through early October 2008, President George W. Bush had received 2,064 pardon petitions and 7,707 commutation requests.[54] The Pardon Attorney's Office has struggled to keep pace with skyrocketing demand, but an influx of resources to combat this challenge is unlikely. As a former pardon attorney observed, "As a general rule, there's nothing in it for a President or an Attorney General to do anything for anybody. . . . They can only be humiliated or embarrassed."[55]

Conclusion

The most controversial clemency actions granted before Watergate are distinguishable from post-Watergate clemency decisions, and presidential use of the clemency power has changed. Controversial clemency decisions of the pre-Watergate era, such as those involving Eugene Debs, Marcus Garvey, Oscar Collazo, and Jimmy Hoffa, followed traditional, well-accepted principles for clemency: they were either carried out as "acts of mercy" for the individuals involved or done "in the public interest."

In the post-Watergate era, presidents have strayed from these principles. Although other factors played important roles in the use of the presidential pardon power, President Ford's pardon of Nixon for "any and all" of Nixon's Watergate crimes was a watershed event in pardon history. In the next chapter, I track the development of Watergate and the Nixon pardon. Then, in the final three chapters of the book, I explore how several of President Ford's successors have abused the presidential pardon power.

4 Watergate, Ford, and the Nixon Pardon

On Sunday, September 8, 1974, President Gerald Ford announced to the press that he had decided to pardon former president Richard Nixon.[1] The Nixon pardon was completely unprecedented: No American president had ever been pardoned. Richard Nixon was the highest-ranking executive branch official ever to receive clemency, and he accepted a full pardon before the American public knew exactly what crimes he had committed. Nixon had resigned from the presidency on August 8, but he was legally exonerated only a month later. Immediately following the pardon announcement, Nixon acknowledged the decision in a statement released from his San Clemente, California, home that stopped short of an apology.[2] President Ford's failure to obtain a full apology from Nixon was one of his biggest mistakes in a series of blunders that made the volatile situation surrounding the Nixon pardon even worse. The public chose to focus primarily on this unprecedented, politically volatile pardon, virtually ignoring Ford's historic agreement with his predecessor regarding the disposition of the Nixon presidential records.[3]

As the story unfolded, various actors in the political environment reacted harshly to the pardon. Mass media outlets, elected officials, and the general public expressed deep anger and resentment at this unexpected end to the Watergate investigation. The pardon contributed heavily to an unfavorable political environment for the GOP: Republicans suffered massive losses in the 1974 midterm elections, and Ford was defeated in 1976.

Three Key Questions

Three key questions emerged from public protests focusing on unfair treatment and cronyism: (1) Did Nixon (or a Nixon representative) and Ford make a "deal" whereby the former resigned as president and left the latter to assume office in exchange for a pardon? (2) Was the Nixon pardon legal? (3) Why did President Ford decide to pardon Richard Nixon at that point, before the former president was even indicted? Each of these questions merits a close examination.

Did Ford and Nixon Make a Deal?

The first question on the minds of Americans concerned President Ford's reason for granting a pardon to Richard Nixon in the first place. President Ford's second press conference as president—his first since the September 8 pardon—was held September 16, 1974, and he faced a barrage of questions from the press. He was asked, for example, whether he and his predecessor had arranged "a deal." Ford denied any deal between Nixon and himself or their staffs. Instead, he articulated a timeline. At the end of his earlier press conference, he stated, he had asked his counsel to conduct a legal inquiry into the president's right of pardon; asked the special prosecutor about the kind of legal action planned against the former president; and learned that criminal proceedings against Nixon—including the indictment, the trial, and so on—would take a year, perhaps longer.[4]

Indeed, a memo from Watergate Special Prosecutor Leon Jaworski to White House Counsel Philip Buchen on this question dated September 4, 1974, speculates that the case would "require a delay, before selection of a jury is begun, of a period from nine months to a year, and perhaps even longer."[5] President Ford told the press that he had also asked his counsel whether Nixon would be able to receive a fair trial. At the end of this process, which required two or three days to complete, he began to consider his options. In his final decision, he told the reporters, he heeded the advice of his staff, who said that his proper "[e]mphasis should be on what's good for the U.S., not the good of Richard Nixon." His main reason for the pardon, he said, was "to heal the wounds throughout the United States."[6]

Was the Nixon Pardon Legal?

Legal scholars Philip Kurland, Edwin Brown Firmage, and R. Collin Mangrum, and investigative journalist I. F. Stone are among those who have argued that at the time of the Nixon pardon, President Ford lacked the constitutional and legal authority to grant clemency in the manner that he did.

There are five main arguments weighing against the constitutional and legal validity of the Nixon pardon: (1) that the Nixon pardon thwarted the intent of the Constitution's "impeachment" exception in Article II, Section II, Clause 1; (2) that President Ford was not allowed to pardon Nixon before he had been convicted of a crime; (3) that the Nixon pardon was void for lack of specificity regarding Nixon's particular offenses; (4) that President Ford failed to follow the pardon attorney's regulations and pardoned Nixon despite his ineligibility for consideration under those rules; and (5) that the president's decision to pardon Nixon violated the Watergate special prosecutor's charter.

Did the Nixon pardon frustrate the purpose of the "impeachment exception" in Article II, Section II, Clause 1, which was intended to limit the pardon power? I believe this argument fails for two key reasons: First, the plain language of the Constitution does not support it; and second, the "spirit" of the impeachment exception does not support it. The "except in cases of impeachment" clause only covers the political process of impeachment, not criminal prosecutions. Since Nixon had only faced potential criminal prosecution and not political prosecution via impeachment (at least, not yet), the "except in cases of impeachment" clause did not forbid President Ford from pardoning him before the impeachment process started. So this argument fails on the "plain language" of the Constitution.

It also fails on the alternate line of reasoning that falls back on the "spirit" of the impeachment clause to question the legality and validity of the pardon. Why? The pardon was clearly contemplated by the "letter" of the pardon clause, which unquestionably trumps the "spirit" of the impeachment clause. What is more, the pardon did not take away Congress's power to impeach the former president—Congress simply failed to follow through after he resigned from office.[7] Thus, the Nixon pardon did not thwart the intent of the language in the Constitution limiting the president's pardon power.

The second argument, that President Ford was not allowed to pardon his predecessor before the disgraced former president had been convicted of, or at least charged with, a crime, can also be disposed of rather quickly. The Supreme Court determined explicitly in Ex parte Garland, recognized again in Ex parte Grossman, and acknowledged indirectly in Brown v. Walker that presidents could indeed grant pardons before legal proceedings had been started.[8] Watergate Special Prosecutor Jaworski was so convinced that the pre-indictment pardon of Nixon was on solid constitutional ground that he declined to challenge its validity.[9] Thus, the Nixon pardon—

although granted before legal proceedings against Nixon had been initiated—did not violate the Constitution for this reason.

The third argument made by Nixon pardon opponents was that the pardon was void because of its vagueness; that is, it failed to specify exactly what offenses it excused. However, despite the English common law practice, which was to include specific offenses in the king's pardon, the American framers did not adopt this practice, nor has American case law found the specificity of offenses pardoned to be a prerequisite to a valid pardon.[10] As will be discussed later, President Ford made a quick decision, which he then acted on before every one of Richard Nixon's potential criminal violations had been identified.[11] He did not need to provide a laundry list of offenses before pardoning him. Thus, the Nixon pardon could not be invalid for failing to specify Richard Nixon's offenses.

The fourth and fifth arguments against the Nixon pardon were more straightforward in that their resolution depended on whether the executive's use of his constitutional powers was restricted by regulations implemented by his own branch of government. Argument number four, that the Nixon pardon was invalid because President Ford pardoned Nixon without following the usual administrative pardon process, was completely without merit. Executive branch regulations cannot restrict the president's constitutional powers, period. The Pardon Attorney's Office exists for the convenience of the president and does not restrict the president's constitutional powers. Pardon Attorney Lawrence Traylor noted at the time that it was the president's constitutional right to pardon and that the president could choose not to involve the Pardon Attorney's Office in the decision-making process (although he also pointed out that Presidents Harry Truman, John Kennedy, and Lyndon Johnson had rarely issued presidential pardons without adhering to the "normal" procedures).[12]

The proposition that a president's constitutional powers trump the Pardon Attorney's Office is clear enough, but what about the special prosecutor's charter? The fifth argument, that the Nixon pardon was invalid because it violated the charter, also fails. Compelling arguments have been made that the pardon power takes precedence over the special prosecutor. As one scholar pointed out, "No statutory regulation or executive branch policy enacted under a congressional statute can nullify or override the president's constitutional authority. No president can agree to forfeit his right to exercise a constitutionally prescribed duty such as the power to pardon." Given a choice between a president's constitutional power to pardon and the special prosecutor's duty as part of the executive branch to investigate someone, the former will trump the latter. Thus, none of the five arguments—the strongest legal and constitutional complaints made by critics of the Nixon pardon—could seriously challenge President Ford's legal and constitutional authority to issue the Nixon pardon.[13]

A separate legal question involved President Nixon's power to issue a "self-pardon." Pardon experts have speculated about whether Nixon could have issued a "self-pardon" to eliminate his legal issues on his way out of the Oval Office, and thus whether this option would be open to other presidents.[14] No president has ever attempted to pardon himself. Still, what were the prospects of a Nixon self-pardon?

The *Washington Post* highlighted the self-pardon possibility and solicited the opinions of a number of legal experts in 1974. Several well-respected legal scholars, such as Solicitor General Robert Bork, former pardon attorney Reed Cozart, and Pardon Attorney Lawrence Traylor, argued that a self-pardon was constitutionally possible.[15] The most persuasive arguments for allowing a self-pardon are drawn from the debates (or lack thereof) of the framers and the text of the Constitution itself. Except in cases of impeachment, the reasoning goes, the framers gave the president the nearly unlimited constitutional power to pardon and never forbade self-pardons. Because the self-pardon was never discussed at the Constitutional Convention, one may interpret that silence to mean that the framers did not oppose the possibility. In fact, a self-pardon may have been an "occasional abuse" the framers accepted to create a stronger presidency. Finally, other Supreme Court pardon precedents suggest that a self-pardon would not be found unconstitutional.[16]

However, other experts, including former attorney general Elliot Richardson, clemency scholar Ronald Goldfarb, and Harvard professor Raoul Berger, have contended that a self-pardon was not constitutionally permissible.[17] There are at least four arguments supporting this point of view. First, and most compelling, is the argument that allowing a president to pardon himself would "violate a basic tenet of adjudication: the granting of a pardon requires the exercise of judgment and no person may sit in judgment upon himself. A President can no more pardon himself than could a judge render a decision in his own case."[18] This principle is particularly compelling: As James Madison wrote in Federalist No. 10: "No man is allowed to be a judge in his own cause, because his interest would certainly bias his judgment, and, not improbably, corrupt his integrity."[19] Second, unlike the English king, a president's political power ends, and he then becomes unaccountable to the people. A self-pardon would only be the departing president's "plunder . . . after a career-ending disgrace," according to one legal scholar. Third, the framers' intent with the "except in cases of impeachment" exception was to check the president when Congress was prosecuting someone. Thus, the argument is that the Constitution implicitly—if not explicitly—forbids self-pardons. Finally, some case law suggests that a self-pardon would not be supported in the courts. For example, *Schick v. Reed* (1974) forbids "variations of [the pardon power] that 'offend' the Constitution." Other cases show that self-judging is frowned upon and that upholding the rule of law is key to our government, further supporting the argument that a self-pardon would be constitutionally untenable.[20]

The correct answer about whether a self-pardon would be constitutional, according to University of Chicago professor Philip Kurland, is, "Obviously there's no answer." Stanford University professor John Kaplan said, "I can make the arguments on either side. But the only way to find out if Nixon can (pardon himself in advance) is to wait until he does. . . . Anybody who tells you that he can think of what the answer is, just doesn't know what he's talking about."[21] A definitive answer to the self-pardon question has never been established.

The foregoing discussion shows that President Ford possessed the legal and constitutional power to pardon Richard Nixon. However, just because the president could do so did not mean that the public believed that he *should* have done so. The fact that Nixon had received a full pardon and that he had not apologized for his offenses (and that the public will probably never learn the full extent of those offenses) prompted many to question the timing of the decision in addition to its appropriateness.

Why Now?

The third key question on the minds of many Americans right after the announcement of the Nixon pardon was: "Why now?" Why bring back memories of Watergate now that the Nixon years were history?

The timing of the pardon was probably influenced by three factors. The first is that Ford most likely did not completely grasp the consequences of his earlier public statements.[22] Ford noted in his memoirs—written, of course, with the benefit of hindsight—that he did indeed realize before announcing the pardon that his prior responses could have been interpreted as implying that he was not going to issue a pardon at that time, and that "it would also seem to some in the press that I'd made statements that were contradictory." However, he "wasn't prepared for the allegations that the Nixon pardon prompted."[23] Another, similar blunder did not help Ford's credibility: The day after Acting Press Secretary John Hushen suggested that more Watergate-related pardons might be forthcoming, President Ford backtracked and said that the requests for Watergate pardons would not receive special treatment and would go through the regular pardon application process.[24] Two mistakes on timing regarding such sensitive issues and in such close succession contributed to the perception that Gerald Ford was a well-meaning man who was simply in over his head.

Another possibility is that President Ford foresaw that the public reception of his surprising pardon announcement would be harsh, but proceeded anyway because of other reasons. One of these "other reasons"—indeed, a likely key to the timing of the Nixon pardon—was reported by Rowland Evans and Robert Novak, who wrote that "several Ford advisers" believed that "somebody got to Ford" and convinced him that Richard Nixon was in such poor physical and mental health that he would not live through prosecution.[25]

Who would have the proximity to Richard Nixon and Gerald Ford to persuasively make this argument? One candidate was former Nixon chief of staff General Alexander M. Haig Jr. According to "a longtime friend of Nixon," Haig convinced President Ford on August 29 of Richard Nixon's "alarming state" of physical and mental health and thereby persuaded the president to grant an immediate pardon.[26] At the time, both Ford and Haig denied that Haig had tried to influence the Nixon pardon decision.[27]

Other evidence relating to the pardon announcement itself suggests that Nixon's mental and emotional health was a more important factor than Ford was willing to admit when he wrote A Time to Heal. First, President Ford referred to the suffering of Richard Nixon and his family in the pardon proclamation itself, signaling to the American public that personal worries for the former president—instead of purely constitutional concerns—were motivating his decision. On the morning of the pardon, President Ford added the words "threatening his health" to Robert Hartmann's final draft line "as he tries to reshape his life," indicating that Nixon's health was on his mind and part of the rationale for the pardon.[28]

As Philip Buchen and former Ford military aide Bob Barrett stated in an interview conducted years after the Nixon pardon, the "act of grace" or "act of mercy" rationale of *United States v. Wilson* was apparently another factor that influenced the pardon decision.[29]

A third key factor—and one that may have helped President Ford make up his mind to pardon Richard Nixon quickly—was that Watergate Special Prosecutor Leon Jaworski had uncovered roughly ten different areas of "possible criminal liability" for Nixon. Nixon could have been indicted for all of them.[30] A memo containing a list of potential allegations against the former president from Watergate Deputy Special Prosecutor Henry Ruth to Jaworski was made public by Philip Buchen at his September 10, 1974, press briefing.[31] In light of the circumstances, even Jaworski did not believe that Richard Nixon could receive "a prompt, fair trial" and supported a pre-indictment pardon for the former president.[32]

The truth is that some combination of all three factors probably led to the quick pardon decision. President Ford knew that he would take a public relations hit, but he figured that the press would react angrily whenever he announced the decision, "so it might as well be now."[33]

Reaction to the Pardon

The Nixon pardon sent shockwaves of anger and disbelief through American society. Except for a few key Ford advisers, no one knew that the Nixon pardon was imminent. Some of the harsh reaction to the pardon can be attributed to a public relations problem that President Ford was unable to work around, as will be discussed later.

To more fully convey the magnitude of anger at the Nixon pardon, I have divided the reactions into various segments: the immediate public response; the responses of the White House staff, the press, and Congress; and polling numbers. The impact of these checks on the president contributed to the movement for an independent counsel statute, which itself later provided several of Ford's successors with political cover for self-serving pardons.

Immediate Public Response

Almost immediately, the White House was snowed in under "an avalanche of criticism."[34] On Monday, September 9, phone calls to the White House were "heavy," running about 50–50 pro and con; telegrams (arriving at a rate of 600 to 700 per hour) were 6 to 1 against the pardon.[35] By

February 28, 1975, the White House had received approximately 250,000 telephone calls, mailgrams, and letters, with a ratio of those disagreeing with the Nixon pardon to those supporting it of 2 to 1.[36]

The White House Staff

Within the White House, the immediate impact of the pardon claimed one of President Ford's most valuable staffers, Press Secretary Jerald ter-Horst. TerHorst, a former Washington, D.C., bureau chief of the *Detroit News*, as well as a man who was well liked by the White House Press Corps (and whose support the new president would unquestionably need in the days to come), resigned in protest just before the pardon announcement was made, although it was nine hours until news of the resignation was released.[37] Upset at being kept in the dark about the pardon until the day before it was issued, he stated that he could not "credibly defend" the Nixon pardon and contended that the lack of pardons for Vietnam draft evaders and the other Watergate defendants clashed with his view that "mercy like justice must be evenhanded."[38]

The Press

"The son of a bitch pardoned the son of a bitch!" exclaimed Carl Bernstein to Bob Woodward in a phone call on the day of the Nixon pardon.[39] This sentiment was shared by much of the press. The "surprise" of the "stunning" Nixon pardon "dominated" the networks on the evening of the pardon, September 8, 1974.[40] CBS, NBC, and ABC dedicated almost two-thirds of their early evening broadcasts to the world reaction to the Nixon pardon.[41] Like members of Congress, "most TV commentators" offered "sharp criticism" or "question[ed] the timing" of the pardon; there was a "wide view that the honeymoon's over," as well as "considerable speculation a 'deal' was struck despite [White House] denials."[42] A deal—the presidency in exchange for a pardon—would have been an illegal quid pro quo transaction.

As White House Chief of Staff (later Vice President) Richard Cheney noted in a memo from October 1977, the Nixon pardon had indeed ended Ford's extremely brief "honeymoon" period as president.[43] According to CBS's Roger Mudd, Gerald Ford "heard himself booed for the first time as President" in Pittsburgh the day after the pardon.[44] By Wednesday, September 11, the *Washington Post* had received 253 letters on the Nixon pardon decision: 248 against it and 5 for it.[45] *Newsweek* received more than 550 letters and telegrams regarding the pardon in the week that followed—only 7 were positive.[46] Even the president's hometown newspaper, the *Grand Rapids Press*, criticized the pardon decision.[47]

Congress

With the resignation of Richard Nixon, the general attitude in Congress was "to heave a great sigh of relief that the ordeal was over and let him go in peace."[48] Senate Minority Leader Hugh Scott (R-PA) had made a public appeal for mercy to be shown to Richard Nixon: "He's been hung, and it doesn't seem to me [that] in addition he should be drawn and quartered."[49] Republicans in particular looked forward to a fresh start with President Ford, "a Mr. Clean good guy" at the helm of the ship of state.[50] This dynamic changed dramatically following the Nixon pardon.

Following President Ford's stunning clemency decision, about twenty resolutions and bills were introduced by members of the House seeking additional information about Watergate.[51] Senator Walter Mondale (D-MN) proposed a constitutional amendment that would allow Congress, with a two-thirds vote of each house, to overrule a pardon decision.[52] Senator William Proxmire (D-WI) introduced a resolution to restrict clemency eligibility only to those who had already been convicted of a crime.[53]

Breaking ranks from his fellow Democrats, Senator Hubert Humphrey (D-MN) stated: "The pardon is right. It is the only decision President Ford could make."[54] However, more typical of Democrats' reactions was that of Senator Mondale, who assessed the Nixon pardon as the "worst possible decision" and said that despite the fact that no one wished for Nixon to go to jail, "to grant pardon for unspecified crimes and acts is unprecedented and creates [the] spectacle of [a] 2-track system."[55]

Long-Term Public Response

Four days after the pardon, a *New York Times* article declared, "President Ford's decision to pardon Richard M. Nixon and to consider pardons for other alleged Watergate conspirators has sapped his support among the general public." Proving what was hinted at earlier, a special Gallup poll revealed that Ford's job-approval rating had "fallen from 71% to 49% in a matter of three weeks," with 60 percent of poll respondents pointing at pardon developments as hurting their perception of the president.[56]

Perhaps most significantly, the drop in the polls reflected a trend. On October 7, 1974, almost a month after the pardon, a Harris survey found that nearly two-thirds of the American public (60 percent to 33 percent) believed that Ford was "wrong to give [a] full and complete pardon to former President (Richard) Nixon." The pollster observed that "public opposition to the pardon runs so deep that the memory of it is [un]likely to disappear any time soon and may very well hang a long-term cloud over the Ford administration."[57] By October 14, President Ford's Harris poll numbers were even worse: 67 to 29 percent disapproved of the Nixon pardon, and the president's overall job rating was 49 percent negative to 45 percent positive.[58] On October 21, his Nixon pardon numbers rebounded a bit, with 59 percent to 35 percent believing the Nixon pardon was not "the right thing" to do.[59] A Gallup poll reported on October 31 showed that the president's job-approval rating had crept up to 55 percent approval, with 28 percent disapproving.[60]

Ford's Public Relations Problem

One key problem presented by the Nixon pardon was how to manage public reaction to it. This challenge was particularly daunting considering the president's difficulty in communicating the reasoning behind his decision to his own staff. Only a few key staffers knew of Ford's plan to issue the pardon beforehand, and no one in the press office had any idea what his thoughts on the issue were or even knew the pardon was in the works.[61] When staffers became aware of the situation, the president considered—but ultimately disregarded—their advice.

Notably, White House media adviser Robert Hartmann tried to warn his boss that the public was not prepared for an immediate Nixon pardon, especially given Ford's prior public posturing. Hartmann's fear—that the pardon seemed to contradict Ford's state of mind as publicly expressed up until the moment that the pardon was actually issued—seems reasonable, and a review of Ford's public statements leading up to the day of the pardon confirms that a contradiction certainly existed.

When asked at his vice presidential confirmation hearing whether he believed the next president had the power to prevent Richard Nixon from being indicted and prosecuted, vice presidential nominee Gerald Ford had answered, "I do not think the public would stand for it."[62] On August 9, 1974, after Ford was sworn in as president, his new press secretary, Jerald terHorst, responding to a reporter's query about whether the new president was now leaning toward "immunity" for Richard Nixon, stated, "I can assure you [that he is not]."[63]

At his first presidential press conference on August 28, 1974, President Ford's statements had led listeners, particularly the journalists covering the event, to conclude that even after becoming president, he still had no plans to issue a pardon to Richard Nixon anytime soon. At that press conference, Ford answered a query about a possible Nixon pardon as follows: "There have been no charges made, there has been no action by the courts, there has been no action by any jury. And *until any legal process has been undertaken,* I think it is unwise and untimely for me to make any commitment."[64] Later on, in that same press conference, President Ford again seemed to indicate that any pardon decision would wait until some legal steps had been taken:

> Q: Are you saying, sir, that the option of a pardon for former President Nixon is still an option that you will consider, depending on what the courts will do?
>
> The President: Of course, I make the final decision. And *until it gets to me,* I make no commitment one way or another.[65]

These statements were reported in the *New York Times* the following day in an article subtitled "Ford Says He Will Decide Nixon Case after Legal Process Runs Its Course."[66] A *Washington Post* article on the press conference, "Decision Deferred," began as follows:

> President Ford hinted strongly yesterday at his first White House news conference that he would consider a pardon for former President Nixon *if charges are brought against him in the courts.* The President said he believed that the American people think, as he does, that Mr. Nixon has suffered enough. *However, the President said that he will make no decision regarding a pardon before any legal process takes place.*[67]

According to historian Barry Werth, after the press conference President Ford recognized that he was caught off-guard and became angry about the number of questions about Richard Nixon. He thought to himself, "God dammit, I am not going to put up with this. Every press conference from now on, regardless of the ground rules, will degenerate into a Q&A on, 'Am I going to pardon Mr. Nixon.'"[68] Eleven days later, on September 8, Ford backtracked from his previous public statements, noting that, as president, questions "do not look at all the same as the hypothetical questions that I have answered freely and perhaps too fast on previous occasions."[69] He pardoned Richard Nixon that same day, before any legal proceedings had been started against the former president.

President Ford's flip-flop no doubt surprised the American public. It also caught reporters completely off guard, and—perhaps still smarting from missing the Watergate story—they may have overreacted. The president's positive press coverage took a nosedive as "journalists who, for four weeks, had written that Ford did everything right as president immediately revised their interpretations of his leadership. The contrast could hardly have been more stark. A single presidential act fundamentally changed Ford's press image—from that of an honest, open, and accessible chief executive to that of a deceptive, secretive, even Nixonian chief executive." The press's critical tone lingered long past what White House staffers later identified as the key turning points in the president's press relations—the Nixon pardon and the terHorst resignation—and colored the president's press coverage for the remainder of his term.[70]

Hungate Subcommittee Testimony

The explanations that President Ford offered at his second presidential press conference on September 16 did little to allay the concerns of the American public. Three weeks later, to address the multitude of questions still swirling around him, he agreed to become the first president (or at least the first president since Abraham Lincoln in 1862[71]) to appear in front of a congressional committee, in this case, the House Judiciary Committee's Subcommittee on Criminal Justice, headed by Representative William Hungate (D-MO). In front of television cameras, he would answer questions about the Nixon pardon posed by members of Congress.[72]

After a 43-minute opening statement, Ford answered questions for almost an hour. Here, as reported by NBC, the president again emphasized that his reason for pardoning Nixon was less out of concern for his predecessor's health and more "to try to get the United States focusing on serious problems." A summary of his testimony said that "he was convinced at the time of the pardon, and he is convinced now, that if there were no pardon the attention of the people would have been diverted from the problems facing the country."[73] Ford admitted to lying to the public as vice president, confessing that he had continued to defend Nixon even after he learned that his predecessor had probably committed impeachable offenses. The reason he had defended Nixon, he said, was that he did not wish for the press to conclude that he wanted Nixon to resign so that he could gain the presidency.[74]

Regarding rumors of a "deal" with Nixon, President Ford insisted that "there was no deal, period, under no circumstances."[75] Two crucial points were:

> At no time after I became President on August 9, 1974, was the subject of a pardon for Richard M. Nixon raised by the former President or by anyone representing him. Also, no one on my staff brought up the subject until the day before my first press conference on August 28, 1974.[76]

> Nobody made any recommendation to me for the pardon of the former President.[77]

Even the Hungate hearing testimony did not put rumors of a "deal" to rest, however.

1974 Midterm Elections

Before the "deal" story thread can be continued, we will stop to acknowledge the 1974 midterm elections. President Ford's position going into this election cycle was precarious. The Nixon pardon had damaged his popularity. He had misled the public, withheld information, and conducted less than the "open administration" he had promised.[78] In September 1974, in a poll asking whether respondents believed "Ford has or has not told the country the whole truth" about the Nixon pardon, 29 percent answered "has," and 71 percent answered "has not," a discouraging result for a politician trying to make the country forget about Richard Nixon.[79]

Though President Ford would have to wait until 1976 to face the electorate, many of his fellow Republicans did not have that luxury. In the 1974 elections, Republicans were defeated in droves: Democrats gained forty-nine seats in the House and, initially, four Senate seats.[80] A Time magazine postelection wrap-up placed the blame for the Republican bloodbath squarely at the feet of President Ford, noting that among "the direct causes" of the Republican drubbing was the Nixon pardon. The pardon also "cut off any coattails that [Ford's] accession might have offered to beleaguered Republicans."[81]

"Deal" Questions Return

An article by Bob Woodward and Carl Bernstein published in the *Washington Post* on December 18, 1975, called into question several of President Ford's earlier assertions regarding the lack of a "deal." The thrust of the piece was that Ford had contradicted earlier public statements regarding his reasons for the pardon. According to sources, he actually pardoned Richard Nixon because of "urgent pleas" from Nixon's key staffers. What is more, Ford left out several key facts in his earlier public statements on the Nixon pardon.

First, on August 28, 1974 (the date of Gerald Ford's first presidential press conference)—ten days before the pardon announcement—Ford had privately assured Alexander Haig that Richard Nixon would be pardoned. Second, former Nixon counsel Leonard Garment had written a memo to Philip Buchen on August 28, 1974, asking for a pardon for Nixon, implying that the former president might become suicidal if confronted with criminal prosecution.[82] Though the sources were unsure whether President Ford had seen the memo, they accused Haig of using its contentions to try to sway Ford. Raymond Price Jr., a former Nixon speechwriter, had prepared a statement (attached to the Garment memo) announcing the Nixon pardon for Ford's use at his first presidential press conference, a statement that obviously was never used on that day.[83]

These revelations contradict two statements made by President Ford to the Hungate subcommittee. They are, to repeat:

> At no time after I became President on August 9, 1974, was the subject of a pardon for Richard M. Nixon raised by the former President or by anyone representing him. Also, no one on my staff brought up the subject until the day before my first press conference on August 28, 1974.[84]

> Nobody made any recommendation to me for the pardon of the former President.[85]

In the same *Washington Post* article, Woodward and Bernstein said Buchen acknowledged that President Ford now "recall[ed] that he talked with Haig about the pardon from time to time"—potentially as early as August 28, 1974. Despite what President Ford and Haig had implied previously, however, Haig now acknowledged that he had actually discussed a Nixon pardon with Ford, but refused to get into specifics with the reporters. Ford denied having ever seen the Garment memo, and no copy of it was located in the files of the president or in Buchen's or Haig's files.[86]

In an internal memo from Buchen to White House spokesman William Greener the next day, Buchen bristled at what he characterized as "not accurate" statements attributed to him by Woodward.[87] Buchen acknowledged receiving the Garment memo, but insisted that he had returned his copy to Garment before the president had seen it.

Accordingly, in a *Washington Post* article published the same day, President Ford stuck to his earlier characterization, denying that he had assured Haig of a Nixon pardon on August 28, 1974. Instead, the president argued that on August 28 he and Haig had only discussed the questions about a Nixon pardon that Ford had answered at his first presidential press conference earlier that day. Woodward and Bernstein, citing "three reliable sources" and earlier statements by Haig and Buchen that seemed to hint at a more "substantive discussion," stood by their contention that President Ford and Haig had had a "substantive discussion" about a Nixon pardon and that Ford had assured Haig that Nixon would be pardoned.[88] The Garment memo issue had apparently been dropped by this point.

Representative Elizabeth Holtzman (D-NY) used the *Washington Post* revelations as a springboard for requesting additional hearings to further discuss the pardon situation. However, the House Judiciary Subcommittee on Criminal Justice decided to end any further investigation into the Nixon pardon on February 19, 1976. This 4–3 vote carried over a motion by Holtzman to interview Buchen, Haig, and others related to the Nixon pardon.[89]

President Ford Comes Clean

In *A Time to Heal*, President Ford finally admitted—contrary to his earlier public remarks—that Haig had initiated the idea of a pardon for Richard Nixon on August 1, 1974, a week prior to the former president's resignation, again raising questions of whether the pardon was the price for Nixon's resignation.[90] Fred Buzhardt, who had been spurred to action by Nixon himself, had apparently asked Haig to meet with Ford.[91] Buzhardt had provided Haig with two pieces of paper, one that provided details on the presidential pardon power, the other containing formal pardoning language that could be used to issue a Nixon pardon, if President Ford had a mind to do so.[92] The pieces of paper may have been written by Buzhardt or Nixon's Watergate lawyer, James St. Clair—each has been accused of authorship at some point.[93]

President Ford's recollection was that on that day, while he was still vice president, Haig approached him with the news that the "smoking gun" White House tape from June 23, 1972, that would end the Nixon presidency was imminent. Haig also told Ford that a president can pardon someone even before "criminal action" has been taken against that person.[94] Vice President Ford interpreted Haig's statements as constituting an offer for a "quid pro quo": A pardon would be President Nixon's price for resigning.[95] Vice President Ford declined to make a recommendation and told Haig that he would have to speak with his wife, Betty, before he responded.[96] At the time, Ford did not state his belief to Haig that a pardon granted in exchange for resignation was inappropriate, and he later worried that his silence following Haig's comment may have implied his agreement.[97]

Later that evening, the vice president and Haig shared a telephone call at about 1 A.M., although who called whom and what was discussed are still unclear even today. Ford wrote in *A Time to Heal* that Haig had called him essentially to say "nothing has changed. The situation is as fluid as ever."[98] But to Hartmann and Ford's national security adviser, John Marsh, the vice president apparently admitted having called Haig and said he had told Haig "they should do whatever they decided to do; it was all right with me."[99]

Although Ford insisted that he never explicitly agreed to "a deal," Hartmann and Marsh saw the situation's dangerous implications. They scolded the vice president for his handling of the situation, then brought in well-respected lobbyist Bryce Harlow to help decide what to do next. Following Harlow's advice, Vice President Ford called Haig and read him a disclaimer saying that their prior conversation "yesterday afternoon" (leaving out—whether unintentionally or not—mention of the 1 A.M. phone call) was hypothetical, and nothing discussed should be taken into account if President Nixon were indeed to resign.[100] Haig agreed.[101]

Even years after Ford had returned to private life, Haig continued to insist that a deal was never in the cards: "At no time did I ever suggest in any way an agreement or 'deal' that Mr. Nixon would resign in exchange for a pardon from Mr. Ford."[102] In President Ford's Hungate subcommittee testimony, he stated that he and Haig had definitely not made a "deal"—however, Ford was never asked whether Haig had ever *offered* a deal (and consequently, never testified on the question).[103] "It was a deal," Gerald Ford remarked in 1997, "but it never became a deal because I never accepted." The difference, in Ford's mind, was that Haig had proposed a pardon to benefit Richard Nixon, whereas Ford's decision to actually grant clemency a month later was for the good of the country. It was a decision that President Ford made with a clear conscience.[104]

Was a deal actually agreed to by Gerald Ford and Richard Nixon (through Haig or not)? A conclusive answer would require a more in-depth understanding of their relationship. One view, as expressed by Nixon aide Alexander Butterfield, is that "Nixon had Ford totally under his thumb. He was the tool of the Nixon administration—like a puppy dog. They used him when they had to—wind him up and he'd go 'Arf, Arf.'"[105] Of course Butterfield was fired by President Ford from his position as Federal Aviation administrator, which may explain his perspective.[106] Representative H. R. Gross (R-IA), a conservative, told Clark Mollenhoff, "I have seen Jerry Ford operate for twenty-five years. Jerry Ford will deal on anything, and don't forget it."[107] Bob Woodward suspected that some sort of unspoken agreement was in place, which may explain why Ford appeared "less than fully candid" in his explanations. However, he also acknowledged that even without a "deal" in place, the pardon was probably "inevitable" under the circumstances.[108]

Historian Stephen Ambrose pointed out a number of reasons to believe that—absent a revision of the story from either Ford or Haig (or an audio recording)—it is unlikely that the two "cut a deal" for a Nixon pardon. First, Nixon and Ford were professionally close, but they did not have a strong personal relationship. Second, Nixon had a history of treating Ford poorly, and the latter received the vice presidency not because of Nixon's favor (he preferred his former treasury secretary, John Connally), but because House Republicans strongly supported him for vice president (or because Nixon knew Ford would agree to pardon him, depending on one's interpretation of events). Third, Ford enjoyed the support of Congress and the public at the beginning of his term as president, while obviously Nixon did not. Finally, each man most likely understood that the reality of the circumstances facing President Ford would require him to pardon Nixon. Haig may have spoken to Ford less to strike a deal, which might have provoked an angry response and pushed the president in the opposite direction, than to make sure Ford understood that the pardon power could be used pre-indictment and—given the circumstances—would probably have to be used quickly.[109]

Absent hard evidence of any explicit deal between Nixon and Ford, the more likely reason for Haig's interactions with Ford is that Nixon wanted to make certain that his successor understood the political realities and could clearly see that the best option available to him was a swift pardon.

The 1976 Presidential Campaign

By summer, Jimmy Carter enjoyed what appeared to be an insurmountable lead going into the presidential election. President Ford trailed Carter by 33 points in the July Gallup poll and by 39 points in the August Harris survey.[110] By the end of August, 59 percent of poll respondents believed it "was wrong to pardon Richard Nixon" to 33 percent who did not, establishing the Nixon pardon as a presidential campaign issue.[111] Despite little time to prepare to run for reelection and a strong primary challenge from Ronald Reagan, the Ford campaign succeeded in turning the tide against the Carter team before ultimately falling just short of victory. Exit poll data showed that 7 percent of voters backed candidate Carter over candidate Ford because of "Watergate."[112] President Ford lost the popular vote to Jimmy Carter by only 2 percent—48 percent to 50 percent—and lost the electoral vote 240 to 297.[113]

Conclusion

The Nixon pardon showed future presidents how much a single clemency decision could affect their public standing, and—coincidentally or not—future presidents have generally waited until the end of their final term in office before unleashing their own controversial pardons. As will be explained in the chapters to come, several of President Ford's successors have abused the clemency power to excuse executive branch officials or reward supporters. Even more important, Ford's controversial decision may have exposed a weakness in the framers' plan to trust public officials and then, in rare cases, to remove corrupt ones from their positions via impeachment.

Perhaps the most regrettable consequence of the Nixon pardon is that it was the first time a chief executive had used the pardon power to essentially stop an outside investigation into the behavior of his own (or his predecessor's) executive branch. Coming on the heels of the Vietnam War,

Watergate contributed to a loss of public confidence in the president's ability to investigate the executive branch. Congress's solution to this problem, the independent counsel statute, created a political opening for presidents looking to cut off outside investigations into executive branch behavior. They found that they could use the clemency power as a shield against judicial investigation.

5 Special Counsel Investigations, Pre- and Post-Watergate

The executive branch has always been trusted to investigate alleged wrongdoing in all three branches of the federal government and, if necessary, to prosecute those who have committed offenses. Indeed, it is the executive branch's constitutional responsibility to perform these duties. Although this arrangement may seem awkward in cases of executive branch wrongdoing, the framers knew that not every conflict of interest in the Constitution could be eliminated: Judges, for example, were not forbidden from determining their own salaries, and Congress was not stopped from excusing itself from its own legislation—so why shouldn't members of the executive branch be investigated and, if necessary, prosecuted by the branch of government assigned those responsibilities, even if it was their own?[1]

Consistent with this line of reasoning, the framers gave the president the "executive power" and the responsibility to "take care" that the laws were executed. They probably would not have been surprised that their decision to entrust the executive with the responsibility to investigate wrongdoing in the other branches of government could aid a future president attempting to derail an investigation of his own wrongdoing. In fact, as noted earlier, they anticipated this very issue in their discussions. The framers were satisfied that impeachment, along with Congress's indirect pressure points on the president, provided a sufficient check.

The first part of this chapter examines four notable pre-Watergate investigations into the executive branch by outside prosecutors.[2] These investigations involved the Whiskey Ring, the Oregon Land Frauds, Teapot Dome, and the Income Tax Scandal. A brief look at the history of these pre-Watergate executive branch investigations shows that outside investigations into executive branch behavior for most of U.S. history since the founding were capably undertaken by attorneys general, the Justice Department, or other reliable officials.[3] Excluding President Ulysses Grant's interference in the Whiskey Ring prosecutions, I suggest that in each of these investigations, the presidents involved (Theodore Roosevelt, Calvin Coolidge, and Harry Truman) resisted the temptation to interfere with the outside prosecutor. The restraint shown by these past presidents is consistent with the framers' intentions that the clemency power be used either as a kingly "act of grace" or for "the public welfare"—not to excuse the president's men.

Watergate and the "Saturday Night Massacre" shook the public's confidence in allowing presidents to investigate themselves. The independent counsel statute—Congress's attempt to limit the president's role in executive branch investigations—did not make presidents behave more appropriately when being investigated. In an examination of the independent counsel statute's history, I describe how it actually provided a political opening for the president to thumb his nose at a Congress (usually a Congress dominated by the opposite party) pursuing an executive branch investigation. The statute has not been renewed since its lapse in 1999; nevertheless, I argue that the Scooter Libby investigation shows that partisan lines in the sand are still in place, and that the independent counsel's lasting legacy—its introduction of political considerations into judicial investigations—is alive and well.

Pre-Watergate Executive Branch Investigations by Outside Prosecutors

Before the independent counsel statute was passed, only four presidents had needed to employ a special prosecutor to look into allegations of executive branch misbehavior. President Ulysses Grant named the first "special counsel," John Brooks Henderson, to prosecute moonshiners caught up in the Whiskey Ring scandal.[4] President Theodore Roosevelt named Francis Heney and Charles Bonaparte to investigate illegalities in the General Land Office and Post Office, respectively. President Calvin Coolidge named (and the Senate confirmed) Atlee Pomerene and Owen Roberts as special counsel to investigate the Teapot Dome scandal.[5] Pomerene and Roberts were the only ones ever appointed in this manner.[6] Finally, during the "tax scandals" of the Truman administration, the attorney general bowed to congressional desires and implemented a departmental regulation that led to the appointment of Newbold Morris as "special assistant to the attorney general" to investigate apparent corruption in tax collections within the federal government.[7]

The Whiskey Ring Scandal

When President Grant appointed John Brooks Henderson as special counsel to investigate the Whiskey Ring (or Whiskey Frauds) in 1875, it marked the first time a special federal prosecutor had been named to look into alleged executive branch abuses.[8] Orville Babcock, President Grant's personal secretary and "closest associate," was one key administration figure accused of serious misconduct.[9]

Grant, a Republican Civil War hero and the resounding winner in 1868 over Democrat Horace Greeley for the presidency, nevertheless endured a scandalous administration.[10] In 1871, the Whiskey Ring—the brainchild of Internal Revenue Service supervisor John McDonald—was born as a means to raise money for the Republican Party by tapping illegal whiskey income for campaign dollars. Members of the conspiracy sold more whiskey than they reported to the U.S. Treasury, and everyone in the chain—producers, distributors, tax agents—received a piece of the action. By 1873, the Whiskey Ring had cost the United States about $1.5 million per year. In 1874, a new treasury secretary, Benjamin Bristow, was appointed to clean up the mess. Over the next year, John McDonald and others were arrested and Orville Babcock was indicted by a grand jury, but the formerly supportive Grant performed an about-face on the investigation once Babcock became a target.[11]

Although Grant was not perceived as personally corrupt, his standing suffered from his dogged loyalty to his friends. He believed Babcock's plea of innocence, and he feared that Bristow—who apparently had presidential aspirations—and the prosecutors were out to get him (Grant).[12] Accordingly, he moved to protect Babcock and himself. When prosecutor Henderson accused Babcock of obstructing justice, and attacked Grant in a closing argument made against another Whiskey Ring defendant, Attorney General Edwards Pierrepont fired Henderson, who had only been on the job for seven months.[13] Ten days before Babcock's trial, Grant ordered Pierrepont to command prosecutors not to offer immunity to criminals for turning state's evidence. This had the effect of limiting the evidence available to the prosecutors trying to convict Babcock. Grant even contemplated showing up in court to testify on Babcock's behalf, although he settled for just submitting a deposition he had given in the White House. Babcock—alone among the key St. Louis Whiskey Ring defendants—was acquitted, and historians agree that he escaped because of Grant's deposition.[14]

Grant and his successor pardoned several Whiskey Ring figures. Of the major players in the scandal, those receiving clemency included William O. Avery, formerly chief clerk of the U.S. Treasury, and William McKee, a proprietor of the St. Louis Globe, in November 1876; Grant pardoned John McDonald in January of the next year.[15] President Rutherford B. Hayes pardoned Revenue Agent John A. Joyce in December 1877.[16]

The president had plunged into the legal system to protect his aide, and ultimately, perhaps, himself. Had Babcock not escaped conviction, thanks largely to Grant's intervention, it is reasonable to suppose that Grant would have pardoned him too. This case is an exception to the later practice: Until Watergate, no other president had intervened in an independent judicial investigation of the executive branch to rescue a close executive aide.

Decades earlier, President Thomas Jefferson had used clemency to attempt to convict his former vice president, Aaron Burr, of treason. Jefferson told government prosecutor George Hay to use a pardon to coax witness Erick Bollman to testify against Burr. Bollman refused. Jefferson also sent "some other blank pardons" to Hay to be used "at [Hays's] discretion."[17] Still, such forays into the legal system by presidents are rare. Several presidents have had opportunities to interfere with judicial prosecutions, but they have usually resisted the temptation.

Oregon Land Frauds

Although his own executive branch aides were not in the line of fire during the Oregon Land Frauds investigation, President Theodore Roosevelt's "hands-off" approach led to the prosecution of high-ranking Republican allies. Roosevelt decided to allow Special Prosecutor Francis J. Heney to pursue, indict, and convict two fellow Republicans: Oregon Senator John H. Mitchell, for land fraud, and U.S. Attorney John H. Hall, for conspiracy (Mitchell died while his case was on appeal; Hall was later pardoned by President William Howard Taft). Roosevelt fought pressure from Oregon Republicans to fire Heney, and he encouraged Heney not to fear a Republican backlash for doing a thorough investigation.[18] He even used the clemency power to further the investigation by pardoning Stephen Puter, a key "land grabber" who turned and cooperated in the Mitchell prosecution.[19]

Roosevelt resisted the temptation to use his influence or constitutional powers to intervene in Heney's investigation, even if to spare prominent members of his own party from prosecution. His quick action in appointing special prosecutors—Heney here, and Charles Bonaparte to address a separate Post Office scandal—helped preserve Roosevelt's reputation and showed that executive branch scandals could be adequately addressed by a president who confronted the problems head-on and acted in good faith.

Teapot Dome

Teapot Dome was a Harding administration scandal that—because of the president's untimely death—became President Calvin Coolidge's problem. Scoring a preemptive strike on his Democratic opposition, Coolidge appointed two special prosecutors: Owen Roberts and Atlee Pomerene, who won convictions against Secretary of the Interior Albert Fall and oil executive Harry Sinclair. Fall and Sinclair were the only ones convicted, but they had plenty of company among the ranks of the fallen. Coolidge asked for Attorney General Harry Daugherty's resignation and replaced him with Harlan Fiske Stone. Daugherty, never convicted of a crime stemming from the scandal, apparently sat on his hands while knowing of corrupt dealings.[20]

Fall has the inglorious distinction of being the first Cabinet member convicted of commiting a felony in office.[21] He was accused of supporting special interests and not adequately enforcing conservation laws. Edward Doheny, an oil executive, testified that Fall had accepted payments as a reward for giving federal Navy oil reserves to private oil interests. In addition to Fall, Secretary of the Navy Edwin Denby earned the taint of scandal. Never charged with a crime, Denby resigned for fear of embarrassing President Coolidge.[22]

The "only defendant convicted in a criminal case resulting directly from Teapot Dome," Fall was on his way to prison in 1931 and as such was politically radioactive.[23] Despite pleas from Fall's friends,[24] President Herbert Hoover—who faced reelection in 1932—passed on granting him clemency.[25]

Income Tax Scandal

In the early 1950s, President Harry Truman's administration faced charges of tax-fixing at the Tax Division of the Department of Justice and the Bureau of Internal Revenue. Truman named a special prosecutor to ferret out wrongdoing, selecting Newbold Morris as special assistant to Attorney General Howard McGrath and ordering him to investigate. Morris, intending to thoroughly investigate the situation, got into trouble for exceeding his mandate by attempting to hand out a 16-page survey that asked for personal financial information from all federal government employees. McGrath soon fired him for his aggressive actions; Truman then fired Mc-Grath for dismissing Morris too quickly.[26]

For unrelated reasons, Truman decided not to run for reelection in 1952. Though it may not have mattered, Truman, unlike Nixon after him, did not actually do anything wrong, and Morris was perceived to have over-reached.[27] Truman was careful not to pardon anyone of consequence, although several of his allies and friends were swept up in the investigation. Later, in 1962, Truman successfully persuaded President John Kennedy to pardon Matthew Connelly, Truman's appointments secretary.[28] Connelly was the only member of Truman's White House staff to be charged with a crime. Truman's head of the tax division of the Justice Department, Theron Lamar Caudle, was charged and convicted in the same case as Connelly.[29] Apparently without Truman's support, Caudle was pardoned by President Lyndon Johnson in 1965.[30] Truman did persuade President Johnson in 1967 to pardon James P. Finnegan, a district collector stationed in St. Louis, Missouri, for the Bureau of Internal Revenue and—perhaps more importantly—a friend of Truman's.[31]

Watergate and the Saturday Night Massacre

Watergate—and President Gerald Ford's use of the pardon power to end the scandal—received more attention and criticism than the actions of Presidents Grant, Roosevelt, Coolidge, and Truman. And no wonder. President Ford granted a full pardon to his predecessor, Richard Nixon, before Nixon was indicted and in circumstances where Nixon would almost certainly have been criminally prosecuted for his role in the Watergate cover-up. Upon closer examination, though, it becomes clear that President Ford faced very difficult circumstances.

President Grant had set aside judicial and constitutional concerns to save his friend Orville Babcock and would likely have pardoned him. President Ford initially fumbled the Nixon pardon by mentioning, in his pardon remarks, not only his constitutional responsibilities, but also his concern for the former president's health. Ford would have been on firmer ground if he had relied solely on the traditional constitutional justifications mentioned earlier, but he would have needed some time to strike the proper balance. Despite his earlier muddled explanation for the Nixon pardon, President Ford always claimed to have acted for the good of the country rather than for the good of Richard Nixon. Whatever friendship Ford and

Nixon may have shared, it did not appear to be an overriding factor in the Nixon pardon. President Ford believed the Nixon quagmire interfered with his presidential duties and wanted to focus on other pressing issues.

Like Calvin Coolidge, President Ford was left with a predecessor's scandal that had to be cleaned up before he could face the electorate. President Ford felt that the only way he could govern effectively was to pardon Richard Nixon (unlike Warren Harding, Nixon did not ease his successor's dilemma by dying). President Ford faced the voters for his clemency decision as the framers intended, and the electorate punished the GOP for Watergate by awarding dozens of congressional seats to Democrats in 1974 and then denying Ford's presidential bid two years after that.

President Truman was fortunate enough to have two sympathetic Democratic successors to pardon his allies who were swept up in the Income Tax Scandal. Truman apparently did not feel comfortable enough to do the "dirty work" of pardoning Connelly, Caudle, and Finnegan on his own. President Ford, with time and circumstances working against him, did his own "dirty work" by pardoning Richard Nixon.

It took a number of years for the controversy to fade, but President Ford's reputation survived the Watergate ordeal more or less intact. Even Ford's harshest critics eventually agreed that the Nixon pardon had been a defensible decision, as I point out in the conclusion. Still, this was the first clemency case in which a president used the pardon power in circumstances where he was almost certainly protecting his predecessor from judicial and political prosecution. The pardon shook the public's trust in President Ford and reminded observers of Nixon's jarring Saturday Night Massacre.

The basic facts of what came to be known as the "Saturday Night Massacre" are complex, with a number of different figures involved in a series of events that occurred in quick succession on October 20, 1973. It came at a time when the press and the public suspected President Richard Nixon of having committed federal crimes in the Watergate scandal, but as yet had little knowledge of exactly what had occurred. In May 1973, Nixon's attorney general, Elliot Richardson, had created the Office of Watergate Special Counsel. Archibald Cox, who was named special prosecutor, tried to use his investigative powers to secure tape recordings from the White House. Nixon refused to produce the requested materials and ordered Richardson, on October 20, to terminate Cox. Instead of firing Cox, Richardson resigned. His successor, Deputy Attorney General William Ruckelshaus, also refused to fire Cox and was himself terminated before he could resign. Solicitor General Robert Bork—third in line at the Department of Justice—then obeyed Nixon's order to fire Cox. These incidents caused a firestorm of public protest.[32]

Public dissatisfaction over the "massacre" was intense: Western Union deemed the flood of telegrams sent to Washington, D.C., after Cox's termination to be "the heaviest volume on record."[33] Well-respected institutions and individuals, such as the director of the American Bar Association, *Time* magazine, and the AFL-CIO, urged Nixon's impeachment.[34] Criticism continued until a new special prosecutor—Leon Jaworksi—was named to continue the investigation.[35] Eventually, bowing to public pressure, Nixon turned over the requested materials. One recording, of a June 23, 1972, conversation, became the "smoking gun" that showed Nixon's culpability in covering up illegal activities and prompted his resignation. In the end, Watergate shattered public confidence in the chief executive, and Congress believed that legislation was needed to tweak the arrangement provided by the framers.

Post-Watergate Special Counsel Investigations

Following Cox's dismissal, Congress considered legislation that would create a special prosecutor named by a court. Members began to deliberate on a legislative response to the Saturday Night Massacre right away. In the fall of 1973, two key bills—H.R. 11401 and S. 2611—were proposed to address the matter. They represented a change of perspective for Congress regarding responsibility for appointing special prosecutors. Instead of relying on the president or the attorney general to appoint a special prosecutor, or even trusting the president to act with the approval of the Senate, these bills proposed to transfer the power to appoint and remove a special prosecutor from the executive branch to the judicial branch. As the congressional hearings on these bills reveal, the underlying rationale was that the executive branch could not be trusted to investigate itself in certain circumstances.[36] By 1977, Congress and the new president, Jimmy Carter, had agreed that major changes were needed.

On October 26, 1978, President Carter signed into law the Ethics in Government Act, albeit with a sunset provision that required reauthorization every five years.[37] The "independent counsel statute," as it was commonly called, set into statutory language for the first time a set of specific procedures and circumstances for investigating alleged wrongdoing by the executive branch. In a break from past procedure, the statute allowed a special division of the U.S. Court of Appeals for the D.C. Circuit, upon the attorney general's request, to appoint a temporary special prosecutor.[38] By dividing the responsibility for implementing a special prosecutor in this manner, members of Congress were attempting to balance the executive's need to ensure the execution of the laws with Congress's desire for an independent investigation of the executive branch.[39]

The independent counsel statute supplemented the president's responsibility to investigate executive branch wrongdoing. Still, instead of providing a less biased way to investigate the executive branch, it gave presidents political cover, enabling them to excuse aides or supporters caught up in investigations as victims worthy of presidential clemency.

The first special prosecutor investigations under the 1978 act were of Timothy Kraft and Hamilton Jordan, two Carter administration figures who were accused of using cocaine. The independent counsel statute was triggered in these two cases despite the fact that neither case was strong enough to warrant investigation by a U.S. Attorney. Ultimately, however, neither Kraft nor Jordan was prosecuted by the special prosecutor.[40]

A Democratic Congress and President Ronald Reagan

The late 1970s saw a Democratic president, Jimmy Carter, investigated by a Democratic Congress only twice. In contrast, by the end of the 1980s, Republican president Ronald Reagan had been investigated seven times by an opposition Congress. The most controversial special counsel investigation was the one charged with looking into the Iran-Contra scandal, although Reagan himself had little to do with Special Counsel Lawrence Walsh's investigation. Walsh deposed Reagan in 1992 and decided that the former president—who later died of Alzheimer's disease—could not remember anything about Iran-Contra.[41]

To his credit, President Reagan did not pardon anyone connected with the investigation. Reagan withstood Republican pressure to pardon the highest-ranking administration figure charged with criminal activity, National Security Council Adviser John Poindexter, who arguably took the bullet meant for Reagan by claiming not to have informed him of the council's illegal activities. Reagan also resisted pardoning Marine Lieutenant Colonel Oliver North, who neglected to dispose of a document containing evidence of the administration's criminal acts.[42] Each man's convictions were eventually overturned on appeal. At the time, though, Reagan did not necessarily have to pardon anyone, as his vice president, George H. W. Bush, was in line to take over as chief executive.

A Democratic Congress and President George H. W. Bush

Iran-Contra questions haunted Bush throughout his presidency, and he finally put them to rest with his Christmas Eve pardons of Caspar Weinberger (secretary of defense), Elliott Abrams (assistant secretary of state), Duane Clarridge (CIA Latin American division head), Robert McFarlane (national security adviser), Alan Fiers (CIA head of the Central American Task Force), and Clair George (CIA chief of Operations Directorate), all of whom were, like Bush himself, former Reagan administration officials.[43]

The timing of the Iran-Contra pardons was fortuitous: Bush had lost his reelection bid to Bill Clinton, and Caspar Weinberger had been reindicted. A White House lawyer revealed on December 11, 1992, that Bush had kept a diary that, according to Special Counsel Lawrence Walsh, may have contained information that would have been useful to Weinberger at trial. The existence of the diary increased the likelihood of Bush being called to testify in Weinberger's case.[44] By pardoning Weinberger, Bush therefore not only kept Weinberger from having to stand trial but also avoided being called in to testify in the case himself. As discussed in the next chapter, the Iran-Contra pardons may have marked the start of a new trend whereby presidents pardon not for traditional reasons of mercy or for the public interest but in order to protect their own personal interests.

A Republican Congress and President Bill Clinton

With Democrat Bill Clinton in the White House and a new Republican majority in Congress, investigations into executive branch behavior continued. In the eight years of the Clinton presidency, several Cabinet officials were targets of independent counsel investigations: Secretary of Commerce Ron Brown, Secretary of Agriculture Mike Espy, Housing and Urban Development Secretary Henry Cisneros, Interior Secretary Bruce Babbitt, and Labor Secretary Alexis Herman.

Unlike his predecessor, however, Clinton did not require the pretext of an independent counsel statute investigation to abuse the clemency power: His clemency offer to members of the FALN, a Puerto Rican Nationalist group, was most likely a political calculation designed to help his wife, Hillary, in her Senate bid, or Vice President Al Gore in his presidential run, by appealing to Hispanics in New York City. Still, the conceit of using clemency to fight off an "overreaching" Congress served Clinton well at the end of his term, when he unleashed his widely condemned "last-minute" pardons.

In the final hours of his presidency, Clinton awarded clemency to Cisneros and former CIA director John Deutch.[45] He also offered clemency to his half-brother, Roger Clinton, and to Whitewater figure Susan McDougal, among others. More importantly, he pardoned fugitive Marc Rich, whose ex-wife had participated in a wide-ranging clemency campaign and had herself contributed almost half a million dollars to Clinton's presidential library.[46]

Morrison v. Olson

Although only in effect intermittently throughout the 1980s and 1990s, the independent counsel statute kept coming back to torment new presidents. It had survived an important legal challenge. In *Morrison v. Olson* (1988), Theodore Olson, a Reagan administration official, challenged the constitutionality of the independent counsel statute, arguing that it violated the Constitution's "appointments" clause of Article II, Section 2, Clause 2, and intruded upon Article III. Alexia Morrison was the independent counsel investigating Olson.

In a 7–1 decision (Justice Anthony Kennedy did not participate; Antonin Scalia alone dissented), the Supreme Court ruled that the independent counsel statute was constitutional. The Court dealt with two appointment clause challenges early on. First, Chief Justice William Rehnquist's majority opinion held that because the independent counsel was an "inferior" rather than a "principal" officer, the appointments clause was not violated. The majority reasoned that the independent counsel was an "inferior" officer for three key reasons: she could be removed by a higher-ranking executive branch official, the attorney general; her responsibilities were limited to investigation and prosecution and did not include policy-making or administrative duties unrelated to her main responsibilities; and she enjoyed only "limited" jurisdiction and tenure. Had the Court found that the independent counsel was a "principal" officer, her appointment would have to come from the president, with the advice and consent of the Senate, and the statute would have failed to meet this constitutional requirement. On the second appointment clause question, the Court decided that, contrary to Olson's assertion, this particular interbranch appointment was constitutional: Congress could vest the power to appoint an independent counsel in a special federal court located outside the executive branch.[47]

The Court found that Article III of the Constitution was not violated by the fact that the independent counsel statute assigned to the Special Division of the U.S. Court of Appeals for the D.C. Circuit the responsibility to appoint, define the jurisdiction of, and even terminate an independent counsel (when an investigation is nearly finished). Finally, the Court found that the provision in the statute preventing the attorney general from dismissing the independent counsel unless "good cause" could be shown did not "sufficiently deprive the President of control over the independent counsel to interfere impermissibly with his constitutional obligation to ensure the faithful execution of the laws," and that the act as a whole did not interfere with the president's ability to exercise his Article II powers. In other words, the independent counsel statute could take away the president's power to unilaterally remove an independent counsel, since, in the Court's opinion, this did not interfere with the president's responsibility to fulfill his constitutional duty to execute the laws. Indeed, in the eyes of the majority, the statute provided the president with adequate control over the independent counsel: She could be fired for "good cause" by the attorney general.[48]

In a blistering dissent, Justice Scalia scolded the majority. Taking issue with the portion of the act's language that required an attorney general to request an independent counsel unless there were "no reasonable grounds to believe that further investigation or prosecution [was] warranted," Scalia argued that political reality essentially required the attorney general to request an independent counsel even when one might not be appropriate under the circumstances.[49] One legal analyst referred to the provision as using "howitzers to combat mice," in that many investigations were begun, but few indictments resulted.[50] In essence, Scalia argued, Congress had used the independent counsel statute to ensnare executive branch officials in order to hurt the president and help itself. Also, under Scalia's strict interpretation of the Constitution, the independent counsel statute unconstitutionally vested executive power in someone other than the president. The majority's suggestion that the president—via the attorney general—maintained "at least *some* control" over the independent counsel, Scalia suggested, was "somewhat like referring to shackles as an effective means of locomotion."[51]

Instead of the remedy presented by the independent counsel statute, Scalia endorsed a separation of powers–based solution, whereby (1) any branch could retaliate against any other branch by using its own unique powers, and (2) the public could rid itself of corrupt officeholders at the ballot box. One key consequence of the independent counsel statute, Scalia continued, was to short-circuit the political check (number 2 above) by instead establishing a hair trigger on investigations. While the president suffered, he noted, it was a consequence-free win-win situation for Congress.[52]

Finally, and perhaps most importantly, Scalia argued that the independent counsel statute actually exacerbated the original problem that it was designed to remedy: a lack of executive accountability. "The difference," he argued, "is the difference that the Founders envisioned when they established a single Chief Executive accountable to the people: the blame can be assigned to someone who can be punished."[53]

While Scalia's point about direct executive accountability is well taken, the majority correctly points out that the independent counsel always remained subject to dismissal by the attorney general. Thus, the president's strongest argument against the independent counsel statute—that it allowed Congress to unfairly pursue executive branch officials—failed to persuade the Supreme Court.

The Independent Counsel Statute: Ripe for Exploitation?

Now that the independent counsel statute has run its course, we can look back and analyze its fairness and effectiveness. As noted above, the Saturday Night Massacre had scared the public, which then urged Congress to act to limit presidential discretion when the executive branch was under investigation. The independent counsel statute was a success insofar as it restored the confidence of the public in the government's ability to investigate itself. What is more, the Supreme Court later held in *Morrison v. Olson* that it was constitutional, and an acceptable mechanism for supplementing the president's authority on those occasions when executive branch conduct was under investigation. Despite these successes, the independent counsel statute was constantly under fire from critics.

Unlike many divisions in politics, the line between those who opposed and those who supported the independent counsel statute depended largely upon who was in the White House at the time of an investigation. From the late 1970s through the Iran-Contra scandal, Republicans generally sympathized with the executive branch. Thus, critics of the statute were, at first, primarily Republicans. Presidents Richard Nixon, Gerald Ford, Ronald Reagan, and George H. W. Bush were Republicans, so this perspective is no surprise. Executive branch sympathizers during this era viewed the independent counsel statute as a weapon created by Congress in an attempt "to render the President blind and lame by restricting his authority to appoint, direct, and remove the officers who wield executive power." They suggested that the statute was "an instrument for undermining the independence of executive officers themselves." According to this point of view, the independent counsel statute was a way for the legislature to "undermin[e] public confidence in the ability of the President and his subordinates to faithfully execute the law, thereby paving the way for the Congress to assume the direction of the administration of the law through its oversight and investigatory powers."[54]

When Bill Clinton became president and Republicans dominated Congress, the arguments remained similar even as the advocates exchanged seats. Arguments against the independent counsel statute during the Clinton years were quite similar to the ones that had been made in the past, with one twist: Now, both parties had taken a turn complaining about the statute and advocating for it. The independent counsel statute may have passed constitutional muster, but it was not terribly successful: Out of twenty independent counsel investigations conducted between 1978 and 1999, only eight resulted in indictments.[55] Both political parties eventually agreed that the statute created more problems than it solved.

In addition, the independent counsel statute created at least one long-lasting problem: Presidents, relieved of direct responsibility for investigations into executive branch behavior, discovered that they could criticize the independent counsel for political advantage. As one scholar pointed out, "Presidents attack their appointees at their own peril, but it is far easier for presidents to attack the investigator appointed by someone else."[56] The independent counsel statute was not renewed when it lapsed again in 1999. Still, the pattern of presidents justifying controversial clemency decisions because of outside investigations into the executive branch—whether by a statutory independent counsel or not—continued into the administration of President George W. Bush.

Conclusion

The framers' imperfect system for detecting executive wrongdoing has been sufficient throughout most of American history. As I demonstrated via case studies of four key pre-Watergate cases—the Whiskey Ring, the Oregon Land Frauds, Teapot Dome, and the Income Tax Scandal—this success was largely due to the attitudes of the presidents serving during the investigation. If the public trusted that the president was behaving appropriately, they often viewed the investigation as legitimate.

Watergate shook the public's confidence in its own institutions, and as a result, the independent counsel statute was enacted. It was an alternative to trusting the president's own direct appointee's investigation into executive branch wrongdoing, and it survived a constitutional challenge in *Morrison v. Olson*. However, the lasting significance of the independent counsel statute has been to create maneuvering room for presidents to use the clemency power to excuse executive branch officials caught up in an investigation.

Although the statute was not reauthorized in 1999, the damage had already been done. Politics has tainted judicial inquiries, and outside investigations into executive branch behavior—whether under the independent counsel statute or not—have provided political cover for post-Watergate presidents to abuse the pardon power. They have done so by using clemency to protect their own executive branch officials and end investigations or to reward political donors. In the next chapter, I will explain why several of the most controversial pardons of the 1990s and 2000s can be considered abuses of the clemency power.

6 Three Recent Presidents and Abuse of the Pardon Power

Our three most recent presidents—George H. W. Bush, Bill Clinton, and George W. Bush—whose years in office spanned a time period that occurred both during and after the years that the independent counsel statute was in force—have abused the pardon power. Rather than pardon as an "act of grace" or "for the public welfare," these three presidents succumbed to the temptation to use clemency for their own personal reasons. President George H. W. Bush was left with President Reagan's Iran-Contra investigation to deal with, but the scandal disappeared with the stroke of Bush's pardon pen. President Bill Clinton used his last year in office to aid his wife's New York Senate bid and his vice president's presidential campaign while also helping along his presidential library fund. The independent counsel statute lapsed in 1999, but the Scooter Libby commutation suggests that the lines between politics and judicial investigation are forever blurred, and that George W. Bush may have allowed Libby to remain out of jail because Libby kept quiet about confidential executive branch communications. This chapter examines the circumstances leading up to these four scandals in detail and explores each president's decision to use the clemency power, the response in the political arena, and the public's reaction.

George H. W. Bush and Iran-Contra

To understand the significance of President George H. W. Bush's use of the clemency power, one must first have a basic grasp of the facts of the Iran-Contra affair and the ongoing controversy it stirred from the Reagan years right up until the eve of the election that Bush lost to Bill Clinton in 1992. President Ronald Reagan, Bush's predecessor, was strongly in favor of (some aides say "obsessed" with) rescuing American hostages in Lebanon. He feared being accused of abandoning them, apparently remembering how Jimmy Carter's inability to free the American hostages in

Iran had paved the way to office for Reagan. He also felt great sympathy for the Nicaraguan contras, the "freedom fighters" whose struggle against their Marxist government Reagan strongly supported.[1]

Once Congress passed the Boland amendments that ended American military assistance to the Nicaraguan contras, Reagan, who wished to continue to aid them, asked his advisers for ideas on how to do so. Apparently with President Reagan's approval, National Security Agency (NSA) Adviser Robert McFarlane and his aide, Marine Lieutenant Colonel Oliver North, cooperated with retired Air Force Major General Richard Secord and the Central Intelligence Agency (CIA) to ship missiles to Iran in exchange for American hostages. More hostages were taken, however, and the deal eventually went sour for both Iran and the United States.[2]

Regarding the contras, McFarlane, John Poindexter (who succeeded McFarlane), North, Secord, and CIA Director William Casey worked together to raise money and assemble "a small, rag-tag private air force" to supply the contras with military aid and provisions. After one of the supply planes was shot down, the story became public and a surviving pilot stood trial. North, aware that he was about to be investigated by the Justice Department, began to shred his files; however, he missed one that showed how arms sales profits were funneled to the contras. Once the two stories were linked, the entire affair became major news. The headline stories continued while Congress investigated during the spring of 1987. Despite televised congressional hearings featuring dozens of witnesses, the two key questions—the scope of President Reagan's involvement and Vice President Bush's knowledge of the events—remained unanswered.[3] A special counsel, Lawrence Walsh, was named to investigate.

The buzz did not last for long. By 1988, despite convictions of key figures such as North, McFarlane, and Poindexter, the public seemed disinterested. Successful appeals by several defendants eliminated their convictions altogether, and the most senior figure to be indicted—Caspar Weinberger—had yet to stand trial.[4] It had, however, been a rough stretch for Weinberger, Reagan's former secretary of defense. On June 16, he was indicted by Walsh on five felony counts for his role in the Iran-Contra investigation. The charges included allegations that he had lied to Congress and obstructed the investigation.[5]

On October 30, 1992—four days before the presidential election between Republican incumbent president George H. W. Bush and his Democratic opponent, Arkansas governor Bill Clinton—Weinberger was indicted again.[6] Walsh's new charge was that Weinberger had made a false statement, an allegation that encompassed Weinberger's "notes on a [January 7,] 1986 White House meeting that contradicted President Bush's often-repeated assertion that he had been unaware at the time, when he was Vice President, that arms sold to Iran were part of an arms-for-hostages swap."[7] Walsh quoted Weinberger's note as follows: "President decided to go with Israeli-Iranian offer to release our 5 hostages in return for sale of 4,000 TOWs to Iran by Israel. George Shultz and I opposed—Bill Casey, Ed Meese and VP favored—as did Poindexter."[8]

According to Walsh, the "VP favored" notation meant that Bush had not been completely forthcoming about what he knew and when he knew it. Weinberger's notes placed Vice President Bush at that January 7, 1986, meeting where Shultz and Weinberger disagreed with selling arms to Iran; the notes also establish that the Reagan officials intended to swap 4,000 TOW missiles for five American hostages, an "arms for hostages" arrangement that Bush had previously said that he only learned about in late 1986.[9]

Despite dangers of Republican criticism regarding the timing of the second indictment, Walsh's investigation proceeded without regard to political consequences. Focused on furthering the investigation, he did not believe that the note, which contradicted five years' worth of claims by Bush that he was "out of the loop," was important, because he believed that the public already understood that Bush was not being truthful about his knowledge of the "arms for hostages" situation. Walsh ignored the warning of his staffer, Steven Ellis, that the timing of the Weinberger indictment "would be a political bombshell."[10] Walsh later admitted that he "had been oblivious to the dramatic effect the quotation would have once it became public."[11] Thus, although Walsh did the right thing by ignoring the political context of his investigation, he ended up becoming a scapegoat for angry Bush supporters.

Once public, the note became ripe for political use. The saga of the note became a media sensation and led news broadcasts.[12] Bill Clinton used Weinberger's note to question President Bush's credibility in the closing days of the presidential election.[13] This charge especially hurt Bush because throughout the campaign he had repeatedly insisted that he had told the special prosecutor everything he knew regarding Iran-Contra.[14] Weinberger's note, according to journalist Bob Woodward, was "the first documented evidence that Bush had known the arms were a direct exchange for hostages and that Bush had been privy to the strong opposition of

Weinberger and Shultz."[15] Although the note did not show any criminal wrongdoing by Bush, it did hurt him politically by revealing that he had apparently been lying all along about his role in the Iran-Contra affair and his knowledge of events.[16]

George H. W. Bush lost his reelection bid to Bill Clinton on November 3, 1992. As his electoral defeat took much of the political sting out of potential consequences, he began considering pardons for various Iran-Contra figures. Rumblings of pardon talk surfaced publicly in November 7, 1992, newspaper reports saying that midlevel Bush administration officials had discussed asking President Bush for a pardon for Weinberger, who enjoyed solid backing from conservatives.[17] Weinberger's trial was to be held on January 5, 1993.[18] Walsh's team speculated that at trial, former presidents Reagan and/or Bush might be called by Weinberger to testify, most likely via videotape.[19]

At the White House's request, Weinberger's attorneys sent a formal pardon request directly to the chief executive.[20] President Bush had written in his diary on Tuesday, December 22, that "the pardon of Weinberger will put a tarnish, kind of a downer, on our legacy."[21] However, on Christmas Eve 1992, after receiving support from White House Counsel C. Boyden Gray and Press Secretary Marlin Fitzwater, as well as assurance from Fitzwater that "the Weinberger indictment . . . shows that Walsh has become vindictive," President Bush had the political cover he needed.[22] He granted clemency to Weinberger and five other Iran-Contra figures.

The Iran-Contra Pardons

The executive clemency that President Bush granted on Christmas Eve 1992 included full pardons for Caspar Weinberger, Elliott Abrams, Duane Clarridge, Alan Fiers, Clair George, and Robert McFarlane, effectively ending the Iran-Contra scandal investigation. The pardon proclamation first focused on Weinberger, whom President Bush praised as "a true American patriot [who] has rendered long and extraordinary service to our country." Reminiscent of Gerald Ford's personal justifications for the Nixon pardon, Bush went on to note that "I am pardoning him not just out of compassion or to spare a 75-year-old patriot the torment of lengthy and costly legal proceedings, but to make it possible for him to receive the honor he deserves for his extraordinary service to our country. Moreover, on a somewhat more personal note, I cannot ignore the debilitating illnesses faced by Caspar Weinberger and his wife."[23]

Regarding the other recipients of executive clemency, President Bush offered the following justifications: They were motivated by "patriotism"; "did not profit or seek to profit" from their activities; had established "a record of long and distinguished service"; and had "already paid a price—in depleted savings, lost careers, anguished families—grossly disproportionate to any misdeeds or errors of judgment they may have committed."[24] In keeping with the second justification, three Iran-Contra defendants, Secord, Albert Hakim, and Thomas Clines, did not receive pardons because they were positioned to make a profit from their activities.[25]

In an apparent attempt to appease the press with his transparency, Bush offered to publicly release his own sworn testimony. He also addressed the larger separation-of-powers issue at stake as he saw it: the political use of the independent counsel statute by a partisan Congress. Taking aim at what he characterized as "the criminalization of policy differences" by Congress, he argued that "the proper target is the President, not his subordinates; the proper forum is the voting booth, not the courtroom." Noting that "the actions of the men I am pardoning took place within the larger Cold War struggle," President Bush attempted to place the pardons within the "healing tradition" of pardoning that occurred after earlier wars, including the Civil War, World War II, and Vietnam.[26] Conspicuously—but not surprisingly—absent was any mention of the Nixon pardon.[27]

Public Reaction

The Iran-Contra pardons were an important enough event to prompt a reaction from many segments of American society: Various media outlets dissected the situation from every angle, political elites provided on-the-record comments to attempt to spin the situation for political advantage, and pollsters queried the public for its reaction to the whole production.

On the day of the pardons, Lawrence Walsh released a statement in which he accused the Iran-Contra pardons of "undermin[ing] the principle that no man is above the law."[28] Weinberger's notes—Walsh revealed for the first time—contained "evidence of a conspiracy among the highest-ranking Reagan administration officials to lie to Congress and the American public."[29] In essence, Weinberger's decision to withhold his notes "possibly forestalled timely impeachment proceedings against President Reagan and other officials."[30]

In addition, Walsh spoke of "President Bush's own misconduct" in failing to disclose and turn over "his own highly relevant contemporaneous notes," actions that Walsh ominously warned would "lead to appropriate action."[31] Bush's diary notes were not discovered by Walsh until December 11, 1992, when the White House first revealed their existence. The Bush diaries were important because, as the *New York Times* noted, there was a chance they would "include evidence that Mr. Weinberger would have been entitled to present in his trial, a possibility that could have led him to seek Mr. Bush's testimony." Thus, President Bush's decision to pardon Weinberger may have been motivated by Bush's desire to avoid having to testify in Weinberger's trial.[32]

In an interview, Walsh said, "The Weinberger trial would have exposed the effort (by senior Reagan administration officials) to protect President Reagan from a confrontation with Congress. We could have showed they concealed his deliberate pursuit of an arms-for-hostages transaction even though he knew the Arms Export Control Act forbade it." Disagreeing with President Bush's "wholly false statement that these are political issues, not criminal," Walsh stated that "making false statements to Congress is a crime."[33]

On February 8, 1993, Walsh presented his report to Congress and revealed evidence that he had planned to use at the Weinberger trial. Despite Walsh's claim of "new and disturbing facts" proving his allegation that senior Reagan aides had lied about what the president knew about an "arms-for-hostages" exchange, one of his representatives said that Walsh had "absolutely no intention" of requesting that Bush or Reagan testify.[34] Neither ever did. Walsh turned in his final Iran-Contra report, and his conclusions were made public on January 18, 1994.

Republicans and Democrats urged competing interpretations of the Iran-Contra scandal. Republicans, on the one hand, framed it as "an institutional dispute about the relative importance of the Congress and the president in the conduct of foreign affairs."[35] The resulting pardons could then be seen in the manner urged by President Bush: as the legitimate end result of a political struggle between the president and Congress. Democrats, on the other hand, portrayed the Iran-Contra dispute as a struggle to uphold the rule of law between a White House hell-bent on following its own agenda and a Congress that was right to investigate the executive branch for disregarding the Boland amendments and keeping crucial facts secret from Congress. To them, the pardons were used as a political weapon to cut off a legitimate independent counsel inquiry.

A majority of the American public sided with the Democrats on the pardon issue. A Gallup poll conducted on December 28, 1992, found that 54 percent disapproved of President Bush's decision to pardon Weinberger if he acted so that Weinberger could not "be prosecuted for his alleged involvement" in Iran-Contra.[36] In an ABC News/*Washington Post* poll conducted in mid-January 1993, only 36 percent of respondents approved of Bush's pardon of Iran-Contra figures, while 56 percent disapproved.[37] A CBS News/*New York Times* poll found that 63 percent disapproved of Bush granting a pardon for Weinberger so that Weinberger could not "be prosecuted for his alleged involvement" in Iran-Contra.[38]

Not lost on the general public was the argument that President Bush may have benefited personally from the pardons by preventing a trial at which testimony contradicting his understanding (or even revealing criminal activity) may have been revealed.[39] A plurality (though nearly a majority) of 49 percent of respondents to a Gallup poll taken in the week following the pardons believed that the main reason Bush had decided to pardon the Iran-Contra defendants was "to protect himself from legal difficulties or embarrassment resulting from his own role in Iran-Contra." The next most popular response (21 percent) was the poll's equivalent to Bush's proffered justification of "moving on," that is, "to put the Iran-Contra affair in the country's past."[40] A majority (51 percent) of respondents to the mid-January ABC News/*Washington Post* poll believed that Congress should hold hearings to investigate the pardons, while 45 percent disagreed.[41]

Here, the most reasonable interpretation of the Iran-Contra pardons was that George H. W. Bush was indeed trying to avoid an embarrassing appearance in court. Despite his attempt to use a public statement to place the pardons into the healing traditions of past wars, Bush failed to persuasively frame them as "acts of grace" or "for the public interest." These proffered rationales seemed to be a stretch when considered alongside the more compelling reason that the public suspected: using the pardon power to make a terribly uncomfortable situation go away, at a time when no political consequences would apply.

Bill Clinton and Clemency

As president, Bill Clinton wielded the clemency power differently than his immediate predecessor (or successor, for that matter). Although several of his top-ranking executive branch officials endured investigations, Clinton never needed to pardon anyone to keep them quiet about top executive branch discussions. Nevertheless, he found several opportunities to abuse the clemency power during his last year in office. A quid pro quo, though strongly suspected, was never conclusively proven in either situation discussed here. Still, the evidence suggests that Clinton attempted to use clemency to purchase votes for his wife and vice president and to reward a generous contributor for donating to his presidential library.

Members of the FALN

In 1999, President Clinton decided to offer conditional clemency to sixteen members of the FALN, the Armed Forces of National Liberation (FALN is the acronym for the group's name in Spanish). The FALN, a Puerto Rican Nationalist group, was responsible for at least 130 bombings between 1974 and 1983, killing 6 people, at minimum, and wounding more than 70. At the time of his decision, the president asserted that the prisoners who had received his conditional clemency offer had been sentenced to excessive prison sentences—some to more than 50 years—even though they had not been directly involved in the acts that injured or killed others. The terms of the clemency offer required each prisoner to swear off acts of violence and agree to parole supervision.[42]

Among those who encouraged the clemency decision were representatives of popular Democratic constituencies, including former president Jimmy Carter; Archbishop Desmond Tutu of South Africa; Martin Luther King Jr.'s widow, Coretta Scott King; and several New York Democrats in the House of Representatives. Though the clemency offer was a potential boon to First Lady Hillary Clinton, enhancing her standing in New York's Puerto Rican community at a time when she was considering a senatorial campaign, the White House said she was not involved with the FALN clemency decision.[43] About 75 percent of the Puerto Ricans living in New York City were registered Democrats.[44]

On August 27, the *New York Times* reported that the federal agencies that had reviewed the FALN clemency petition—including the Federal Bureau of Investigation, the Bureau of Prisons, and U.S. Attorneys in two states—were all against executive clemency for the sixteen prisoners. What is more, the final report to the White House from the Department of Justice listed multiple options for each individual prisoner. The use of this format usually suggested that the agencies involved had expressed varying viewpoints, but in this case, the format was used despite the fact that the agencies in question had unanimously opposed any leniency whatsoever. Also, it was "highly unusual" for a president not to follow the unanimous opinion of such agencies, especially in a case involving a group with a reputation for violent acts. Nevertheless, a White House spokesman said that "the President and his counsel [Charles Ruff] fully understood the range of views on this issue and were not deprived of any advice they needed."[45] The president set a September 10 deadline for the prisoners to accept or reject his clemency offer.[46]

This new information regarding the behind-the-scenes circumstances of the clemency offer brought on considerable criticism from both sides of the political aisle. Even notable Democrats publicly criticized the FALN clemency offer. Senator Daniel Moynihan (D-NY) (whose soon-to-be-vacant Senate seat Hillary Clinton had all but decided to pursue) disagreed with the decision, and Chicago Mayor Richard Daley called it "wrong."[47]

Republicans on the House Government Reform Committee issued subpoenas for relevant White House and Justice Department records while also planning for hearings.[48] President Clinton responded on September 16 by largely refusing to comply with the subpoenas, claiming that executive privilege protected the confidentiality of at least the clemency-related materials.[49] He agreed, however, to provide about 10,000 pages of related documents.[50]

On September 9, the House voted 311–41 in favor of a resolution saying that Clinton "should not have granted clemency to the FALN terrorists." This marked the first time that a congressional resolution had ever been passed to oppose a president's clemency grant.[51] The resolution, though nonbinding, allowed Republicans to keep what they viewed as a political mistake by Bill Clinton in the news.[52] On September 14, the Senate followed suit, voting 95–2 to rebuke Clinton for the clemency offer.[53]

A hearing held on September 21 in front of the House Judiciary Committee revealed the breadth and depth of the federal law enforcement community's opposition to clemency for the FALN. A draft letter prepared for FBI Director Louis Freeh's signature (although unsigned, he testified that it did reflect his position) became the first official proof of the widespread opposition first reported by the *New York Times* on August 27.[54] At a Senate Judiciary hearing held on October 19, a 1996 letter from Pardon Attorney Margaret Love to Charles Ruff formally urging Clinton to deny clemency to Puerto Rican Nationalists was made public. The letter, written on behalf of the Justice Department, was never mentioned by the White House despite the media furor over the FALN clemency offer.[55] The next day, a report written in September 1999, bearing Attorney General Janet Reno's name and warning that the FALN presented an "ongoing threat" to American security, was made public.[56]

Eventually, eleven prisoners accepted President Clinton's clemency offer. They were freed on September 10. Two rejected the offer and remained in prison; one cut a deal to stay for five additional years; and the remaining two—who had completed their confinements—were released from paying fines.[57]

Speaking publicly about the matter for the first time, President Clinton said on September 10 that his wife's possible Senate run had had "absolutely" no effect on his decision to offer commuted sentences to the sixteen FALN prisoners, and that she "didn't know anything about it." He insisted that his goal had been to show mercy toward the sixteen prisoners, whose imposed sentences were out of proportion with their crimes. In reality, he said, those sentences had been a punishment for being associated with the FALN, a group whose other members had killed and wounded to advance a political agenda.[58]

Republicans disagreed with the president's assessment, suggesting in a report from the House Government Reform Committee, which was made public on November 10, that the clemency offer was tied to political considerations. They cited a March 6 e-mail from Jeffrey Farrow, the cochair of Clinton's interagency group on Puerto Rico, to the White House in which Farrow suggested that if clemency were granted, "the V.P.'s Puerto Rican position would be helped," and that the situation was the "top priority" of Representative Luis Gutierrez (D-IL) and "of high constituent importance" to New York Democrats and members of Congress José Serrano (D-NY) and Nydia Velazquez (D-NY). On March 7, White House Deputy Chief of Staff Maria Echaveste forwarded the Farrow e-mail to Charles Ruff.[59] A White House spokesman insisted that political considerations had not influenced the clemency decision, and also denied that Vice President Al Gore or his staff had been involved in the decision.[60] It is worthwhile to note that President Clinton, who had secured a comfortable reelection win over Republican Bob Dole (R-KS) in the 1996 presidential election, made the conditional clemency offer as a second-term "lame duck."

The public was less than impressed with the spectacle. In a USA Today/CNN Gallup Poll conducted September 10–14, 61 percent of the 839 adults polled disagreed with the FALN clemency offer; only 19 percent agreed with it. Sixty percent believed the motivation for the clemency offer was to woo Hispanic support for Mrs. Clinton in New York; just 25 percent believed that the president acted because it was the right thing to do.[61]

President Clinton decided to grant clemency to these members of the FALN in spite of widespread opposition from the law enforcement community. The Farrow e-mail message proved that political considerations—whether benefiting Hillary Clinton or Al Gore—were the driving force behind the decision. As a "lame duck," Clinton calculated correctly that he would be more or less insulated from political consequences for his actions. As it turned out, the FALN clemency controversy was only a warm-up for the debacle of Clinton's final hours as president. The "last-minute" pardons of Marc Rich and others created one final Clinton-era scandal.

The "Last-Minute" Pardons

Aboard Air Force One in January 2001, President Clinton joked to members of the press corps, "You got anybody you want to pardon?"[62] The comment was made in jest, but it foreshadowed the frantic final hours of the Clinton presidency. Burning the candle at both ends, Clinton spent his last days in office furiously completing as much work as possible—finalizing eight national monuments, nominating nine federal judges, authorizing nearly 4,000 pages of new federal regulations, and, of course, contemplating his final clemency decisions.[63] Exhausted but thinking clearly (or not, depending on which Clinton confidants you believe), President Clinton prepared to issue a "unique" group of pardons, set apart by "the amount of back-channel lobbying, the limited scrutiny applied to those seeking clemency, and the number of people who succeeded in obtaining pardons."[64]

At about 10 A.M. on Saturday morning—only two hours before George W. Bush took over the presidency—President Clinton awarded clemency to 176 individuals (140 pardons, 36 commutations).[65] Susan McDougal's name was on the list, as were those of two high-ranking, ex-administration officials: former Department of Housing and Urban Development secretary Henry Cisneros (who had lied to the FBI about hush-money payments to his mistress)[66] and former CIA director John Deutch (who had violated federal law by storing sensitive, classified data on a home computer);[67] Clinton's half-brother, Roger (who had a 1985 drug conviction wiped off his record);[68] and two fugitives from justice named Marc Rich and Pincus Green. Rich and Green had been indicted in 1983 in what was at the time the "largest tax-evasion case in U.S. history," but had been living safe from prosecution in Switzerland.[69] One article noted as an aside that Rich's ex-wife, Denise, was a Democratic Party fundraiser.[70] She would play a much greater role in the days and weeks to come.

Observers were stunned by the number of pardons and commutations. The *Washington Post* accurately described the list of clemency recipients as "extraordinary," and "eclipsing in magnitude and scope the last-minute legal forgiveness dispensed by previous presidents." Red flags began to crop up almost immediately as behind-the-scenes details trickled out. Pardon Attorney Roger Adams said, "I've never seen anything like this," noting, "We were up literally all night as the White House continued to add names of people they wanted to pardon." He added, "Many people on the list didn't even apply for pardons," and said that some of the administration's pardon requests were so late that pardon officials did not have a chance to contact the FBI for record checks.[71] Indeed, the clemency petitions received by the Justice Department during the last three months of the Clinton presidency were the most it had ever received over a three-month period.[72] The pardon attorney did not have the time or the means to adequately deal with this enormous backlog: The office announced in October 2001 that new pardon applications could no longer be accepted and urged applicants to instead appeal to Clinton directly.[73]

This backlog actually worked to the advantage of Marc Rich. Adams later testified that White House officials misled the Justice Department about Rich's fugitive status and tried—at the last minute—to have the pardon attorney create paperwork on Rich suggesting that his application had undergone the normal scrutiny. Had the Rich application gone through the proper channels, Adams noted, it would have been rejected for violating the requirement that applicants serve at least five years before applying for clemency.[74]

The Marc Rich Pardon Campaign

Marc Rich was identified early on as a controversial clemency recipient, but the magnitude of his backstory developed only after weeks of investigation by the *Washington Post*, the *New York Times*, and other newspapers. The key for many clemency recipients, it turned out, was access to Clinton or contact with close Clinton associates. The president had acknowledged heavy reliance on the advice of Rich attorney Jack Quinn, who had been White House counsel and Vice President Al Gore's chief of staff.[75] A "behind-the-scenes campaign" had been waged to obtain a pardon for Rich, a campaign that avoided standard clemency procedures in favor of direct lobbying on the president by Quinn.[76] Quinn later testified that he went directly to Clinton because he knew that Rich's application would be rejected by the Justice Department for violating its guidelines.[77]

Eventually, the full behind-the-scenes campaign was exposed. In Belfast, Northern Ireland, on December 13, 2000, Quinn had approached Clinton aide Bruce Lindsey about Rich's pardon application. Quinn had notified Deputy Attorney General Eric Holder (but not Pardon Attorney Roger Adams or Mary Jo White, the head federal prosecutor in New York) that Rich's pardon application would be sent directly to President Clinton.[78]

Meanwhile, Denise Rich talked with President Clinton on the telephone and wrote a heartfelt letter to support her ex-husband's pardon application. The letter contained the following passages: "I support his application with all my heart" and "I believe with all my heart that this is the right thing to do."[79] She first denied involvement in the pardon decision, then recanted.[80] She insisted that her generosity, with total donations to Democrats totaling $1 million since 1993, was in no way related to her ex-husband's pardon.[81] And yet, since 1998, Ms. Rich had contributed $450,000 to the Clinton presidential library fund.[82] Later still, the public learned that another Rich pardon supporter (and friend of Denise Rich), Beth Dozoretz, had pledged to raise $1 million for the Clinton presidential library.[83]

In reality, the Rich pardon campaign actually began as early as February and March 2000, raising questions about claims by Denise Rich and Beth Dozoretz that their May 2000 contributions to the Clinton presidential library were in no way related to Marc Rich's pardon.[84] Denise Rich's letter was one of dozens from notable elected officials, businesspeople, and nonprofit executives that Quinn and other attorneys working for Rich took to Bill Clinton. The New York Times characterized Rich's letter-writing supporters as "a virtual Who's Who of Israeli society and Jewish philanthropy."[85] Of 71 supporters who signed letters included with Rich's clemency application, 48 were "prominent Israelis" and 8 were "leading American Jews," according to the Post.[86] Through spokesmen, Rich denied giving money to any Israeli election campaigns. However, Jerusalem mayor Ehud Olmert, who supported the Rich pardon, later admitted to receiving a $25,000 political donation from Rich in 1993.[87]

When contacted, several of Rich's letter-writing "supporters" said they had not been told that their kind words toward Rich would be used to secure clemency for him. In fact, only one of six letter writers contacted by the *Times* said they knew their letters might play a role in resolving Rich's legal difficulties. Robert Fink, one of Rich's attorneys, acknowledged that "not everyone was necessarily told it [his/her letter] was going to be for a pardon."[88]

The bottom line was that Rich's campaign had succeeded. His pardon ended a several-year-long standoff between Rich and law enforcement officials, who had refused to agree with Rich's demand that he not face jail time if he agreed to return to the United States to stand trial for the charges against him.[89] Had he been found guilty, Rich could have spent his life in prison.[90] Commenting on his case via a statement released from Jerusalem, Marc Rich said he saw his pardon as "the closing of a cycle of justice and a humanitarian act."[91]

Public Reaction

Clinton's decision to pardon Rich attracted nearly universal disdain. On March 1, 2001, key Clinton aides—Chief of Staff John Podesta and White House Counsel Beth Nolan—testified to the House Government Reform Committee that they had strongly opposed a Rich pardon.[92] Not even close allies such as campaign adviser James Carville or Vice President Al Gore could defend President Clinton's last official acts.[93] President Jimmy Carter characterized President Clinton's handling of the pardon as "one of his most serious mistakes" and said, "I don't think there is any doubt that some of the factors in [Rich's] pardon were attributable to his large gifts. In my opinion, that was disgraceful."[94]

C. Boyden Gray, White House counsel for George H. W. Bush, suggested that his boss had taken the high road on clemency: "We never suggested to anyone that we were open for business." Aside from Weinberger and his fellow Iran-Contra figures who received clemency, every pardon petition sent to President Bush had come through the Justice Department, Gray said.[95] President George W. Bush said that he was "troubled" by the Rich pardon, but that he would not interfere with President Clinton's decision in order to protect the pardon power for himself and his successors.[96]

Senate Majority Leader Trent Lott (R-MS) called the pardon "outrageous" and "clearly indefensible" and suggested the possibility of hearings to learn more about the circumstances.[97] The *Washington Post* described a "near-total absence of Democrats defending" the Rich pardon. "Appalling" was how Representative Barney Frank (D-MA) described the situation, and he suggested that President Clinton had been "insensitive to what is right and wrong" in the Rich matter.[98] Former senator Bob Kerrey (D-NE) said, "This is a real dangerous pardon. You don't pardon a traitor who has paid no price at all. Something got in the way of good judgment."[99] Later, at a Senate Judiciary Committee hearing, Democratic senators Charles Schumer, Richard Durbin, and Russ Feingold joined Republicans in criticizing the Rich pardon.[100]

At a House hearing on the Rich pardon held on February 8, e-mail and other records revealed the "aggressive" nature of the Rich team's efforts to secure a pardon, including its willingness to contact influential people worldwide for support and a shared sense that secrecy was vital to their success.[101] On February 13, the House and Senate committees widened the scope of their investigation into the Rich pardon.[102] Clinton appointee Mary Jo White, the U.S. Attorney in New York, launched a federal criminal investigation into whether Marc or Denise Rich had essentially purchased a pardon.[103] Although such instances are tough to demonstrate, a president may not accept a quid pro quo—that is, grant a pardon in exchange for something of value—a point raised during the Nixon pardon uproar.[104]

According to a mid-February poll, President Clinton's approval ratings had dropped 10 points from the previous week, from 66 percent to 56 percent. The "most significant" factor for the drop was the Rich pardon. Sixty-five percent of Americans disagreed with pardoning Rich, and 55 percent believed Clinton should testify in front of Congress about the Rich pardon.[105]

In an attempt to squelch mounting criticism of his pardon of Marc Rich, President Clinton wrote an editorial for the *New York Times* entitled "My Reasons for the Pardons." The president offered eight specific justifications for the Rich and Green pardons. The first five dealt with the financial nature of the underlying case itself and did not receive significant attention later on.[106] The final three justifications, however, were picked up by the *Washington Post* and further analyzed in the court of public opinion.

In the first of these three justifications, Clinton wrote, "It was my understanding that Deputy Attorney General Eric Holder's position on the pardon application was 'neutral, leaning for.'" Second, he argued that "the case for the pardons was reviewed and advocated not only by my former White House counsel Jack Quinn but also by three distinguished Republican attorneys: Leonard Garment, a former Nixon White House official;

William Bradford Reynolds, a former high-ranking official in the Reagan Justice Department; and Lewis Libby, now Vice President Cheney's chief of staff." Third, he pointed out that "many present and former high-ranking Israeli officials of both major political parties and leaders of Jewish communities in America and Europe urged the pardon of Mr. Rich." Clinton asserted his belief that the Rich pardon "was in the best interests of justice," said the idea that he had pardoned Rich because of Denise Rich's contributions to the Democratic Party and the Clinton Library was "utterly false," and claimed "there was absolutely no quid pro quo."[107]

The holes and inconsistencies in Clinton's explanation became apparent immediately. First, Holder testified that his "neutral, leaning positive" view came about *after* Jack Quinn or White House Counsel Beth Nolan told him of Israeli Prime Minister Ehud Barak's support for a Rich pardon.[108] Second, a correction to the Clinton op-ed ran the next day to clarify that the three Republican attorneys whom Clinton had appeared to cite for support for the Rich pardon were not actually involved in the pardon deliberations at all. Rather, Clinton's somewhat ambiguous phrase "the case for the pardons" used in connection with Republican attorneys Garment, Reynolds, and Libby was only intended to apply to Rich's underlying legal case, and not the case for pardoning Rich.[109]

Clinton's op-ed marked "the first time" he had "addressed the [Rich pardon] controversy with a sustained argument." Critics, however, rightly pointed out that the argument was still incomplete. Morris "Sandy" Weinberg Jr., a former prosecutor who had been involved in the Rich case early on, stated that Clinton's arguments could have been used by Rich and Green themselves in federal court, had they not been fugitives from justice. He also noted that only Rich's attorneys were cited in Clinton's explanation: Curiously omitted were the views of the U.S. government's prosecutors. Finally, Weinberg argued that the president had failed to mention the allegation that Rich and Green, contrary to American law, had conducted business with Iran at a time when it held Americans hostage. He had also omitted how Rich and Green had remained out of reach of the American justice system rather than coming home to stand trial.[110]

Given the harsh criticism leveled at his op-ed, the last thing that Clinton needed was more bad news. Nevertheless, it came. Hugh Rodham—Hillary Clinton's brother—had received $400,000 for his efforts to obtain clemency for Carlos Vignali and Glenn Braswell, both of whom were on the list of final clemency grants. The president and Hillary Clinton asked Rodham to return the money, and he did so.[111] Although Rodham was later cleared of any potential ethics violation by the Florida bar, the political damage had been done.[112] The president's half-brother, Roger, had also tried to lobby for pardons, but he was unsuccessful and did not receive compensation for his efforts.[113]

The Justice Department decided to expand its investigation into the last-minute pardons. Justice Department officials had called upon federal prosecutor Mary Jo White to examine Clinton's final clemency decisions. White—who had been appointed to her position by President Clinton—was chosen over a special counsel after Attorney General John Ashcroft determined that a special counsel would not be needed in light of White's efforts.[114] Of course, this decision by the Bush administration kept the investigation out of Washington, D.C., and under the supervision of a Clinton appointee—two powerful arguments against any accusation that the new administration was "out to get" Clinton.[115] Eventually, the probe ended without a finding of wrongdoing.

The controversy here was not just that Clinton had been lobbied for pardons. It was disturbing enough that he had apparently been lobbied by close family members, at least one of whom had been paid a significant sum of money and ultimately was successful. The more unfortunate legacy of the last-minute pardons is that Marc Rich's successful clemency campaign was more than likely connected to his ex-wife's past Democratic fundraising, her nearly half-million-dollar donations to Clinton's presidential library, and her friend's pledge to raise a million more.

George W. Bush and the Scooter Libby Situation

President George W. Bush, like his father and Bill Clinton before him, faced temptation to use the clemency power for personal reasons. I. Lewis "Scooter" Libby, Vice President Richard Cheney's former chief of staff, was the only person charged with wrongdoing in the first post-1999 special counsel investigation under what is essentially the pre-Watergate system.[116] U.S. Attorney General John Ashcroft recused himself from the investigation in favor of Deputy Attorney General James Comey Jr., who named Chicago-based U.S. Attorney Patrick Fitzgerald to investigate alleged wrongdoing by Bush administration officials in the Valerie Plame–CIA secret identity controversy.[117] As will be shown, the Scooter Libby trial, conviction, and commutation were the culmination of a series of events set into motion several years earlier.

The Sixteen Words

For the first time in decades, a completely unified Republican government (boasting both houses of Congress and the presidency) was seated following George W. Bush's election in 2000. Shortly after he took office, the terrorist attacks of 9/11 focused President Bush's attention on national security issues. With overwhelming public approval numbers, he soon spearheaded a military action in Afghanistan that removed the Taliban from power. At some point, he also set his sights on Iraq.

In his 2003 State of the Union address, President Bush warned that "the British government has learned that Saddam Hussein recently sought significant quantities of uranium from Africa."[118] In a *New York Times* op-ed, Ambassador Joseph Wilson, who had traveled to Niger to investigate the situation, publicly contradicted the president's claim, writing that "it was highly doubtful" that Hussein had attempted to buy uranium from Africa. Wilson raised the possibility that "some of the intelligence related to Iraq's nuclear weapons program was twisted to exaggerate the Iraqi threat."[119]

Journalist Robert Novak further exacerbated the tension. In an op-ed in which he explored the possible Iraqi uranium purchase, Novak identified Ambassador Wilson's wife by her maiden name "Valerie Plame" and described her as a CIA "agency operative on weapons of mass destruction."[120] This was the first time that Plame's secret identity had been revealed publicly, and speculation mounted that Novak's source may have violated the Intelligence Identities Protection Act of 1982 in revealing her identity.[121]

Wilson argued quite publicly that the Bush administration had decided to out his wife's secret identity as a way to punish him for his critical op-ed. In a book published in 2004 entitled *The Politics of Truth*, Wilson speculated that a top administration official—most likely Vice President Cheney's chief of staff, Scooter Libby—had revealed his wife's secret identity to Robert Novak.[122]

The Special Counsel Investigation

Given the mystery surrounding how and from whom Novak obtained Plame's name, and the possibility of criminal acts by a high executive branch official, Comey appointed Fitzgerald to investigate.[123] Deputy Chief of Staff Karl Rove and Libby became Fitzgerald's prime targets because they apparently had been assisting President Bush with the White House's response to criticism of Bush's infamous "sixteen-word" statement on Iraq and African uranium around the same time that Plame's identity was disclosed, leading to speculation that the outing of Plame was meant to undercut Wilson's credibility.[124]

Rove was never indicted. However, a potential indictment of Libby was still a major problem for the Bush administration. Succinctly described as "Dick Cheney's Dick Cheney,"[125] Libby was Cheney's chief of staff and enjoyed multiple appointments; he even had clearance to sit in on "the highest level of White House meetings."[126] At trial, Libby might have been forced to testify about secret—and potentially embarrassing—top-level White House conversations.

Libby testified to the grand jury investigating the situation that he had learned Plame's secret identity from journalists. Accordingly, Fitzgerald's investigation included journalists who had interacted with White House aides. One, Judith Miller, was jailed for refusing to name a confidential source.[127] For some unexplained reason, she waited over a year to seek a waiver from her source, and then spent nearly three months in jail before the source, who turned out to be none other than Scooter Libby, waived their confidentiality agreement so that she could testify.[128] But Libby had signed a "blanket" waiver to journalists a year earlier. Why did she wait over a year to secure a waiver from Libby when he had already signed a "blanket" waiver that applied to her?[129] Miller wrote that despite the "blanket waiver," which she believed to be involuntary, "nothing short of a personal letter and a telephone call would allow me to assess whether Mr. Libby truly wished to free me from the pledge of confidentiality I had given him."[130]

With Libby's explicit waiver and the special counsel's agreement to limit his questioning to Libby, Miller eventually agreed to testify. Miller revealed that she had written the words "Valerie Flame" in her interview notes, but insisted that the name was in a different section of her notebook than her interview notes from a talk with Libby. Also, Miller testified that she had written "Victoria Wilson" in her notebook, an additional apparent reference to Valerie Plame. Miller said she "didn't think" that the notation "Valerie Flame" had come from her conversation from Libby and "didn't know and didn't want to guess" whether Libby was the source for "Victoria Wilson."[131]

The true reason for the delay? Libby had stonewalled in order to run out the clock on the special counsel, successfully ensuring that his eventual indictment would not hurt President Bush's 2004 reelection bid. By claiming that journalists had revealed Plame's identity, Libby knew that the news organizations would try to prevent their employees from testifying.[132] This is exactly what happened with Judith Miller.

The Indictment

On October 28, 2005, Scooter Libby was indicted for five felonies: obstruction of justice, making false statements to FBI investigators (two counts), and lying to a grand jury (two counts); he was not charged with publicly revealing Plame's identity, nor was anyone else.[133] The indictment alleged that he had not learned Plame's identity from journalists; rather, he had used the State Department and CIA to learn more about her. Libby immediately resigned from his White House position.[134]

Scooter Libby pleaded not guilty to obstruction and perjury on November 3, 2005.[135] The situation apparently began to drag down President Bush's standing with the public. A *Washington Post*/ABC News poll released on November 3 showed that Bush's "honest and trustworthy" rating had dropped from May 2004's 53 percent to 40 percent, while his negative rating on that question had risen from 45 percent to 58 percent.[136] Meanwhile, journalist Bob Woodward admitted that he had learned Valerie Plame's identity from a senior Bush administration official several weeks before her identity was revealed.[137] In August, former deputy secretary of state Richard Armitage admitted that he was the government official who had supplied Robert Novak and Bob Woodward with Valerie Plame's secret identity.[138]

The Armitage revelation disproved Joseph Wilson's claim that the administration had outed his wife to punish him for the *New York Times* editorial. Armitage was no lackey of pro–Iraq War administration figures and, as someone who enjoyed gossip, revealed Plame's identity to Novak without even realizing it was classified information. However, Libby and Cheney responded to Wilson's accusations by looking into his wife's role in recommending Wilson for the trip to Niger that had led to the *New York Times* op-ed. Libby then apparently revealed Plame's identity to reporters, and ultimately lied about it to the grand jury, in a failed attempt to discredit Wilson.[139] The special counsel had known from his first day on the job that Armitage was the leaker. Still, he continued to pursue leads in the case for almost two years before indicting Libby for obstruction of justice.[140]

The Trial

At trial, Libby's defense was muted. Libby did not testify or cut a plea deal with prosecutors. Despite his lawyers' plan to call Vice President Cheney to testify, which would have earned Cheney the distinction of being the first sitting vice president to provide testimony in a criminal prosecution,

Cheney never took the stand.[141] As George Washington University Law School professor Jonathan Turley correctly pointed out, "a lot of people view this [investigation] as a subordinate [Libby] taking a bullet for Cheney. . . . He did not call in Cheney to testify, which would have been embarrassing." Turley added, "Libby is the ultimate inside player. He's not the type to cop a plea or turn on Cheney."[142]

The jury sided with the special prosecutor over the accused. On March 6, 2007, Scooter Libby was found guilty of four of the five felonies with which he was charged. He was acquitted on one charge of making false statements to the FBI. He became the most senior executive branch official to be convicted of a felony since the Iran-Contra scandal during the 1980s.[143]

Early Pardon Speculation

That a Libby pardon was in the cards was no surprise to anyone, and speculation percolated on March 6, 2007. The editors of the conservative magazine *National Review* called for a Libby pardon.[144] CNN legal analyst Jeffrey Toobin calculated a timeline of the various legal steps involved in the appeal process: If Libby were to remain out of jail while his appeal was considered, Toobin said, and his legal defense team could "slow [the] process down" enough, then President Bush could pardon Libby just as the president was leaving office in 2009, and Libby could avoid prison altogether. The Libby defense team's strategy would be, as Toobin put it, "running down the clock."[145] The White House refused to comment about a Libby pardon.[146]

Speculation ran rampant as many major media outlets weighed in with their own pardon stories. Journalist Charles Krauthammer made the conservative case for a Libby pardon as follows: "This is a case that never should have been brought, originating in the scandal that never was, in search of a crime—violation of the Intelligence Identities Protection Act— that even the prosecutor never alleged. That's the basis for a presidential pardon. It should have been granted long before this egregious case came to trial. It should be granted now without any further delay."[147]

Those supporting a Libby pardon were in the minority, however. A Gallup poll released on March 16 showed that 67 percent of those polled opposed a pardon, while 21 percent approved.[148] Breaking those numbers down, only 34 percent of Republicans supported a pardon, while just 21 percent of independents and a mere 11 percent of Democrats supported one.

President Bush's first remarks on the Libby verdict were to CNN en Español. He stated, "I'm pretty much going to stay out of it until the course—the case has finally run its final—the course it's going to take."[149] President Bush could expect that a pardon of Libby would be quite unpopular initially. However, given Bush's low public approval rating (33 percent), and the fact that he was generally perceived favorably by Republicans and less so by Democrats and independents, he could assume that a Libby pardon would not hurt his standing among Democrats and independents very much and might even increase his stock with Republicans.[150] Pardon expert Margaret Love suggested that "it is going to be hard for [Bush] to justify pardoning Libby when he has been so unreceptive to requests from ordinary applicants."[151] In this context, and—it is important to note—as a "lame duck" president, it seemed to many observers that it would not be all that surprising if Bush decided to award clemency to Scooter Libby when the timing was right.

The Sentence

On June 5, 2007, Scooter Libby was sentenced by U.S. District Judge Reggie Walton to spend thirty months in prison and pay a $250,000 fine. Libby was also given two years' probation. The judge indicated that he would soon hold a hearing to determine whether Libby should begin serving his sentence right away. The *Washington Post* noted that the sentence was "fairly long . . . for a case involving perjury," and that the sentence was imposed despite more than 150 letters of support from Libby's sympathizers.[152]

Although his trial had exposed the fact that three other Bush administration officials—Rove, Armitage, and former press secretary Ari Fleischer—had also revealed Plame's status as a CIA agent, Libby was the only one who had been charged with a crime. Fitzgerald noted the gravity of Libby's offenses: Libby's decision to lie about what he knew about Plame and the conversations he'd had with reporters had prevented Fitzgerald from learning exactly what went on and why.[153]

Former special counsel for President George H. W. Bush William Otis is credited as the first person to publicly suggest that President Bush "should commute the sentence by eliminating the jail term while preserving the fine."[154] Otis argued in a June 7 editorial for the *Washington Post* that Libby had received "an unusually harsh sentence for a first offender convicted of a nonviolent and non-drug-related crime." He then suggested that "commutation offers a middle ground" by "leav[ing] Libby with the disabilities of a convicted felon." At the same time, the "commutation would alleviate the harshest, and unnecessary, aspects of the sentence."[155] In the *Los Angeles Times*, Margaret Love addressed commutation as well, noting that Bush had granted "only three of more than 5,000 requests for sentence reduction from federal prisoners."[156] A commutation would be an extremely rare event, if the president decided to grant one.

At a hearing held on June 14, 2007, Judge Walton determined that Libby would have to begin to serve his prison sentence even while pursuing an appeal of his conviction. Walton decided that Libby had a very small chance of succeeding on appeal. Thus, the pressure on President Bush to grant clemency of some kind increased greatly: Unless he acted, Scooter Libby would be a prisoner within six to eight weeks, regardless of any appeals he might pursue.[157] On June 27, the U.S. Bureau of Prisons designated Scooter Libby as federal prisoner number 28301-016.[158]

The Commutation

On July 2, two days before a midweek Fourth of July holiday, President Bush left the White House Press Corps in Kennebunkport, Maine, flew back to the White House, and signed a grant of executive clemency for Scooter Libby.[159] The grant commuted Libby's thirty-month prison sentence to zero time behind bars, but left in place the two years of probation and the $250,000 fine.[160]

President Bush had turned away the efforts of Libby's supporters to make his case, instead relying on only a few close advisers—none of whom worked for the Justice Department—to arrive at the decision, in which an insider described the president as having "comfort" that it would not do political damage.[161] A "senior administration official" said that Bush made up his mind to grant the commutation soon after he learned that Libby would not be allowed to remain free while his appeal progressed.[162]

In a statement, the president defended his decision to act before Libby's appeal had been heard. He took great care not to criticize either the special counsel or the jury, noting that "Mr. Fitzgerald is a highly qualified, professional prosecutor who carried out his responsibilities as charged. . . . I respect the jury's verdict." However, he disagreed with the result reached by the process, determining that "the prison sentence given to Mr. Libby is excessive."[163]

Judge Walton refused initial comment on the commutation.[164] Patrick

Fitzgerald declined comment on the president's use of the clemency power, but disagreed with the president's characterization of Libby's sentence as "excessive," instead arguing that Libby's sentence was "consistent with the applicable laws."[165] Fitzgerald contended that Libby had received a fair shake from the criminal justice system. One is hard-pressed to disagree: Both Judge Walton and U.S. Attorney Fitzgerald were appointed to their current positions by President George W. Bush himself.

Public Reaction

Reaction to the Libby commutation was nearly instantaneous and almost totally critical. CNN's Jeffrey Toobin seemed perplexed by Bush's rationale for the pardon, suggesting that "30 months is precisely within the range [of sentence] for obstruction of justice."[166] According to a New York Times study of federal court records, 382 convictions for obstruction of justice had occurred in the previous two years. Of those, 75 percent went to prison, the average prison term was sixty-four months, and the largest group of defendants received prison terms of thirteen to thirty-one months.[167] Then again, the Libby case was hardly typical, given its political context.

Other reactions to the verdict fell along predictable lines. Democrats in Congress expressed their disapproval and attempted to cast the Libby verdict as one small occurrence in the larger context of a failing war in Iraq. Senate Majority Leader Harry Reid (D-NV) suggested that "Libby's conviction was the one faint glimmer of accountability for White House efforts to manipulate intelligence and silence critics of the Iraq war. Now, even that small bit of justice has been undone." House Speaker Nancy Pelosi (D-CA) accused Bush of "condon[ing] criminal conduct."[168]

The Washington Post noted that the day after the commutation, "all but a few Republicans were conspicuously silent."[169] This response was similar to that of the Democrats following the Marc Rich pardon. Mary Lu Carnevale of the Wall Street Journal characterized the conservative reaction as "tepid and terse."[170] Indeed, in an editorial, the Wall Street Journal took Bush to task, characterizing the commutation statement as a "profile in non-courage" and accusing him of "evading responsibility for the role his administration played" in the Libby situation by withholding a full pardon.[171]

Pardon experts were quite critical of the commutation. Margaret Love described the decision as "very unusual," while Ohio State University law professor Douglas Berman called the commutation "hypocritical and appalling," considering the Bush Justice Department's strict stance on federal sentencing.[172] "The Bush administration . . . has repeatedly supported a federal sentencing system that is distinctly disrespectful of the very arguments that Bush has put forward in cutting Libby a break."[173] In this one case, Berman suggested, the president made an exception: "My friend Scooter shouldn't have to serve 30 months in prison because I don't want him to."[174]

What is more, Bush was able to grant clemency to Libby without having to pay any political price himself. By commuting Libby's sentence, President Bush joined President George H. W. Bush and Bill Clinton—his two most recent predecessors—as presidents who made controversial clemency decisions only after they were immune from electoral consequences. As Michigan State University law professor Brian Kalt observed, "to do a pardon at the moment in which the president is the least accountable of his entire term—that's problematic. It's also very tempting, which is why it has happened."[175]

The Aftermath

As an aside, the president's decision presented a unique question for clemency observers. Libby's commutation was granted before he had served a single day in prison, but required Libby to remain on probation for two years, per his original sentence. However, as Judge Walton noted, the statute under which Libby was sentenced, if strictly interpreted, suggested that the probation period could only be imposed once the offender had served some prison time.[176] White House Counsel Fred Fielding reiterated President Bush's intention that Libby was still required to complete a probationary period.[177] The commutation decision had been made on the basis of the presidency's clemency power rather than on the basis of the statute that controls supervised release decisions. Under this rationale, President Bush retained the power to grant Libby a full pardon at a later date, should he choose to do so.[178] On July 11, in the midst of the commutation controversy, the House Judiciary Committee held a hearing to discuss clemency issues.[179] The president declined to participate in the inquiry.[180]

Polls showed that Americans were not pleased with the president's clemency decision. A USA Today/Gallup poll found that only 13 percent believed that the commutation was the correct decision, while 66 percent believed that Bush should not have made any clemency decision at all. Only 6 percent supported a full pardon for Libby, with 15 percent having no opinion. As the poll itself noted, these findings "mirror[ed] earlier Gallup polling on this topic."[181]

Perhaps surprisingly, even Republicans were dissatisfied with the decision: More fell on the side that President Bush should not intervene at all (45 percent) than on the side that favored a full pardon (11 percent). Despite speculation that granting clemency to Libby might help President Bush in Republican circles, the poll showed that only 9 percent of Republicans gained confidence in Bush because of his decision. Almost double that number (16 percent) reported having lost confidence in his leadership. In the poll, Bush's overall approval rating clocked in at a dismal 29 percent.[182]

As the end of President George W. Bush's second term draws near, he is still issuing pardons. Scooter Libby's name has been absent from the list of clemency recipients, as of this writing in November 2008. One effect of granting a commutation rather than a pardon—whether intentional or not—was that Libby was able to continue to remain silent (and, importantly, keep his Fifth Amendment right against self-incrimination intact) as his appeal proceeded.[183] Bush's reluctance to pardon Libby entirely even after the controversy has subsided suggests that he will continue to hold the line, at least until his final hours in office.

Conclusion

Although their stated reasons were complex, there is little doubt that Presidents George H. W. Bush, Bill Clinton, and George W. Bush exercised the clemency power for personal reasons in the situations discussed in this chapter. In the Conclusion, I will analyze how the Ford pardon of Nixon and the clemency decisions discussed in this chapter square with the framers' intentions for the presidential pardon power.

Conclusion

Presidents have generally exercised executive clemency to give average, anonymous Americans another chance. In the past, presidents were occasionally able to make controversial pardoning decisions regarding famous or even notorious individuals with a minimum of public protest. After standing trial, Eugene Debs, James Hoffa, Marcus Garvey, and several Puerto Rican Nationalist Party figures were given commutations apparently because of the political clout of their respective constituencies. Then, in 1974, the Nixon pardon provided a stark example to future presidents of how costly a pardon could be under certain circumstances.

Gerald Ford's pretrial, pre-conviction pardon of Richard Nixon created a public outcry that led to the Ethics in Government Act of 1978 and its key component, the independent counsel statute. Under the statute, presidents no longer directly appointed independent counsel investigators; instead, the special prosecutors working intermittently between 1978 and 1999 were appointed by a special division of the U.S. Court of Appeals for the D.C. Circuit, upon the attorney general's request, usually at the urging of Congress. Freed from direct political accountability by the statute, presidents whose aides or allies were investigated by an independent counsel had political cover to cry foul and used pardons as political weapons to correct perceived injustices. While the constitutional pardon power has remained the same, the larger political context in which it is used—and how it is used—has changed.

What Changed?

As noted in the Introduction, legal scholar Daniel Kobil has argued that public officials with clemency powers are hesitant to use them because they are afraid of creating controversy that could cost them in public standing.[1] The first "pardon paradox" mentioned in the Introduction was that despite enjoying nearly unlimited clemency powers, modern presidents in general have been reluctant to exercise them, even while pushing the boundaries in other areas of executive prerogative. Why is this the case? The simple answer is that the clemency power is unique. In other areas of executive power, presidents have something to gain by pushing the boundaries of appropriate behavior. As history has shown, powers that the president can usurp from Congress (regarding war powers, budgeting, and the like) do not always flow back to Congress.

In the case of the pardon power, however, the president has always had an almost unlimited prerogative. As demonstrated in earlier chapters, the courts rarely review presidential clemency decisions, and they usually prevent Congress from interfering in clemency cases. The president enjoys virtually all of the clemency power, and he does not have to use it. A president does not have much to gain from pardoning: In nearly all cases, the only benefit to a president from pardoning is the grateful thanks of the pardon recipient and his or her family and friends. A president's overall public standing is not usually increased by pardoning, and in granting a pardon, he runs the risk that his decision might backfire. Thus, he does not pardon much: Inactivity actually protects the president from making a mistake with the clemency power.

What about the second "pardon paradox," that Presidents George H. W. Bush, Bill Clinton, and George W. Bush made highly controversial clemency grants to aid executive branch officials or supporters despite their concern for political safety? Every once in a while, a president has a convenient reason and context (the end of his term) in which to offer clemency to someone controversial, as the various presidents of recent years did with Caspar Weinberger, members of the FALN, Marc Rich, and Scooter Libby. In these rare cases, the president's usual desire for political safety is outweighed by a greater benefit, such as protecting aides (and possibly himself) from embarrassing disclosures in court (Bush 1 and 2), or helping along the political prospects of a wife or vice president, or furthering the project of raising funds for a presidential library, at a time when the president is safe from punishment at the ballot box. In each of these cases, the presidents involved bypassed or ignored the pardon attorney apparatus—thereby thumbing their noses at the public—and did what they wanted to do. In each case, a president abused the clemency power because he could do so without risking real punishment.

Aside from fear of impeachment, the next strongest check keeping presidents from abusing the clemency power is the damage a controversy might do to a legacy. Concerned about history's judgment, Ronald Reagan resisted the temptation to pardon Marine Lieutenant Colonel Oliver North or National Security Adviser John Poindexter. George H. W. Bush, as mentioned earlier, worried about his legacy but still decided to pardon Caspar Weinberger. Bill Clinton, who had already been impeached and enjoyed high approval ratings on his way out the door, granted an enormous number of pardons and commutations in his final hours, apparently unconcerned about how this would affect history's judgment of his presidency. As of November 2008, it appears that George W. Bush's presidential legacy is going to be tied to America's role in wars in Iraq and Afghanistan, although the Scooter Libby commutation will earn at least a footnote in many accounts of the Bush years.

I believe that Ford's pardon of Richard Nixon is different from the other controversial clemency decisions analyzed in this study. In the next section, I will argue that Ford's pardon of Richard Nixon—unlike the volatile clemency decisions of his successors—was consistent with the framers' understanding of the clemency power. Still, Ford's mishandling of the situation combined with circumstances beyond his control to make the Nixon pardon an extremely costly decision. Ford did not have many good options, but the one he chose led him down the most politically risky path of all of them.

How Could Ford Have Better Handled the Nixon Pardon?

Could Ford have minimized the political damage he suffered from the Nixon pardon with a better approach? Bob Woodward said in 1999 that "the problem with the pardon was in Ford's execution. To be successful, the pardon required elaborate orchestration. The public, Congress and the media needed to be prepared."[2] Echoing Woodward's argument, Professor John Robert Greene speculated that a different course of action could have allowed the president to dampen the harsh public reaction. According to Greene: "If Ford had waited for another month, had he explained his thought processes to the American people before he made his decision, had he consulted or at least informed Congress, had he not kept it a secret from the press, then the president might have spared himself the violent backlash from a decision made too soon."[3] Are Woodward, Greene, and other critics of Ford correct? This is an inquiry worth undertaking, as it shows how Ford's own decisions, along with circumstances beyond his control, worked together to limit his options.

In several ways, Ford had painted himself into a corner by the way he handled the events leading up to the decision to pardon Nixon and by the way he announced the pardon itself. His decision to tape the pardon announcement at 11 A.M. on a Sunday morning and release it later in the day suggested that he was trying to avoid a large audience and widespread criticism. Furthermore, his failure to obtain a clear apology from Nixon may have suggested that neither president was particularly sorry for Watergate and its aftermath. Ford's clumsy attempt to hide the behind-the-scenes maneuvering regarding the pardon decision-making process came across as disingenuous and potentially dishonest.

Even so, Ford's options at this point, a month into his presidency, were few: Given his concern for eliminating Nixon-related business from his workday, Ford could have stopped holding press conferences, or at least banned Nixon-related queries. He could have tried to govern while allowing Nixon to stand trial. He could have resigned and allowed Nelson Rockefeller to make the call on Nixon. These were all available options. The one he chose was to make the decision to pardon Nixon and bear the consequences himself.

Could Ford have waited another month to pardon Richard Nixon? As explained earlier, the primary factors driving a quick decision on clemency were as follows: Ford did not understand that his public statements seemed contradictory; he was concerned about Nixon's state of mind and lapse into depression and felt he needed to act quickly to prevent further suffering or even suicide; and he knew that the special prosecutor was about to indict Nixon. All of these factors pointed toward the need for a speedy decision.

Could Ford have explained his decision to the public in a manner that would have helped Americans understand the decision and accept it as a necessary step? He took over as president without an electoral coalition (voters and financial backers) or a governing coalition (advisers, foreign leaders, members of Congress, the press) when his present and future success depended on having at least one of these.[4] Ford decided that his best choice was to offer several justifications for the decision.

In hindsight, it seems that Ford might have made some headway if he had offered one consistent rationale for his decision. Instead, once the pardon was granted, he tried to appease many constituencies with conflicting preferences. The pardon proclamation on September 8, 1974; his remarks accompanying the proclamation; his Hungate subcommittee testimony; and his memoirs, as well as the memoirs of his advisers, all speak to different audiences—to Nixon and his lawyers, to the American public, to his critics, and to history, respectively.[5] Instead of brokering compromises between these groups, however, he ended up stoking their disagreements.

Ford also made the mistake of investing himself in the Nixon pardon personally, instead of relying on the institution of the presidency as his backing. His remarks when granting the pardon contained sixty-four references to himself, all referring to his personal decision-making abilities.[6] In doing so, he "unnecessarily and unwisely invested his personal credibility in the Nixon pardon."[7] Also, as noted earlier, Ford personally wrote in a line referring to Nixon's health after Hartmann had handed him a final draft of his pardon announcement.

Harris polling data taken during late September indicate that the public saw the invocation of Nixon's health as largely a ploy to win sympathy: Sixteen percent said the former president's health was "a major consideration" in determining whether his pardon was justified; 27 percent believed it was "a minor consideration"; and 48 percent believed Ford used his predecessor's health situation to "create sympathy" for the former president.[8] Ford essentially invited the public to take out its anger and frustration on him personally, and the public took him up on the offer. This is one area where a change in perspective in the pardon announcement and the speeches that followed may have made a difference.

Part of Ford's problem was his choice of words and the role he assumed in his pardon announcement. Pardon rhetoric requires the president to perform three functions: (1) act as the symbolic head of state; (2) show that the present is a good time to act; and (3) justify the pardon decision as undertaken for the public good. Deviations from this formula can be costly to a president—indeed, it is not the individual serving as president who speaks, it is the institution.[9]

For a president acting as symbolic head of state, Ford was avoiding public scrutiny. As noted earlier, he recorded his pardon announcement at 11 A.M. on a Sunday morning without providing notice to anyone other than a few key staffers that this major announcement was going to be made. His justification for the timing failed, given his public statements that he would not act until legal proceedings had been initiated. Finally, although expected to justify his decision under the Constitution, Ford drew upon his role as a "humble servant of God" and his own individual conscience, not his role as president of the United States, thus undermining his own legitimacy.[10]

Perhaps the most advantageous strategy would have been to cite Federalist No. 74 and argue that he was acting in the public interest to "restore the tranquility of the commonwealth."[11] This was the rationale cited by the court in Murphy v. Ford (1975), an unsuccessful challenge to the Nixon pardon brought by a disgruntled citizen.[12] If he had disregarded Nixon's mental and emotional state, Ford might have risked offending Richard Nixon and those close to the former president. Still, he would have aligned himself with the historically recognized justifications for a pardon. Instead, the pardon announcement failed to follow traditional form, was not linked to conventional justifications, was not solely based on his presidential powers, and was given at an inopportune time of day.

One course of action for Ford would have been to announce to the public that Nixon's acceptance of a pardon was really an admission of guilt and could pave the way for the former president to testify in Watergate trials. According to Burdick v. United States (1915), Nixon's acceptance of the pardon was tantamount to an admission of guilt.[13] However, Nixon's statement acknowledging the pardon had been less than forthcoming about any criminal wrongdoing on his own part, a significant obstacle for Ford to overcome. By not confronting the Nixon statement directly and regularly and not emphasizing Nixon's guilt in his pardon announcement, Ford failed to help Americans grasp the larger significance of Nixon's acceptance of the pardon. Polling data taken on September 9 indicated that only 50 percent understood that Nixon's acceptance of the pardon was an admission of guilt; 32 percent believed that no admission had been made.[14] White House Counsel Philip Buchen made this key point in a press conference on September 10, 1974, answering a question about whether Nixon's acceptance implied guilt with "You can so read it."[15]

Ford knew that the pardon negated Nixon's Fifth Amendment privilege against self-incrimination, and thus that Nixon could be forced to testify.[16] However, emphasizing this fact would have likely prolonged the controversy. By the time he began to speak up about the implications of the pardon, it was too late to change the public's mind. Ford said at his second press conference that "the acceptance of a pardon, I think, can be construed by many, if not all, as an admission of guilt."[17] In front of the Hungate subcommittee, the president repeated his belief that Nixon's acceptance of the pardon was essentially an admission of guilt.[18] In a 1979 interview, former president Ford said that before the pardon, he had been "devoting 25 percent of my time" to Nixon-related matters, but blamed himself for being surprised by the negative reaction to the pardon and then not adequately explaining his reasons for granting it.[19] "I didn't foresee the vehemence. . . . We had to let the healing that is inherent in the American people take over. But I didn't explain that well enough."[20] In hindsight, it was not that Ford did not know what to say, but that he did not know when and how to say it effectively.

What If Ford Had Recruited Congress?

What if Ford had not hidden the Nixon pardon decision-making process from Congress? What if, instead, he had announced his intention to pardon his predecessor in a behind-the-scenes meeting with congressional leaders, and then launched a campaign to drum up congressional support for a "sense-of-Congress" resolution supporting a pardon? Stanley Kutler mused, "Imagine if Ford had asked former congressional colleagues from across the political spectrum—Mike Mansfield, Hugh Scott, Barry Goldwater, Carl Albert, John Rhodes, and Tip O'Neill—to stand with him as he delivered his announcement."[21]

Apparently "two powerful Democrats" believed a resolution could have happened under this scenario. Even without a resolution of support from the entire Congress, according to "one leading House Democrat," advance notice to congressional sympathizers could have created a "backfire" to at least somewhat combat the surprise and anger caused by the sudden pardon decision.[22] Indeed, former Nixon secretary of defense Melvin Laird and former Nixon counselor Bryce Harlow had gone to Senator John Stennis (D-MS) to discuss the prospects of having Republican and Democratic congressional leaders encourage the president to pardon Nixon. The plan enjoyed "strong [bipartisan] support" and was "well along," but even though the president knew about the plan, he refused to discuss his intentions even with his friends.[23]

Ford considered and then rejected the idea of calling congressional leaders ahead of time, finding that "a leak would be calamitous."[24] "I knew the reaction would be bad," he said, "and if I had floated it as a possibility, a hell of a lot of people would have jumped all over me, and then it would have been much harder to do. Because people did not understand then the absolute necessity of doing it then. And the longer it was put off, the worse it would have been."[25] To ensure secrecy, the president "had lined up no surrogates, no congressional or party elders, no cabinet secretaries or editorialists or anyone else who could rally support, blunt criticism, and share the heat."[26]

What If Ford Had Lobbied the Press?

Although one may wonder why Ford decided not to lay any groundwork with the press, it is important to recognize that the press was even less likely to be helpful than the Democratic Congress. Whatever the character of Nixon's successor—stellar reputation for honesty and integrity or not—that person was going to be put under the microscope by the White House Press Corps, which was still smarting from having missed "the big story" of Watergate a few months earlier to two unknowns from the *Washington Post*. A major decision such as a pardon for a disgraced president was not going to be well received in the environment of the time, even if Ford had tried to court the press in advance of his pardon announcement.[27] The press had a sore nerve for being lied to by the prior president, and now his replacement was perceived to be doing the same thing—and worse, giving the hated Nixon a "get out of jail free" card. Still feeling the pain inflicted by Richard Nixon and Watergate, the press would most likely have lashed out at what it perceived to be a similar hurt inflicted by Gerald Ford.

The sensitivity was so widespread that few of the reporters who felt betrayed by Nixon recognized those same feelings permeating their coverage of Ford. One who did was David Broder of the *Washington Post*. Asking "Where the devil is our sense of perspective?" Broder castigated his colleagues for trying to bring Ford along on "a roller coaster ride—elevating him to paragon status for no good reason and then condemning him utterly when, in our view, he makes his first mistake."[28] Another voice in the wilderness was William Raspberry, who advised that "to keep harping on [the pardon] is a waste. Worse than a waste: It's counterproductive."[29] Unless more journalists secretly agreed with Broder and Raspberry, Ford had few potential allies to give him the benefit of the doubt.

In the big picture, it probably would not have mattered much even if Ford had managed to rally both Congress and the press to his side. The public would not have understood or been easier on him, in all likelihood. The American people had taken Ford's earlier public statements to mean that a pardon for Nixon was an uncomfortable decision to be made sometime down the road. Citizens were not yet ready to hear Ford grant a pardon, let alone to hear him justify it in part on the former president's failing health, especially given Nixon's lukewarm statement of contrition. Many were also unhappy that Ford appeared so elusive about the behind-the-scenes maneuvering that led up to this important act of clemency. Had Ford justified the pardon on strictly constitutional grounds, perhaps the firestorm would have abated a bit, but just how much we will never know for certain.

The Country Comes around to Ford's Point of View

Eventually, conventional wisdom shifted to recognize that pardoning Nixon was the right thing to do. In June 1976, while Ford was campaigning for election to the presidency in his own right, Gallup polls revealed that only 35 percent of Americans believed that he had done the right thing by pardoning Nixon, while 55 percent believed the pardon was not the right thing to do. Twenty-six years later, an ABC News poll found that "the right thing" respondents had grown to 59 percent, while "the wrong thing" respondents had dropped to 32 percent.[30]

Even Ford's most prominent critics gradually came to see things his way. On May 21, 2001, the John F. Kennedy Library honored Gerald Ford with its "Profile in Courage" award for issuing the Nixon pardon.[31] At the library, Senator Edward Kennedy (D-MA) said, "I was one of those who spoke out against his action then. But time has a way of clarifying past events, and now we see that President Ford was right. His courage and dedication to our country made it possible for us to begin the process of healing and put the tragedy of Watergate behind us."[32] Bob Woodward said in 1999 that over the years, he had "become more and more convinced that Ford made the correct decision in pardoning Nixon."[33] Carl Bernstein admitted that in the aftermath of Watergate, "the American system worked—including Gerald Ford's pardon of Nixon, that allowed the country to move on."[34]

The Nixon Pardon in Context

A brief look at Alexander Hamilton's words from Federalist No. 74, and the Supreme Court cases United States v. Wilson and Biddle v. Perovich, suggests that—despite Ford's mishandling of his public presentation of the Nixon pardon—the decision itself was consistent with the original rationales offered for the presidential pardon power. As Hamilton noted, "in seasons of insurrection or rebellion," the president has the power to pardon to "restore the tranquility of the commonwealth."[35] Watergate was a constitutional crisis, and Ford was on solid historical, legal, and constitutional ground in granting the pardon. Under the circumstances, a Nixon trial had the potential to tear the government apart and prevent the new president from concentrating on the many other responsibilities he had inherited a month earlier. There is little chance that Ford could have protected his party or himself from intense criticism for pardoning Richard Nixon. Public anger for Watergate was simply too overwhelming for any president in Ford's position to hold off for very long, especially with an indictment looming.

All of that said, however, Ford might have been able to save himself some grief if he had based the Nixon pardon solely on the rationale expressed in *Biddle v. Perovich* and argued that he was only pardoning Nixon for "the public welfare."[36] By referencing Nixon's health in his pardon proclamation, the president drew upon the "act of grace" rationale of *United States v. Wilson*, an unwise move considering Nixon's overwhelming unpopularity and the fact that he was getting away with whatever crimes he had committed before even standing trial.[37]

Unlike George H. W. Bush, Bill Clinton, and George W. Bush, whose circumstances I will compare and contrast with Ford's momentarily, Ford absorbed the criticism and the political consequences of his clemency decision, as the framers intended. As Hamilton pointed out, the framers vested the pardon power in "a single man" because "the sense of responsibility is always strongest in proportion as it is undivided."[38] In other words, the public would know whom to blame for a pardon that angered them. Despite the public's turnaround over time, voters did just that by punishing congressional Republicans at the ballot box in 1974 and Ford himself in 1976.

The Iran-Contra Pardons in Context

The public had a ready frame of reference for the Iran-Contra pardons, as the Nixon pardon fiasco had raised and answered some of the bigger questions regarding the presidential pardon power. As the most controversial single pardon ever granted—and the only pardon ever granted to a former president—the Nixon pardon was the logical measuring stick by which to evaluate future volatile pardons, particularly those of executive branch officials.

There was no question that President George H. W. Bush had the legal power to grant the Iran-Contra pardons, even pre-indictment. Also, the timing of the Iran-Contra pardons worked out well for Bush. While many had questioned Ford's decision to pardon former president Nixon so soon after taking office, Bush had the luxury of waiting until after he had lost his reelection bid to grant his pardons. Unlike Ford, Bush did not have to answer pointed questions about whether he had made a "deal." Although testifying in Weinberger's case would have been embarrassing to President Bush, at the time the question of a quid pro quo was not seriously pursued, and it eventually faded away.

The Nixon and Iran-Contra pardons shared some similarities. They were both politically charged pardons made under the shadow of an outside prosecutor's investigation. Also, both Ford and Bush were trying to find a way to deal with scandals that broke during their predecessors' second terms. In granting the pardons, both men opted to act without the involvement of the Pardon Attorney's Office, apparently to keep the decision-making process a secret. Neither Richard Nixon nor Caspar Weinberger stood trial before being pardoned.

There are two crucial dissimilarities between the situations, though. One was that Ford was looked upon with suspicion as an unelected replacement for his disgraced predecessor, whereas Bush was not. Bush had earned election on his own, and Iran-Contra—for all of its unfortunate characteristics—was not comparable to Watergate. Although Reagan violated federal law in pursuing the arms-for-hostages deal, and Bush probably lied about what he knew and when he knew it, neither was in as precarious a position as Richard Nixon, whose criminal indictment and impeachment for abuse of power were all but inevitable. Compared to the widespread public anger and loss of trust in government brought on by Watergate and fueled again by the Nixon pardon, the reaction to the Iran-Contra scandal was somewhat less severe. There were three factors ameliorating the public's response: (1) The stakes were not as great as those existing after Watergate; (2) a new president of the opposing party was set to take office; and (3) owing largely to factors 1 and 2, Bush had the opportunity to make two key strategic decisions that laid the groundwork for the pardons.

Hoping to avoid fallout similar to that brought on by the Nixon pardon, Bush met with his advisers to come up with ways to minimize the public damage that he expected the pardons of Weinberger et al. to inflict.[39] First, he tried to find Democratic allies in Congress to provide political cover. Weinberger's attorney, Robert Bennett, and longtime Weinberger associate William Clark[40] were able to sway two key Democrats in the House of Representatives—Speaker Thomas Foley (D-WA) and Representative Les Aspin (D-WI), Clinton's nominee for secretary of defense—who then let White House officials know that they would not oppose a Weinberger pardon. Other Democrats either supported a pardon without prompting, such as

Senator Dennis DeConcini (D-AZ), or, like Senator Sam Nunn (D-GA), steered clear.[41] As discussed earlier, Ford chose not to try to rally Democrats in Congress behind his decision to pardon Richard Nixon before making his announcement; then, when public outrage continued for weeks afterward, he took the highly unusual step of appearing before Congress for questioning. Bush's approach was to nip controversy in the bud, and it worked fairly well.

Second, unlike Ford, President Bush tried to prepare the press for the pardons. Bush apparently used a November 7, 1992, newspaper piece about pardon discussions by administration officials as a trial balloon. Then his staffers tested the waters with journalists to gauge their reaction. In his pardon proclamation statement, Bush offered to release his own testimony, thereby quelling public demand for additional disclosure.[42] Ford, of course, kept everything secret until just before the announcement.

The other crucial dissimilarity between the Nixon and Iran-Contra pardons was timing, an important variable that worked against Ford and in Bush's favor. Bush was able to put off a pardoning decision until he had already lost his reelection bid and was on his way to retirement. He would not suffer political consequences for his final pardons, save incidental damage to his legacy. The political timing of the Christmas Eve pardons was "impeccable," since few dissenting voices remained in Washington, D.C., over Christmas, and the television and newspaper audiences for Christmas Eve and Christmas morning were quite small.[43] Under the circumstances, any eruptions of public outrage would be muted and likely die down quickly. In contrast, Ford knew in early September that President Nixon was almost certain to face criminal charges. With a Nixon indictment looming, he did not have the luxury to wait until late December to act. Ford had been president for one month before pardoning Nixon, and arguably could not have waited much longer.

Moreover, although it was a major scandal, Iran-Contra was not in the same league as Watergate because it did not cause the same crisis of confidence in government. Ford faced a situation that fit into the framework of the clemency power devised by the framers and the Supreme Court in Federalist No. 74, *United States v. Wilson*, and *Biddle v. Perovich*. "In seasons of insurrection or rebellion," the framers had written, the president has the power to pardon to "restore the tranquility of the commonwealth."[44] The situation that President Bush faced was not as serious as the one facing Ford in 1974:

People had not lost faith in governmental institutions to the same degree. Bush had lived with an ongoing Iran-Contra investigation throughout his term as president. He had been perfectly able to run the country—even winning the first Gulf War—while Lawrence Walsh investigated potential wrongdoing within the Bush administration. Bush did not grant the Iran-Contra pardons until his term of office was essentially over. If the situation had been dire enough that Bush needed to pardon the Iran-Contra defendants to give himself an opportunity to govern, he may well have pardoned the Iran-Contra defendants right away. So the Nixon pardon fit squarely within the framers' intentions, whereas the Iran-Contra pardons did not.

Like Ford, President Bush made the mistake of basing at least the Weinberger pardon on the "act of grace" rationale of *United States v. Wilson.* Weinberger and Bush were longtime friends, and Weinberger had serious health issues at the time. Their relationship thus had some elements in common with the Nixon-Ford relationship. It should not have come as a surprise, then, that instead of citing *Biddle v. Perovich* and justifying the Weinberger pardon as for "the public welfare," Bush attempted to gain sympathy for Weinberger personally.[45] This may have worked with Republicans, but Democrats and independents were not so impressed. However, Bush enjoyed less restrictive circumstances than Ford had after Watergate. The forty-first president learned from the thirty-eighth president's mistake and had time to make sure that the pardons would be palatable to key political elites and journalists before he issued them.

The framers vested the pardon power in "a single man" because that man, the president, would always be answerable to the public for clemency decisions.[46] This is the crux of the public's dissatisfaction with the Iran-Contra pardons: Not only did President Bush wait to pardon the Iran-Contra defendants until he had lost his reelection bid, but he pardoned an accused before trial and under circumstances where his own involvement was far from clear. As legal scholar Laurence Tribe observed, "the framers did not intend the power to pardon to enable a president to cover his own tracks."[47] In Bush's case, the public perception was that perhaps a pardon was the cost of Weinberger's silence. This is a reasonable interpretation, given the circumstances. As Samuel Dash, former chief counsel to the Senate Watergate Committee, put it, "Bush's action cheapened the pardon power using it as little more than a sham to protect those who had demonstrated loyalty to the White House in the Iran-Contra scandal."[48]

The Clinton Pardons in Context

Riding a crest of high public opinion following his impeachment by the House and his acquittal by the Senate, President Clinton felt the harsh sting of public disapproval over his clemency offer to members of the FALN, a Puerto Rican Nationalist group, which was likely made to help Hillary Clinton's New York Senate bid, Vice President Al Gore's presidential campaign, or both. His popularity ratings still fairly strong, Clinton approached the end of his presidency in 1999. He waited until his final hours in office to get back at Independent Counsel Kenneth Starr when he pardoned dozens, including a number of former administration officials.

What did President Clinton do wrong in the FALN and last-minute pardon cases? For one thing, he opened himself up to charges of cronyism and favoritism by granting pardons without following the Justice Department's normal pardoning procedures. By avoiding the normal screening process that the public had grown to trust, Clinton signaled that such pardons could be less than fairly awarded.[49] As unexpected as the FALN clemency situation was, the Marc Rich pardon emerged as a paradigm of how the public can be blindsided by a clemency applicant who works informal channels to reach the president directly. The fact that Rich's ex-wife had donated a million dollars to Democratic causes, and almost half a million dollars to Clinton's presidential library, further angered the public. These cases showed how presidents can make bad decisions when cut off from the protection of the pardon attorney and faced with temptations such as these.

How do President Clinton's controversial pardons match up with those of President Ford and President Bush? As noted earlier, the Nixon pardon controversy and, later, the Bush Iran-Contra pardons established that Clinton had the legal power to pardon all of the clemency recipients, even Marc Rich, who had yet to face trial. Similar to the Iran-Contra pardons, Clinton's FALN and last-minute clemency decisions were made by a president enjoying his final days in office as a "lame duck." Although Bush faced questions about whether he had purchased Weinberger's silence with a pardon, Clinton, like Ford, faced intense media scrutiny over whether there had been a quid pro quo in each case. The FALN situation raised questions because of the political aspirations of Hillary Clinton and Al Gore. Later, the revelation that Marc Rich's wife and her friend had been major Democratic donors affected the public response to the last-minute pardons.

Clinton's controversial clemency decisions regarding members of the

FALN and his last-minute pardons thus joined the Nixon and Iran-Contra pardons of his predecessors as examples of clemency decisions made for the president's personal benefit. Like the controversial pardons of Ford and Bush, Clinton's last-minute pardons were at least indirectly related to a second-term scandal (although, in Clinton's case, it was his own second term that had hatched the scandals, not his predecessor's). All three presidents operated without the pardon attorney's active involvement, although Clinton attempted to either avoid or obtain the office's rubber stamp at the end of the process.

Like Bush, Clinton had some room to operate. None of the Clinton scandals—even impeachment—scarred him as much as Watergate had wounded Ford, in terms of popularity. Also, like Bush, Clinton made his final pardons literally within hours of the conclusion of the final investigation into his conduct. Unlike Bush, though, Clinton probably did not gain any protection from potentially incriminating testimony through his last-minute clemency decisions (although with Susan McDougal we may never know everything). Nor did he have the comfort of knowing he had freed the country from the spectacle of a former president standing trial, as Ford did. Thus, the stakes were not as great for Clinton as they were for Ford after Watergate: A new president of the opposing party (in this case, George W. Bush) was set to take office, and—owing largely to these factors—Clinton also had the opportunity to try to lay the groundwork for the controversial pardons he had been preparing.

However, unlike Bush, Clinton failed to take adequate steps to prepare the country for his pardons. Although it is unlikely that Republicans in Congress would have given him any leeway, Clinton could have taken advantage of his skill with the media to try to spin the pardons before they were granted. Like Ford, Clinton chose not to do so. This may have been a missed opportunity. If Clinton had been more forthcoming with representatives of the media or consulted with members of Congress, his last-minute pardons might not have met with so much criticism.

Where do the last-minute pardons fall on the scales established by Federalist No. 74, *United States v. Wilson*, and *Biddle v. Perovich*? As noted earlier, Alexander Hamilton said that "in seasons of insurrection or rebellion," the president has the power to pardon to "restore the tranquility of the commonwealth."[50] Unlike Ford, President Clinton did not face a serious crisis in the public's confidence in its governmental institutions. Rather, he had dealt with scandal investigations throughout his term as president. He was perfectly able to run the country even while facing impeachment. Clinton did not grant the FALN or last-minute clemencies until his term of office was essentially over. If the situation had been dire enough that he had needed to pardon Puerto Rican Nationalists or Marc Rich et al. to give himself an opportunity to govern, presumably he would have pardoned everyone earlier on. Like Bush's Iran-Contra pardons, Clinton's FALN and last-minute pardons do not seem to fit the framers' intentions in this regard. Indeed, a *New York Times* editorial astutely pointed out that in the case of Rich, "bestowing undeserved beneficence on a fugitive accused of evading $48 million in taxes and illegally trading with Iran in oil during the hostage crisis is hardly what the Constitution's framers had in mind."[51]

Clinton did not try to pretend that the pardons were an "act of grace," as expressed in *United States v. Wilson*, either. His argument that the last-minute pardons served "the best interests of justice" rang hollow in light of the fact that his public explanation basically blamed others for the Marc Rich pardon.[52] An argument that the last-minute pardons satisfied *Biddle v. Perovich* and its "public welfare" rationale would also fall short, considering that Clinton's strongest justification had to do with the possibility of recovering money from Rich in civil court. Not even Clinton's strongest allies could support what was quite possibly an illegal payoff for presidential library donations. The framers intended that the president would always remain answerable to the public via unlimited eligibility for the presidency.[53] They never intended that a "lame duck" president would be able to make decisions without regard for political consequences.

Defenders of George H. W. Bush and Bill Clinton may contend that the presidents were at the mercy of an opposition Congress that felt free to use the independent counsel statute as a political weapon against the presidency. Nonetheless, abusing the clemency power in this manner is inconsistent with the framers' intentions. Even assuming the worst motives on the part of Congress, the president is not justified in exercising the clemency power to excuse executive branch aides or to reward supporters and contributors.

The Libby Commutation in Context

Inevitably, for years into the future, President George W. Bush's commutation of Scooter Libby's prison sentence will be mentioned in the same breath as the controversial pardons granted by Gerald Ford, George H. W. Bush, and Bill Clinton. Like these predecessors, George W. Bush made the

Libby commutation decision without relying on the Pardon Attorney's Office. This approach was a striking departure from his prior and subsequent practice—as of November 2008, Bush had granted 171 pardons and 8 commutations,[54] and the Libby commutation was one of the few that had originated in the White House.[55]

No one questioned whether Bush had the presidential power to commute Libby's sentence, but the timing and circumstances of the decision brought back memories of the Iran-Contra pardons and Clinton's last-minute pardons: All of these clemency decisions were made by second-term "lame duck" presidents, stemmed from a second-term scandal, and were made by presidents for the benefit of their predecessors'—or their own—executive branch officials.

The Libby commutation's closest parallel among these options is probably the Iran-Contra affair. "That [Iran-Contra] was really a vindication of his political people. They were doing their job to protect the presidency. This case is not as serious, but there is a similar premise for issuing a pardon," offered Margaret Love.[56] Unlike Caspar Weinberger, Scooter Libby had at least been charged, convicted, and sentenced. On the surface, this distinguishes him from the clemency recipients who never had their crimes considered by the judicial system (Nixon, Weinberger, and Rich, most notably). However, Libby was convicted of crimes that involved being evasive and providing incomplete information, and in some cases, simply lying. In a way, it is difficult to argue that Libby's trial resolved the extent of his offenses, given that the prosecutor was never given enough material from Libby to determine what those offenses might be.

Like his father and Bill Clinton, George W. Bush had some room to operate so that he could select an opportune time to grant clemency. Unlike Clinton, whose popularity remained steady even through impeachment, Bush saw his popularity stagnate and remain low through much of his second term. Polls predicted that the Libby commutation would probably not do much additional damage. Although Libby had been indicted back in October 2005, Bush was able to wait on a commutation decision until July 2007, at which point Libby had been tried and sentenced.

As with Iran-Contra, the Libby commutation may have protected the president from potentially embarrassing revelations from a former colleague with knowledge of sensitive issues. However, for George W. Bush, as for Clinton and the elder Bush, the stakes were not as great as those faced by Ford in 1974. What is more, neither President Bush nor his vice president will be president past January 20, 2009, a factor giving them much leeway in the decisions they make in their final months as president and vice president.

George W. Bush certainly knew that the clemency decision would be very unpopular, thanks to polls that anticipated the scenario that eventually played out. He did not make many behind-the-scenes moves to prepare the country for the Libby commutation; then again, it probably would not have made much difference if he had attempted to do so. The Democratic majority in Congress came into office harshly critical of Bush and very uncooperative and would likely have remained so had Bush searched for Democratic support for a commutation. An attempt to "go public" to drum up public support would have likely failed, given Bush's prickly relationship with the media and the public at the time. With little to gain and an unsympathetic political environment, it is no surprise that Bush did not try to rally Democrats in Congress behind his decision, or even agree to appear before Congress for questioning, as Ford had more than thirty years earlier.

Where does the Libby commutation fall on the scales established by Federalist No. 74, *United States v. Wilson*, and *Biddle v. Perovich*? Unlike President Ford, President Bush did not face a serious crisis in the public's confidence in its governmental institutions. The Valerie Plame investigation was serious, but in the end no one was even charged with leaking her secret identity. Nobody argued that commuting Libby's sentence would have any widespread public benefit. Indeed, President Bush was harshly criticized for granting clemency to Libby when, political ramifications aside, Libby's situation was analogous to that of hundreds of clemency applicants that Bush had ignored.

Was the Libby commutation decision made for the "public welfare," as *Biddle* contemplates? Bush did not argue in his clemency grant that commuting Scooter Libby's sentence had any larger ramifications for the nation. Declaring that the investigation and trial were legitimate, Bush found fault with only the prison term, which he considered "excessive." Was it an "act of mercy" consistent with *Wilson*? Although Bush did not say so, this is really the most likely rationale. Where he ran into difficulty was his own track record. Why would he spare Scooter Libby from prison when his other commutations—out of thousands of applications—numbered fewer than ten?

The framers assumed that presidents would have to face the nation and bear the consequences of their clemency decisions. As Hamilton noted in Federalist No. 74, the framers vested the pardon power in "a single man" because "the sense of responsibility is always strongest in proportion as it is undivided."[57] Here, like his two most recent predecessors, President Bush avoided responsibility for his clemency decision. And, like Clinton, the second Bush clearly took advantage of his end-of-term immunity. As the Libby investigation demonstrates, the changes to the political environment that took place after Watergate appear to still be in effect, even though memories of the independent counsel statute have faded since 1999.

Politics and the Pardon Power

A main theme of this book has been that modern presidents have taken advantage of the clemency power in controversial ways. Two of them made decisions under cover of the political safe haven created by the independent counsel statute. The main reason that George H. W. Bush and George W. Bush were able to make their controversial clemency decisions is that the political context in which outside investigators (whether appointed by means of an independent counsel statute or not) have examined the executive branch has become much more politically charged in recent decades than it was in the pre-Watergate era.[58]

Broadly speaking, the political context in which modern presidents must evaluate clemency cases is different from that of just thirty years ago. Today, presidents must decide whether to award pardons, and to whom, under the watchful eye of the modern mass media. Clemency decisions almost never provide any real political boost, and they almost always require the president to risk political capital. These risks, while always a concern for presidents, are magnified by the Internet, scientific polling techniques, twenty-four-hour cable television, and so on. Modern presidents are much more visible and subject to fluctuations in their political standing than presidents were in earlier times. They may decide to "go public" to raise support for administration programs, and are expected by the press and the public to communicate regularly, particularly in cases where justifications are demanded for controversial decisions.[59]

The give-and-take between presidents and the public is a good—and necessary—interaction. In a system where public officials depend on securing public approval to win reelection, voters need to know how to assign praise or blame at the ballot box. In granting the chief executive a strong clemency power, the framers assumed that the president would always remain accountable to the public for clemency decisions. Political accountability was the linchpin that allowed the check-and-balance system to function, not only in regard to pardons, but in every other area of government as well.

Presidents have adapted their use of the clemency power in recent years to take advantage of political circumstances. In most cases, they have avoided pardoning, opting instead to protect their political capital. On rare occasions, when the safety of not pardoning has been outweighed by a greater concern, presidents have abused the clemency power by excusing executive branch associates or rewarding supporters. George H. W. Bush and George W. Bush exploited an opening created by the independent counsel statute to avoid taking direct responsibility for executive branch investigations, and then used the clemency power as a political weapon to end investigations. Bill Clinton, like both his predecessor and his successor, abused the clemency power, but in his case it was to drum up votes and reward a presidential library donor.

The Nixon pardon and the independent counsel statute left a legacy that affected the clemency practices of later presidents. Each of the presidents discussed in this Conclusion received some personal benefit from their clemency decisions. The framers intended pardons to be motivated by mercy for the offender or made in the public interest, not used in the service of the president's private interest. However, only the Nixon pardon, given by a president eligible for and seeking election, had lasting political consequences. Presidents George H. W. Bush, Bill Clinton, and George W. Bush did not need to take political consequences into account when making their clemency decisions because they would never have to face the electorate again.

Epilogue: Reform Needed?

The separation of powers and the system of checks and balances were meant to ensure that the pardon power would be "a broad, final check on the entire legal and judicial system,"[60] and it was intended at the founding of the nation that presidents would always be responsible to the public for their decisions. In recent years, some have questioned whether these constitutional arrangements are sufficient. Our latest three presidents have made clemency decisions in which they have taken advantage of the pardon power. All three presidents (or their supporters, at least) argued that their favored people were victims of politically motivated prosecution and/or punishment. As the Libby inquiry showed, the blending of the lines between politics and justice that characterized the independent counsel era may be permanent, and it is questionable whether any future investigation by a special counsel—regardless of party—will be considered fair and legitimate by both sides.

Although the pardon power belongs to the president alone, most of these controversial clemency decisions were sprung on the public without warning. The Iran-Contra pardons and Libby commutation did not go through the normal process established by the Office of the Pardon Attorney, where applicants must wait years before applying, then wait while their application is processed, their case investigated, and a positive recommendation reached. Many of the Clinton pardons were rushed through or even rubber-stamped at the last minute.

Presidential sympathizers have argued that Congress used the independent counsel statute to attack the president,[61] and that presidents have then used the powers of their office to strike back.[62] Nevertheless, the controversial and self-serving clemency actions by our latest three presidents are not what the framers had in mind for the clemency power. The Anti-Federalists were very concerned that chief executives might be tempted to use clemency to cover up executive branch wrongdoing or for their own personal benefit. All three presidents analyzed here are guilty of using the clemency power for self-serving reasons, possibly even to complete an illegal quid pro quo transaction.

Presidents have broad authority to pardon, but the proper motives for pardon (an "act of grace" or "for the public welfare") are well established both in law and practice. The examples of Presidents Grant, Roosevelt, Coolidge, and Truman are instructive, at least in the limited context of how to treat investigated executive branch officials. Presidents before Watergate usually showed restraint in these sensitive circumstances, whereas more recent presidents have not. The framers did not create the president to be an American king, and he should not use the clemency power as if he is one. In the long run, presidential abuse of the pardon power will undermine public confidence in the president and our Constitution. Accordingly, one might ask, Is it time to amend the Constitution?

A number of reforms have been suggested to involve Congress in clemency decisions or otherwise limit the clemency power. One widely discussed plan proposed shortly after Watergate by Senator Walter Mondale

(D-MN) would have amended the Constitution to allow Congress to override a presidential pardon by a two-thirds vote of the House and Senate. Acknowledging that the framers had considered but declined to give Congress a role in granting pardons, Mondale nevertheless contended that they would not have objected to Congress reviewing the president's clemency decisions.[63] Another plan put forward by a legal scholar suggested amending the Constitution to prevent presidents from pardoning after they or their party had lost a reelection bid. Representative Barney Frank (D-MA) proposed a similar solution in a constitutional amendment banning a president from using the pardon power "from a month before a presidential election until the next inauguration day."[64]

However, reform proposals purportedly necessary to preserve the separation of powers would actually throw off the existing balance of powers and go against the separation-of-powers doctrine.[65] The framers, who believed the clemency power should be as broad as possible, entrusted it in the Constitution to the president alone. As Alexander Hamilton wrote in Federalist No. 74, "the benign prerogative of pardoning should be as little as possible fettered or embarrassed," and "one man appears to be a more eligible dispenser of the mercy of the government than a body of men."[66] The framers were very clear in their debates about preventing the legislature from interfering with the president's pardon power.

The framers' reasons for granting this all-but-unlimited power to the president included the fact that they wanted to provide a check on the justice system. Clemency was thus seen as an act of mercy toward an individual offender that was intended to serve the public welfare. However, as Hamilton noted, the "principal argument" for entrusting the president with a potent clemency power was that "in seasons of insurrection or rebellion, there are often critical moments when a well-timed offer of pardon to the insurgents or rebels may restore the tranquility of the commonwealth; and which, if suffered to pass unimproved, it may never be possible afterwards to recall." Hamilton added, "The dilatory process of convening the legislature, or one of its branches, for the purpose of obtaining its sanction to the measure, would frequently be the occasion of letting slip the golden opportunity."[67]

In other words, the framers wanted the president to be able to use the clemency power to defuse volatile situations that required one person to act quickly and then bear the consequences of that decision. Over time, that key expectation has been fulfilled, particularly after the Civil War and various other wars throughout American history. The controversial clemency decisions discussed in Chapter 3 regarding various movement leaders also fall into this category.

The framers were also aware that their decision to lodge the clemency power in the presidency carried with it real risk of abuse. They debated, and discarded, alternatives that would have involved Congress in the clemency process. Although these alternatives may have given another branch of government some control over presidential clemency decisions, they would have undermined the very principles that the framers identified as key to the framework they devised: The clemency power, they believed, should be as potent as possible, entrusted to one individual, and used quickly to defuse volatile situations.

Assuming that presidents would act in good faith, the framers were confident that impeachment would be an adequate check for egregious abuses of the clemency power. Nevertheless, recent presidents have exploited the pardon power for personal reasons. Despite complaints from the public, from the press, and from other elected officials, not one of these self-interested clemency decisions has yet triggered an impeachment inquiry.

These recent self-interested clemency decisions may indeed reveal a weakness in the framers' design—but I believe it is not a fatal flaw. The best way to address self-interested clemency decisions is not to wish for a better system, but to trust the framers' design and fully use the protections already provided to combat executive abuse of power. When abuses occur, Congress should put all its options on the table, including the one reserved for the most serious situations: the impeachment clause in Article II, Section 4, of the Constitution.

Past practice has taught us that extra vigilance is required during the final days of a presidential term, because it is then that the temptation to abuse the clemency power is strongest. Rather than wring our collective hands and grumble about which cronies or supporters will receive executive clemency as a president departs, we need to decide, as a nation, that last-minute clemency abuses will not be tolerated. When a president abuses the clemency power, we need to decide that his actions will trigger real sanctions. The judgment of history should be harshly critical of presidents who make self-interested clemency decisions. It is only by punishing presidents who exploit the clemency power that we can uphold the rule of law, and—ultimately—preserve and defend our Constitution.

APPENDIX
NOTES ON SCHOLARSHIP

Since the founding of the United States, nearly all scholarly writing on the pardon power has focused on its historical and legal aspects and appeared in legal publications. The specialized literature (excluding magazine and newspaper articles) published on the clemency power can be broken into two general categories: (1) legal opinions, articles, notes, and case comments published or posted online by legal scholars ("Legal Scholarship"); and (2) a few notable books, book chapters, and articles published or posted online by political scientists ("Political Science Scholarship").

Legal Scholarship

Legal scholarship on the pardon power focuses primarily on a dozen or so cases[1] that together explain the forms, nature, acceptance, extent, effect, and limits of the pardon power. Only a smattering of law review articles on the presidential pardon power were published before World War II.[2] Although a couple of book-length analyses of the pardon power were published around that time,[3] it was not until the pardon of Richard Nixon in 1974 that a significant number of legal scholars were spurred—either directly or indirectly—to action.[4]

The controversial pardons of George H. W. Bush may explain a spike in the number of pardon-related articles written in the early 1990s.[5] More recently, Bill Clinton's controversial pardons in 1999 and 2001 probably stimulated another wave of pardon scholarship.[6] If nothing else, Clinton's pardoning practices likely convinced the publishers of the *Federal Sentencing Reporter* to devote their entire November/December 2000 and January/February 2001 double issue to federal and state pardons.

Of all law review articles focused on the clemency power, the most useful (and among the lengthiest) works are by William Duker, Daniel Kobil, and Brian Hoffstadt. Recent clemency information is available from three terrific electronic sources: Ohio State University law professor Douglas Berman's Sentencing Law and Policy blog,[7] University of Pittsburgh School of Law professor Bernard Hibbitts's Jurist Web site, and Rock Valley College political science professor P. S. Ruckman Jr.'s Pardonpower .com blog.[8]

Political Science Scholarship

Two key works to understanding the clemency power concern the framers' original intentions for Article 2, Section 2, Clause 1.[9] Aside from works focusing on the framers, the two most significant early publications on the pardon power were written in 1939 and 1941, although only the 1941 book can be considered a true political science work.

In 1939, a team of editors directed by the U.S. attorney general and funded by a grant from the Works Progress Administration published a four-volume set entitled *The Attorney General's Survey of Release Procedures*, which featured an entire volume dedicated to state and federal pardons. This 323-page work explored such issues as the history of pardoning, its development, limits, effect, and other related issues. Just two years later, a dissertation written by aspiring Ph.D. candidate Willard H. Humbert, entitled *The Pardoning Power of the President*, magnificently traced the American president's pardon power from its English roots to its development through American case law, applying quantitative techniques to get at how the power has been used. These two works remain the standard today for political scientists studying the pardon power, although each requires some supplementation with more recent works.

Strangely, the intensely political nature of the Nixon pardon in 1974 did not encourage political scientists to try to place the decision into the framework of the modern presidency. Given the attention paid by political scholars to how other important presidential powers have evolved in the modern era, this omission is perplexing. Controversial pardons by George H. W. Bush and Bill Clinton also failed to generate much political science scholarship.

Until quite recently, only a small number of scholarly articles on the pardon power have been written by political scientists, and the scope has been narrow.[10] The most useful recent political science writing regarding the pardon power has been undertaken by David Adler,[11] Mark Rozell,[12] and P. S. Ruckman Jr.[13] Ruckman in particular has done yeoman's work on clemency, and only a few other clemency studies have emerged in recent years.[14] Especially when compared with the legal pardon power literature, political science scholarship in this area is severely lacking in amount and substance. Political scientists have shied away from the pardon power, leaving monolithic legal and historical analyses to fill a void in the literature that should be filled by dynamic political analysis.

I suggest that principles pulled from political science literature on the presidency can explain the relationship between the pardon power and the modern presidency. That relationship, which is inadequately explained by current political science literature, is the focus of this book.

NOTES

Introduction

1. Gerald Ford, "Proclamation 4311, Granting Pardon to Richard Nixon," *Public Papers of the Presidents*, 61: September 8, 1974, 103.

2. Ibid.

3. Jerald terHorst, *Gerald Ford and the Future of the Presidency* (New York: Third Press, 1974), 230. Also see Robert Hartmann, *Palace Politics* (New York: McGraw-Hill, 1980), 266.

4. John Robert Greene, *The Presidency of Gerald R. Ford* (Lawrence: University Press of Kansas, 1995), 52.

5. terHorst, *Gerald Ford and the Future of the Presidency*, 228.

6. Perhaps coincidentally, an article by Timothy Ingram published in the June 30, 1974, *Washington Post* had speculated that a Nixon self-pardon "could contain the phrase 'crimes, if any,'" and that the president could avoid enumerating his offenses by simply excusing "all" offenses he may have committed since becoming president. The purpose behind the "blunt[ed]" language would be to counteract the fact that "a pardon generally implies guilt." This language is, of course, very similar to that of the actual Nixon pardon.

7. Ford was not running for "reelection" because he had assumed the presidency under the Twenty-Fifth Amendment and had not actually won a presidential campaign.

8. The Justice Department in the executive branch usually investigates wrongdoing in all three branches of the federal government. Under the independent counsel statute, the president was no longer directly responsible for appointing investigators to look into executive branch wrongdoing.

9. Margaret Love deserves credit for this term. See Margaret Love, "The Pardon Paradox: Lessons of Clinton's Last Pardons," *Capital University Law Review* 31 (2003): 185.

10. Louis Fisher, *Congressional Abdication on War and Spending* (College Station: Texas A&M University Press, 2000).

11. Richard Stevenson, "Washington Talk: A Presidential Power This President Uses Rarely," *New York Times*, December 25, 2002.

12. See Samuel Kernell, *Going Public*, 4th ed. (Washington, DC: CQ Press, 2007).

13. See Jeffrey Tulis, *The Rhetorical Presidency* (Princeton, NJ: Princeton University Press, 1987).

Chapter 1. The Pardon Power and the Constitution

1. U.S. Constitution, art. 2, sec. 2, cl. 1.

2. Charles Berger notes that nothing in the Constitution requires that an

offense be committed before it may be pardoned. However, he points out that case law (Ex parte Garland and Ex parte Grossman, discussed in the next chapter) has clarified that an offense must have been committed before a president may exercise the clemency power to excuse it. See Charles Berger, "The Effect of Presidential Pardons on Disclosure of Information: Is Our Cynicism Justified?" Oklahoma Law Review 52 (1999): 172–175.

3. See In re Bocchiaro, 49 F. Supp. 37, 38 (D.C.N.Y. 1943): "Since the crime charged here was not an offense against the United States, the President has not the power of pardon . . . and it lies only in the state."

4. U.S. Constitution, art. 2, sec. 2, cl. 1.

5. Kathleen Moore, Pardons (New York: Oxford University Press, 1989), 15.

6. For excellent analyses of the pardon power's past, see Willard Humbert, The Pardoning Power of the President (Washington, DC: American Council on Public Affairs, 1941); Wayne Morse et al., The Attorney General's Survey of Release Procedures, vol. 3 (Washington, DC: Government Printing Office, 1939); Daniel T. Kobil, "The Quality of Mercy Strained: Wresting the Pardoning Power from the King," Texas Law Review 69 (1991): 569; and William Duker, "The President's Power to Pardon: A Constitutional History," William & Mary Law Review 18 (1977): 475.

7. Moore, Pardons, 16; Kobil, "Quality of Mercy," 583.

8. Ibid. According to Kathleen Moore, these privileged few included athletes, actors, and "disgraced rulers." See Moore, Pardons, 16.

9. Moore, Pardons, 16–17; Kobil, "Quality of Mercy," 584. See, generally, Jonathan Truman Dorris, Pardon and Amnesty under Lincoln and Johnson (Chapel Hill: University of North Carolina Press, 1953).

10. Kobil, "Quality of Mercy," 585.

11. Kathleen Moore, "Pardon for Good and Sufficient Reasons," University of Richmond Law Review 27 (1993): 282.

12. Kobil, "Quality of Mercy," 585.

13. Duker, "Constitutional History," 487–488.

14. Kobil, "Quality of Mercy," 587.

15. James Jorgensen, "Federal Executive Clemency Power: The President's Prerogative to Escape Accountability," University of Richmond Law Review 27 (1993): 351. The "Act of Settlement" can accurately be assigned to either 1700 or 1701 because of an alteration in how bills were assigned a name.

16. Duker, "Constitutional History," 496.

17. Kobil, "Quality of Mercy," 588.

18. Duker, "Constitutional History," 488, 497–501.

19. John Locke, Second Treatise of Government, C. B. Macpherson, ed. (Indianapolis: Hackett, 1980), 83–84.

20. Baron de Montesquieu, The Spirit of the Laws, vol. 1, Thomas Nugent, trans. (New York: Hafner Press, 1949), 92–93: "So many are the advantages which monarchs gain by clemency, so greatly does it raise their fame and endear them to their subjects, that it is generally happy for them to have an opportunity of displaying it."

21. William Blackstone, Commentaries on the Laws of England, adapted by Robert Malcolm Kerr, vol. 4 (Boston: Beacon Press, 1962), 467–468. Blackstone also wrote: "To him therefore the people look up as the fountain of nothing but bounty and grace; and these repeated acts of

goodness, coming immediately from his own hand, endear the sovereign to his subjects, and contribute more than anything to root in their hearts that filial affection, and personal loyalty, which are the sure establishment of a prince."

22. James Wilson, "Executive Department, Lectures on Law, 1791," in Philip Kurland and Ralph Lerner, eds., *The Founders' Constitution*, vol. 4 (Chicago: University of Chicago Press, 1987), 20.

23. Joseph Story, *Commentaries on the Constitution*, vol. 3, secs. 1488–1498 (1833), in Philip Kurland and Ralph Lerner, eds., *The Founders' Constitution*, vol. 4 (Chicago: University of Chicago Press, 1987), 26.

24. *Youngstown Sheet & Tube Co. v. Sawyer*, 343 U.S. 579, 635 (1952).

25. Alexander Hamilton, James Madison, and John Jay, *The Federalist Papers*, Clinton Rossiter, ed. (New York: Mentor, 1999), 290.

26. Stephen Carter, "The Iran-Contra Pardon Mess," *Houston Law Review* 29 (1992): 884.

27. Jerry Carannante, "What to Do about the Executive Clemency Power in the Wake of the Clinton Presidency?" *New York Law School Law Review* 47 (2003): 347. For the Supreme Court's articulation of these principles, also see *Ex parte United States*, 242 U.S. 27, 41–42 (1916).

28. Kobil, "Quality of Mercy," 590.

29. John Feerick, "The Pardoning Power of Article II of the Constitution," *New York State Bar Journal* 47 (1975): 9.

30. Kobil, "Quality of Mercy," fn. 125.

31. Humbert, *Pardoning Power*, 15.

32. Feerick, "The Pardoning Power of Article II," 9.

33. Max Farrand, *Records of the Federal Convention of 1787*, vol. 2, 171–172, available online via the Library of Congress's American Memory Collection, http://memory.loc.gov/ammem/amlaw/lwfr.html (accessed 8/26/07).

34. Farrand, *Records*, vol. 2, 411, 419.

35. Ibid., 426.

36. Ibid., 563–564.

37. Ibid., 626–627.

38. Ibid., 627.

39. Feerick, "The Pardoning Power of Article II," 10.

40. Richard J. Ellis, *Founding the American Presidency* (Lanham, MD: Rowman & Littlefield, 1999), 221–222; Herbert J. Storing, *The Complete Anti-Federalist*, vol. 2 (Chicago: University of Chicago Press, 1981), 67, 142, 151, 348.

41. Farrand, *Records*, vol. 3, 218.

42. Duker, "Constitutional History," 504; Todd David Peterson, "Congressional Power over Pardon and Amnesty: Legislative Authority in the Shadow of Presidential Prerogative," *Wake Forest Law Review* 38 (2003): 1231; Ashley Steiner, "Remission of Guilt or Removal of Punishment: The Effects of a Presidential Pardon," *Emory Law Journal* 46 (1997): 966.

43. James Iredell, "North Carolina Ratifying Convention, July 28, 1788," in Philip Kurland and Ralph Lerner, eds., *The Founders' Constitution*, vol. 4 (Chicago: University of Chicago Press, 1987), 17.

44. Hamilton et al., *Federalist Papers*, 386–387.

45. Ibid., 392.

46. Ibid., 415–416.

47. Ibid., 417.

48. Kobil, "Quality of Mercy," 589.

49. Jorgensen, "Federal Executive Clemency Power," 354–355.

50. For an excellent analysis of several key points of struggle between the executive and legislative branches, see

the classic work in the field: Louis Fisher, *Constitutional Conflicts between Congress and the President*, 5th ed. (Lawrence: University Press of Kansas, 2007).

51. U.S. Constitution, art. 2, sec. 2, cl. 2.

52. Ibid.; also see Michael Gerhardt, *The Federal Appointments Process* (Durham, NC: Duke University Press, 2003).

53. U.S. Constitution, art. 2, sec. 3.

54. U.S. Constitution, art. 2, sec. 1, cl. 1.

55. See Kenneth Mayer, *With the Stroke of a Pen* (Princeton, NJ: Princeton University Press, 2001) (executive orders); Mark Rozell, *Executive Privilege*, 2d ed. (Lawrence: University Press of Kansas, 2002); and Lawrence Margolis, *Executive Agreements* (New York: Praeger, 1986).

56. U.S. Constitution, art. 2, sec. 2; also see Louis Fisher, *Presidential War Power*, 2d ed. (Lawrence: University Press of Kansas, 2004).

57. U.S. Constitution, art. 1, sec. 7; see also Robert Spitzer, *The Presidential Veto* (Albany: State University of New York Press, 1988).

58. U.S. Constitution, art. 2, sec. 3.

59. Kobil, "Quality of Mercy," 576, 577.

60. See *Osborn v. United States*, 91 U.S. 474, 478 (1876): "The power to pardon offences must be held to carry with it, as an incident, the power to release penalties and forfeitures which accrue from the offences." See also Kobil, "Quality of Mercy," 595.

61. Kobil, "Quality of Mercy," 578.

62. Ibid., 576–577.

63. Kevin Krajick, "The Quality of Mercy," *Corrections*, June 1979, 51.

64. 28 USCS Secs. 509–510 (2005); 28 CFR 0.35 (2005).

65. See, generally, John Burke, *The Institutional Presidency*, 2d ed. (Baltimore: Johns Hopkins University Press, 2000); and Stephen Hess, *Organizing the Presidency*, 3d ed. (Washington, DC: Brookings Institution Press, 2002).

66. John Stanish, "The Effect of a Presidential Pardon," *Federal Probation* 42 (1978): 3; Grover Cleveland, Executive Order 30-1, June 16, 1893, available online at http://cisweb.lexis-nexis.com/histuniv/data/10/pdf/P-10-EO-00043.pdf (accessed 8/26/07).

67. Stanish, "Presidential Pardon," 3; 13 Stat. 516 (1865).

68. Stanish, "Presidential Pardon," 3; 26 Stat. 946 (1891).

69. Stanish, "Presidential Pardon," 3.

70. Reed Cozart, "Clemency under the Federal System," *Federal Probation* 23 (1959): 3.

71. Reed Cozart, "The Benefits of Executive Clemency," *Federal Probation* 32 (1968): 34.

72. Brian Hoffstadt, "Normalizing the Federal Clemency Power," *Texas Law Review* 79 (2001): 591.

73. 28 CFR 0.36 (2005).

74. Carl Cannon and David Byrd, "The Power of the Pardon," *National Law Journal* 32 (2000): 776.

75. 28 CFR 1.5 (2005).

76. P. S. Ruckman Jr., "'Last-Minute' Pardon Scandals: Fact and Fiction," http://www.rvc.cc.il.us/facelink/pruckman/pardoncharts/Paper2.pdf (accessed 8/26/07), 7, 12.

77. 28 CFR 1.1 (2005). A military offender is directed to apply to the secretary of the military department with original jurisdiction over that offender's court-martial trial.

78. 28 CFR 1.4 (2005).

79. 28 CFR 1.2 (2005). The five-year

waiting period is one major result of changes in the "Rules Governing Petitions for Executive Clemency" approved by President Ronald Reagan on May 18, 1983. Notably, the revisions "lengthen[ed] the eligibility waiting period for pardon applicants to a minimum of five years, with a minimum of seven [years] required for more serious crimes," such as violent crimes, narcotics law violations, and income tax violations, among others, while also "increas[ing] the categories of crimes requiring the longer eligibility period" (see 48 FR 22290, Sec. 1.2). As P. S. Ruckman notes, the waiting period was changed back to five years for all offenses by President Bill Clinton. See P. S. Ruckman Jr., "President-Centered and Presidency-Centered Explanations of Federal Clemency," http://www.rvc.cc.il.us/facelink/pruckman/pardoncharts/Paper1.pdf (accessed 8/26/07), fn 10.

80. 28 CFR 1.2 (2005).

81. 28 CFR 1.3 (2005).

82. 28 CFR 1.6 (2005).

83. Margaret Love, "Of Pardons, Politics, and Collar Buttons: Reflections on the President's Duty to Be Merciful," *Fordham Urban Law Journal* 27 (2000): 1484, 1508.

84. Ibid., 1510–1511.

85. Margaret Love, "The Pardon Paradox: Lessons of Clinton's Last Pardons," *Capital University Law Review* 31 (2003): 188, 216.

86. Love, "Reflections," 1511.

87. William Taft, *Our Chief Magistrate and His Powers* (New York: Columbia University Press, 1925), 123.

88. See Comments, "The Pardoning Power of the Chief Executive," *Fordham Law Review* 6 (1937): 256.

89. U.S. Constitution, art. 5.

90. U.S. Constitution, art. 2, sec. 4.

91. Peterson, "Congressional Power," 1260.

92. Louis Fisher, "Congressional Investigations: Subpoenas and Contempt Power," *Congressional Research Service Report*, April 2, 2003.

93. Peterson, "Congressional Power," 1260.

94. Tom Squitieri, "House Rebukes Clinton on Clemency for FALN Members; Senate Is Scheduled to Vote on Its Own Resolution Monday," *USA Today*, September 10, 1999.

95. Louis Fisher, *The Politics of Executive Privilege* (Durham, NC: Carolina Academic Press, 2004), 220, 222.

96. On July 11, 2007, the House Judiciary Committee held a hearing entitled "Use or Misuse of Presidential Clemency Power for Executive Branch Officials."

97. Mark Rozell, "In Defense of President Ford's Pardon of Richard M. Nixon," in *Gerald R. Ford and the Politics of Post-Watergate America*, Bernard Firestone and Alexej Ugrinsky, eds. (Westport, CT: Greenwood Press, 1993), 48.

98. Edward Corwin, *The President: Office and Powers, 1787–1984*, 5th ed. (New York: New York University Press, 1984), 201.

99. Jorgensen, "Federal Executive Clemency Power," 361.

100. Mark Rozell, "President Ford's Pardon of Richard M. Nixon," in *Triumphs and Tragedies of the Modern Presidency*, David Abshire, ed. (Westport, CT: Praeger, 2001), 97.

Chapter 2. Executive and Legislative Clemency Power

1. Daniel Kobil, "The Quality of Mercy Strained: Wresting the Pardoning Power

from the King," *Texas Law Review* 69 (1991): 597–598 (emphasis added). Kobil writes, "The courts . . . have not entirely refused to limit the exercise of the clemency power via the judiciary. Instead, courts . . . treat the President's *reasons* for using the power as sacrosanct, but recognize that courts may review and invalidate some pardons because of their impermissible *effect*."

2. Leonard Boudin, "The Presidential Pardons of James R. Hoffa and Richard M. Nixon: Have the Limitations on the Pardon Power Been Exceeded?" *University of Colorado Law Review* 48 (1976): 6–7.

3. *Hoffa v. Saxbe*, 378 F. Supp. 1221, 1244 (D.D.C. 1974).

4. Henry Weihofen, "Pardon: An Extraordinary Remedy," *Rocky Mountain Law Review* 12 (1939–1940): 113.

5. Mark Strasser, "Some Reflections on the President's Pardon Power," *Capital University Law Review* 31 (2003): 144.

6. Margaret Love, "Of Pardons, Politics and Collar Buttons: Reflections on the President's Duty to Be Merciful," *Fordham Urban Law Journal* 27 (2000): 1485.

7. Christopher Joyner, "Rethinking the President's Power of Executive Pardon," *Federal Probation* 43 (1979): 19.

8. *United States v. Wilson*, 32 U.S. 150, 160 (1833): "As this power had been exercised, from time immemorial, by the executive of that nation whose language is our language, and to whose judicial institutions ours bear a close resemblance; we adopt their principles respecting the operation and effect of a pardon, and look into their books for the rules prescribing the manner in which it is to be used by the person who would avail himself of it."

9. Ibid., 160–161 (emphasis added).

10. Kobil, "Quality of Mercy," 594. According to Kobil, "implicit in Marshall's definition is the notion that the executive can dispense such 'grace' in any form, at any time, and for any reason, in all cases except impeachment."

11. *United States v. Wilson*, 32 U.S. 150, 161 (1833).

12. Ibid., 163.

13. G. Sidney Buchanan, "Nature of a Pardon under the United States Constitution," *Ohio State Law Journal* 39 (1978): 48–49.

14. *Biddle v. Perovich*, 274 U.S. 480, 485 (1927).

15. Ibid.; David Garland, ed., "The President's Power of Commutation," *New York Law Review* 5 (1927): 401.

16. *Biddle v. Perovich*, 274 U.S. 480, 486 (1927) (emphasis added).

17. William Howard Taft, *Our Chief Magistrate and His Powers* (New York: Columbia University Press, 1925), 121.

18. Carl Cannon and David Byrd, "The Power of the Pardon," *National Law Journal* 32 (2000): 776.

19. *Hoffa v. Saxbe*, 378 F. Supp. 1221, 1231–1232 (D.D.C. 1974).

20. Kobil, "Quality of Mercy," 595.

21. *Ex parte Garland*, 71 U.S. 333, 380 (1866).

22. *Ex parte Grossman*, 267 U.S. 87, 120 (1925): "The executive can reprieve or pardon all offenses after their commission, either before trial, after trial, during trial or after trial, by individuals, or by classes, conditionally or absolutely, and this without modification or regulation by Congress."

23. *Ex parte Garland*, 380–381 (emphasis added).

24. Samuel Williston, "Does a Pardon Blot Out Guilt?" *Harvard Law Review* 28 (1915): 649–650.

25. Ibid., 651.

26. Ibid., 651–652 (emphasis added).

27. See *Boyd v. United States*, 142 U.S. 450 (1892).

28. See *Carlesi v. New York*, 233 U.S. 51 (1914).

29. *Bjerkan v. United States*, 529 F.2d 125, 126–127 (C.A. Ill. 1975).

30. Ibid., 126–128; Williston, "Does a Pardon Blot Out Guilt?" 653: "The true line of distinction seems to be this: The pardon removes all legal punishment for the offense. Therefore if the mere conviction involves certain disqualifications which would not follow from the commission of the crime without conviction, the pardon removes such disqualifications. On the other hand, if character is a necessary qualification and the commission of a crime would disqualify even though there had been no criminal prosecution for the crime, the fact that the criminal has been convicted and pardoned does not make him any more eligible."

31. *Bjerkan v. United States*, 529 F.2d 125, 128 (C.A. Ill. 1975) (emphasis added): "Thus, the fact of *conviction* after a pardon cannot be taken into account in subsequent proceedings. However, the fact of the *commission* of the crime may be considered. Therefore, although the effects of the *commission* of the offense linger after a pardon, the effects of the *conviction* are all but wiped out."

32. See *Ex parte Grossman*, 367 U.S. 87 (1925).

33. Ibid.

34. Charles Berger, "The Effect of Presidential Pardons on Disclosure of Information: Is Our Cynicism Justified?" *Oklahoma Law Review* 52 (1999): 175, 176.

35. William F. Duker, "The President's Power to Pardon: A Constitutional History," *William & Mary Law Review* 18 (1977): 528.

36. James Jorgensen, "Federal Executive Clemency Power: The President's Prerogative to Escape Accountability," *University of Richmond Law Review* 27 (1993): 361.

37. Brian M. Hoffstadt, "Normalizing the Federal Clemency Power," *Texas Law Review* 79 (2001): 594–595; *Ohio Adult Parole Authority v. Woodard*, 523 U.S. 272, 289 (1998).

38. *United States v. Noonan*, 906 F. 2d 952, 953, 955, 956, 958–959 (C.A. 3, 1990).

39. *In re North*, 62 F.3d 1434, 1435 (C.A. D.C., 1994).

40. Ibid., 1435–1437 (emphasis added).

41. As pointed out by Ashley M. Steiner in "Remission of Guilt or Removal of Punishment: The Effects of a Presidential Pardon," *Emory Law Journal* 46 (1997): fn 24, "The D.C. Court of Appeals (D.C.) is the equivalent of a state high court for the District of Columbia. The U.S. Court of Appeals for the District of Columbia Circuit, or D.C. Circuit (D.C. Cir.) is the federal appeals court.

42. *In re Abrams*, 689 A.2d 6, 7 (D.C. 1997).

43. Ibid., 7, 10–11: "Suppose that an alcoholic surgeon performs an operation while intoxicated. He botches the surgery. The patient dies. The surgeon is convicted of manslaughter and is sentenced to imprisonment. The President grants him a full and unconditional pardon. According to

Abrams, the surgeon now has the right, as a result of the pardon, to continue to operate on other patients, without any interference from the medical licensing authorities. The proposition that the alcoholic but pardoned surgeon (or, by analogy, a habitually inebriated and unsafe airline pilot) cannot be disciplined is, in our view, altogether unacceptable and even irrational, and it has been emphatically rejected by the courts" [citations omitted].

44. *United States v. Wilson*, 32 U.S. 150, 161 (1833).

45. *Ex parte Wells*, 59 U.S. 307, 308 (1855).

46. Ibid., 307–309, 314. The pardon stated: "I have granted, and do hereby grant unto him, the said William Wells, a pardon of the offence of which he was convicted—upon condition that he be imprisoned during his natural life; that is, the sentence of death is hereby commuted to imprisonment for life in the penitentiary of Washington."

47. Ibid., 315: "For the power to offer a condition, without ability to enforce its acceptance, when accepted by the convict, is the substitution, by himself, of a lesser punishment than the law has imposed upon him, and he cannot complain if the law executes the choice he has made."

48. Kobil, "Quality of Mercy," 594–595.

49. *Schick v. Reed*, 419 U.S. 256, 257–258 (1974).

50. Harold Krent, "Conditioning the President's Conditional Pardon Power," *California Law Review* 89 (2001): 1696.

51. *Schick v. Reed*, 419 U.S. 256, 258–259 (1974).

52. Ibid., 263–264: "The conclusion is inescapable that the pardoning power was intended to include the power to

commute sentences on conditions which do not in themselves offend the Constitution, but which are not specifically provided for by statute."

53. Ibid., 267.

54. Ibid., 266: "A fair reading of the history of the English pardoning power, from which our Art. II s. 2, cl. 1, derives, of the language of that clause itself, and of the unbroken practice since 1790 compels the conclusion that the power flows from the Constitution alone, not from any legislative enactments, and that it cannot be modified, abridged, or diminished by the Congress."

55. Ibid., 267.

56. Boudin, "The Presidential Pardons of James R. Hoffa and Richard M. Nixon," 25, 27.

57. See Patrick R. Cowlishaw, "The Conditional Presidential Pardon," *Stanford Law Review* 28 (1975): 156; S. Elizabeth Gibson, "Presidential Pardons and the Common Law," *North Carolina Law Review* 53 (1975): 790, 785–786, 793; Kobil, "Quality of Mercy," 596.

58. Krent, "Conditional Pardon Power," 1670, 1694–1695, 1697–1698.

59. *Hoffa v. Saxbe*, 378 F. Supp. 1221, 1223–1224 (D.D.C. 1974).

60. Ibid., 1233.

61. Kobil, "Quality of Mercy," 600.

62. *Hoffa v. Saxbe*, 378 F. Supp. 1221, 1236 (D.D.C. 1974).

63. Ibid., 1237–1238: "It is clear that the crimes for which Mr. Hoffa stood convicted were directly related to his participation in union activities. The public, of course, has a strong interest in the integrity of union activities inasmuch as unions exert great influence on the economic life of the nation and on the welfare of individual members of unions. Within this context, the President was

clearly justified in exacting as a condition of Hoffa's release the assurance that he would not participate directly or indirectly in the management of union activities until 1980, the time at which his judicially imposed sentences would have otherwise expired."

64. Kobil, "Quality of Mercy," 599.

65. Krent, "Conditional Pardon Power," fn 299.

66. Henry Weihofen, "Legislative Pardons," *California Law Review* 27 (1939): 374, 386.

67. Jorgensen, "Federal Executive Clemency Power," 360.

68. Weihofen, "Legislative Pardons," 377.

69. Todd David Peterson, "Congressional Power over Pardon and Amnesty: Legislative Authority in the Shadow of Presidential Prerogative," *Wake Forest Law Review* 38 (2003): 1268.

70. Peterson, "Congressional Power," 1241. Also see Harrop Freeman, "An Historical Justification and Legal Basis for Amnesty Today," *Law & Social Order* 1971 (1971): 520.

71. See *Armstrong v. United States*, 80 U.S. 154 (1872).

72. Confiscation Act, ch. 195, Sec. 13, 12 Stat. 589 (1862). See also Leonard Boudin, "The Presidential Pardons of James R. Hoffa and Richard M. Nixon: Have the Limitations on the Pardon Power Been Exceeded?" *University of Colorado Law Review* 48 (1976): 14–17.

73. Freeman, "Historical Justification," 520.

74. Abraham Lincoln, Proclamation of Amnesty, December 8, 1863, in *Compilation of the Messages and Papers of the Presidents, 1789–1897*, ed. J. D. Richardson (Washington, DC: Government Printing Office, 1907), 7:

3414–3416; Abraham Lincoln, Proclamation of Amnesty, March 26, 1864, in Richardson, *Papers of the Presidents*, 7: 3419.

75. Andrew Johnson, Proclamation of Amnesty, May 29, 1865, in Richardson, *Papers of the Presidents*, 7: 3508–3510; Andrew Johnson, Proclamation of Amnesty, September 7, 1867, in Richardson, *Papers of the Presidents*, 8: 3745–3747; Andrew Johnson, Proclamation of Amnesty, July 4, 1868, in Richardson, *Papers of the Presidents*, 8: 3853–3854; Andrew Johnson, Proclamation of Amnesty, December 25, 1868, in Richardson, *Papers of the Presidents*, 8: 3906.

76. Jonathan Dorris, *Pardon and Amnesty under Lincoln and Johnson* (Chapel Hill: University of North Carolina Press, 1953), 25.

77. 12 Stat. 502 (1862).

78. 13 Stat. 424 (1865).

79. *Ex parte Garland*, 71 U.S. 333, 335–336, 375, 376 (1866).

80. Ibid., 377, 379–380 (emphasis added).

81. Ibid., 380–381.

82. *Armstrong's Foundry*, 73 U.S. 766, 766–768 (1868).

83. 12 Stat. 319 (1861).

84. *Armstrong's Foundry*, 73 U.S. 766, 769 (1868): "We think it clear that the statute regarded the consent of the owner to the employment of his property in aid of the rebellion as an offence, and inflicted forfeiture as a penalty. The general pardon of Armstrong, therefore, relieved him of so much of the penalty as accrued to the United States."

85. *United States v. Padelford*, 76 U.S. 531, 532, 533 (1869).

86. Abraham Lincoln, Proclamation of Amnesty, December 8, 1863, in

Richardson, *Papers of the Presidents*, 7: 3414–3416.

87. *United States v. Padelford*, 76 U.S. 531, 533–534, 539 (1869).

88. Dorris, *Pardon and Amnesty*, 402.

89. 12 Stat. 820 (1863); *United States v. Padelford*, 76 U.S. 531, 534 (1869).

90. *United States v. Padelford*, 76 U.S. 531, 535 (1869).

91. 15 Stat. 75, Sec. 3 (1868). For more on *Padelford* and *Klein*, see Gordon Young, "Congressional Regulation of Federal Courts' Jurisdiction and Process: U.S. v. Klein Revisited," *Wisconsin Law Review* 1981 (1981): 1189.

92. *United States v. Padelford*, 76 U.S. 531, 543 (1869): "At the time of the seizure of the petitioner's property he was purged of whatever offence against the laws of the United States he had committed by the acts mentioned in the findings, and relieved from any penalty which he might have incurred. . . . If, in other respects, the petitioner made the proof which, under the act, entitled him to a decree for the proceeds of his property, the law makes the proof of pardon a complete substitute for proof that he gave no aid or comfort to the rebellion."

93. *United States v. Klein*, 80 U.S. 128, 131–132 (1871).

94. Dorris, *Pardon and Amnesty*, 404; *United States v. Klein*, 80 U.S. 128, 132 (1871), Young, "U.S. v. Klein Revisited," 1197–1198.

95. *United States v. Klein*, 80 U.S. 128, 132, 133 (1871).

96. 14 Stat. 377 (1867).

97. *United States v. Klein*, 80 U.S. 128, 145 (1871); 16 Stat. 235 (1870).

98. *United States v. Klein*, 80 U.S. 128, 138–139, 141–142 (1871).

99. Ibid., 147. In *Armstrong v. United States*, 80 U.S. 154 (1871), Hibernia Armstrong tried to claim the proceeds of cotton that was confiscated and sold, with its proceeds deposited into the U.S. Treasury. Although she did not actively aid the rebellion, she had fled the Union Army with thirty or forty slaves to prevent the Union from emancipating them. Without addressing Armstrong's loyalty, the Court held that President Johnson's final amnesty proclamation of December 25, 1868, had unconditionally pardoned every Confederate or Confederate sympathizer, including Armstrong.

100. *United States v. Klein*, 80 U.S. 128, 148 (1871): "[Under this provision,] the court is required to receive special pardons as evidence of guilt and to treat them as null and void. It is required to disregard pardons granted by proclamation on condition, though the condition has been fulfilled, and to deny them their legal effect. This certainly impairs the executive authority and directs the court to be instrumental to that end."

101. Ibid., 147.

102. *Carlisle v. United States*, 83 U.S. 147, 148–149, 150–151 (1872).

103. *Pargoud v. United States*, 80 U.S. 156 (1871).

104. *Carlisle v. United States*, 83 U.S. 147, 153 (1872): "It must be regarded as settled in this court that the pardon of the President, whether granted by special letters or by general proclamation, relieves claimants of the proceeds of captured and abandoned property from the consequences of participation in the rebellion and from the necessity of establishing their loyalty in order to prosecute their claims."

105. Ibid., 155–156.

106. *Osborn v. United States*, 92 U.S. 474, 478 (1876).

107. *Osborn v. United States*, 92 U.S. 474 (1876); Dorris, *Pardon and Amnesty*, 416. Osborn was a U.S. marshal who was partially in charge of holding Brown's proceeds. He stood to lose money if the Supreme Court agreed that Brown's proceeds should be returned, and thus he opposed the circuit court's decision to return Brown's proceeds by appearing as a party to the Supreme Court case. Brown represented the U.S. government in front of the Supreme Court. See "United States Supreme Court," *New York Times*, December 16, 1875.

108. *Osborn v. United States*, 92 U.S. 474, 475 (1876); Dorris, *Pardon and Amnesty*, 416–417.

109. *Osborn v. United States*, 92 U.S. 474, 476 (1876).

110. *Knote v. United States*, 95 U.S. 149, 156 (1877).

111. *Osborn v. United States*, 92 U.S. 474, 476 (1876): "The effect of pardon was to restore to its recipient all right of property lost by the offence pardoned, unless the property had, by judicial process, become vested in other persons, subject to such exceptions as were prescribed by the pardon itself; that until an order of distribution of the proceeds was made in these cases, or the proceeds were actually paid into the hands of the party entitled as informer to receive them, or into the treasury of the United States, they were within the control of the court, and that no vested right to the proceeds had accrued so as to prevent the pardon from restoring them to the petitioner."

112. Ibid., 477 (1876): "It is of the very essence of a pardon that it releases the offender from the consequences of his offense. . . . Unless rights of others in the property condemned have accrued, the penalty of forfeiture annexed to the commission of the offence must fall with the pardon of the offence itself, provided the full operation of the pardon be not restrained by the conditions upon which it is granted. The condition annexed to the pardon of the petitioner does not defeat such operation in the present case."

113. *Knote v. United States*, 95 U.S. 149, 149–152 (1877); Andrew Johnson, Proclamation of Amnesty, December 25, 1868, in Richardson, *Papers of the Presidents*, 8: 3906.

114. *Knote v. United States*, 95 U.S. 149, 152 (1877): "The question presented for determination in this case is, whether the general pardon and amnesty granted by President Johnson, by proclamation, on the 25th of December, 1868, will entitle one receiving their benefits to the proceeds of his property, previously condemned and sold under the confiscation act of 1862, after such proceeds have been paid into the treasury."

115. Ibid., 153.

116. Ibid., 154: "If, for example, by the judgment a sale of the offender's property has been had, the purchaser will hold the property notwithstanding the subsequent pardon. And if the proceeds of the sale have been paid to a party to whom the law has assigned them, they cannot be subsequently reached and recovered by the offender. The rights of the parties have become vested, and are as complete as if they were acquired in any other legal way."

117. Ibid.

118. Ibid.: "Where, however, property condemned, or its proceeds, have not thus vested, but remain under control of the Executive, or of officers subject to his orders, or are in the custody of the

judicial tribunals, the property will be restored or its proceeds delivered to the original owner, upon his full pardon."

119. Ibid.

120. Ibid., 154: "Moneys once in the treasury can only be withdrawn by an appropriation by law. However large, therefore, may be the power of pardon possessed by the President, and however extended may be its application, there is this limit to it, as there is to all his powers,—it cannot touch moneys in the treasury of the United States, except expressly authorized by act of Congress. The Constitution places this restriction upon the pardoning power."

121. Peterson, "Congressional Power," 1249–1250.

122. *Hart v. United States*, 118 U.S. 62, 64, 65 (1886).

123. 14 Stat. 571 (1867). April 13, 1861, is the date that Fort Sumter fell.

124. 14 Stat. 571 (1867); *Hart v. United States*, 118 U.S. 62, 65–66 (1886).

125. Ibid., 67: "[Even] [i]f the joint resolution had said nothing on the subject of a pardon, no pardon could have had the effect to authorize the payment out of a general appropriation of a debt which a law of congress had said should not be paid out of it. The pardon cannot have such effect ascribed to it merely because the joint resolution says that it shall not have such effect. It was entirely within the competency of congress to declare that the claims mentioned in the joint resolution should not be paid till the further order of Congress."

126. Ibid.

127. *The Laura*, 114 U.S. 411, 411–412, 413 (1885).

128. Ibid., 414: "But is that power exclusive, in the sense that no other

officer can remit forfeitures or penalties incurred for the violation of the laws of the United States? This question cannot be answered in the affirmative without adjudging that the practice in reference to remissions by the secretary of the treasury and other officers, which has been observed and acquiesced in for nearly a century, is forbidden by the constitution."

129. Ibid., 415–416; Hoffstadt, "Normalizing the Federal Clemency Power," 612.

130. Peterson, "Congressional Power," 1271.

131. *Brown v. Walker*, 161 U.S. 591, 591–592, 593 (1896). Buchanan, "Nature of a Pardon," 42.

132. Buchanan, "Nature of a Pardon," 42–43.

133. *Brown v. Walker*, 161 U.S. 591, 601 (1896) (emphasis added).

134. Buchanan, "Nature of a Pardon," 43.

135. *Brown v. Walker*, 161 U.S. 591, 599, 638 (1896).

136. Kobil, "Quality of Mercy," 615.

137. See, generally, Peterson, "Congressional Power," especially pp. 1269, 1278–1280.

138. Max Farrand, *Records of the Federal Convention of 1787*, vol. 2, 627, available online via the Library of Congress's American Memory Collection, http://memory.loc.gov/ammem/amlaw/lwfr.html (accessed 8/29/07).

139. *Public Citizen v. U.S. Dept. of Justice*, 491 U.S. 440, 485–486 (1989): "Where the Constitution by explicit text commits the power at issue to the exclusive control of the President, we have refused to tolerate *any* intrusion by the Legislative Branch. For example, the Constitution confers upon the President

the 'Power to grant Reprieves and Pardons for Offenses against the United States, except in Cases of Impeachment.' . . . Where a power has been committed to a particular Branch of the Government in the text of the Constitution, the balance already has been struck by the Constitution itself. It is improper for this Court to arrogate to itself the power to adjust a balance settled by the explicit terms of the Constitution."

140. *Ohio Adult Parole Authority v. Woodard*, 523 U.S. 272, 276 (1998).

141. Krent, "Conditional Pardon Power," 1710. O'Connor's concurrence read in relevant part: "I believe that the Court of Appeals correctly concluded that some minimal procedural safeguards apply to clemency proceedings. Judicial intervention might, for example, be warranted in the face of a scheme whereby a state official flipped a coin to determine whether to grant clemency, or in a case where the State arbitrarily denied a prisoner any access to its clemency process." See *Ohio Adult Parole Authority v. Woodard*, 523 U.S. 272, 289 (1998).

142. Strasser, "Some Reflections," 157–158. Strasser wrote: "While the President making a coin toss on national television to determine whether an individual would receive a pardon or the President expressly refusing to issue a pardon to anyone of a particular race or sex would violate existing guarantees, these are simply not the kinds of cases that might reasonably be expected to occur."

Chapter 3. Clemency before Watergate

1. Margaret Colgate Love, "The Quality of the President's Mercy," *New York Times*, December 19, 2002.

2. "List of Amnesty or Pardons' Proclamations in American History," undated, Folder: "Clemency—List of Amnesty or Pardon Proclamations in History," Philip Buchen Files, 1974–1977, Box 4, Gerald R. Ford Library.

3. See *United States v. Vigol*, 28 F. Cas. 376 (1795); *United States v. Mitchell*, 26 F. Cas. 1277 (1795).

4. George Washington, Pardon warrant for John Mitchell and Philip Vigol, 1795. Document 00114B2B.TIF. Compact disc set of Microfilm Set T967. Office of the Pardon Attorney. Department of Justice.

5. James D. Richardson, *Messages and Papers of the Presidents*, vol. 1 (Washington, DC: Government Printing Office, 1896), 184 (accessed 6/25/08 via HeinOnline).

6. P. S. Ruckman Jr., "Executive Clemency in the United States: Origins, Development, and Analysis (1900–1993)," *Presidential Studies Quarterly* 27 (1997): 251, at 254.

7. P. S. Ruckman Jr., "Policy as an Indicator of 'Original Understanding': Executive Clemency in the Early Republic (1789–1817)," unpublished paper, available at http://www.rvc.cc.il.us/faclink/pruckman/pardoncharts/Paper7.pdf (accessed 11/15/05); P. S. Ruckman Jr., "Seasonal Clemency Revisited: An Empirical Analysis," unpublished paper, on file with author.

8. "Wilson Refuses to Pardon Debs," *New York Times*, February 1, 1921.

9. "Denies President Cabled about Sentence of Debs," *New York Times*, April 3, 1919.

10. "Wilson Refuses to Pardon Debs," *New York Times*, February 1, 1921.

11. "Debs, Minus Guard, Visits Washington to Plead His Case," *New York Times*, March 25, 1921.

12. "President Is Expected to Pardon Debs When Freeing Other War Offenders Friday," *New York Times*, December 21, 1921.

13. "Daugherty's Report on Release of Debs," *New York Times*, December 31, 1921.

14. "Harding Frees Debs and 23 Others Held for War Violations," *New York Times*, December 24, 1921.

15. "Will Be Deported Soon," *New York Times*, November 24, 1927.

16. "Marcus Garvey, 60, Negro Ex-Leader," *New York Times*, June 12, 1940.

17. "Garvey Convicted in Black Line Fraud," *New York Times*, June 19, 1923; "Garvey Sentenced to 5 Years in Jail," *New York Times*, June 22, 1923.

18. "Garvey Sentenced to 5 Years in Jail," *New York Times*, June 22, 1923.

19. "2,000 Negroes Ask Bail for Garvey," *New York Times*, July 2, 1923.

20. "Plead for Marcus Garvey," *New York Times*, July 17, 1923.

21. "Garvey to Be Freed for Deportation," *New York Times*, November 24, 1927; "Will Be Deported Soon," *New York Times*, November 24, 1927.

22. "Assassin Spared by Truman in Gesture to Puerto Rico," *New York Times*, July 25, 1952; "President Resting," *New York Times*, November 2, 1950.

23. "President Resting," *New York Times*, November 2, 1950.

24. "Oscar Collazo, 80, Truman Attacker in '50," *New York Times*, February 23, 1994.

25. "Blair House Assassin Guilty, Death Sentence Is Mandatory," *New York Times*, March 8, 1951.

26. "Truman Assassin Sentenced to Die," *New York Times*, April 7, 1951; "Assassin Spared by Truman in Gesture to Puerto Rico," *New York Times*, July 25, 1952.

27. "Assassin Spared by Truman in Gesture to Puerto Rico," *New York Times*, July 25, 1952; Harry S Truman Library & Museum, http://www.trumanlibrary.org/truman-3.htm (accessed 9/9/07).

28. Fred Graham, "Nixon Commutes Hoffa Sentence, Curbs Union Role," *New York Times*, December 24, 1971.

29. Ibid.

30. George Edwards and Alec Gallup, *Presidential Approval: A Sourcebook* (Baltimore: Johns Hopkins University Press, 1990), 61.

31. Joseph Treaster, "Hoffa Ruled 'Presumed' Dead," *New York Times*, December 10, 1982.

32. Leslie Maitland, "62 Getting Reagan's Gift of Forgiveness," *New York Times*, December 25, 1982.

33. Kevin Krajick, "The Quality of Mercy," *Corrections*, June 1979, 51.

34. Leslie Maitland, "62 Getting Reagan's Gift of Forgiveness," *New York Times*, December 25, 1982.

35. Jerry Carannante, "What to Do about the Executive Clemency Power in the Wake of the Clinton Presidency?" *New York Law School Law Review* 47 (2003): 352.

36. See Jeffrey Tulis, *The Rhetorical Presidency* (Princeton, NJ: Princeton University Press, 1987); Samuel Kernell, *Going Public*, 4th ed. (Washington, DC: CQ Press, 2007).

37. Sheryl Gay Stolberg, "Containing Themselves; Whoop, Oops and the State of the Political Slip," *New York Times*, January 25, 2004; Michael Shear and Tim Craig, "Allen on Damage Control after Remarks to Webb Aide," *Washington Post*, August 16, 2006; Larry Sabato, *Feeding Frenzy* (Baltimore: Lanahan, 2000).

38. Harold J. Krent, "Conditioning the President's Conditional Pardon Power," *California Law Review* 89 (2001): 1703.

39. Carannante, "What to Do about the Executive Clemency Power," 349.

40. See Richard E. Neustadt, *Presidential Power* (New York: Free Press, 1990).

41. Margaret Love, "The Pardon Paradox: Lessons of Clinton's Last Pardons," *Capital University Law Review* 31 (2003): 192.

42. Krajick, "Quality of Mercy," 48.

43. Love, "Pardon Paradox," 193.

44. Jonathan Rauch, "Pardon Libby? Maybe, but Not Alone," *Reason*, April 2, 2007, http://www.reason.com/news/show/119424.html (accessed 7/27/07).

45. Daniel Kobil, "The Quality of Mercy Strained: Wrestling the Pardoning Power from the King," *Texas Law Review* 69 (1991): 603.

46. Margaret Love, "Of Pardons, Politics and Collar Buttons: Reflections on the President's Duty to Be Merciful," *Fordham Urban Law Journal* 27 (2000): 1495–1497.

47. Lawrence Walsh, *Firewall* (New York: W. W. Norton, 1997), 469.

48. Willard Humbert, *The Pardoning Power of the President* (Washington, DC: American Council on Public Affairs, 1941), 118, 120. Humbert's work is a classic in the clemency field with few, indeed any, peers.

49. Brian Hoffstadt, "Normalizing the Federal Clemency Power," *Texas Law Review* 79 (2001): 572.

50. Ibid., 573–574.

51. Krent, "Conditional Pardon Power," *California Law Review* 89 (2001): 1677–1678.

52. Richard Willing, "More Seeking President's Pardon," *USA Today*, December 24, 2002.

53. U.S. Department of Justice, Federal Bureau of Prisons, Weekly Population Report, July 3, 2008. Available at http://www.bop.gov/locations/weekly_report.jsp (accessed July 3, 2008).

54. U.S. Department of Justice, Office of the Pardon Attorney, "Presidential Clemency Petitions by Administration: 1945 to Present," updated October 8, 2008, on file with author.

55. David Johnston, "Pardons: Having to Say You're Sorry," *New York Times*, September 12, 1999.

Chapter 4. Watergate, Ford, and the Nixon Pardon

1. Gerald R. Ford, the President's Daily Diary, September 8, 1974, 9/8/74–9/10/74, Folder: 9/8–15/74, Staff Secretary's Copy, Box 61, Gerald R. Ford Library; Gerald Ford, 1974, Pardon warrant for Richard Nixon, Documents 00175965.TIF, 0017596B.TIF, Compact disc set of Microfilm Set T967, Office of the Pardon Attorney, Department of Justice.

2. Statement by former president Richard Nixon, September 8, 1974, Folder: Nixon Pardon—Nixon Statement 9/8/74, Box 34, Philip Buchen Files, Gerald R. Ford Library: "Looking back on what is still in my mind a complex and confusing maze of events, decisions, pressures and personalities, one thing I can see clearly now is that I was wrong in not acting more decisively and more forthrightly in dealing with Watergate. . . . I know that many fair-minded people believe that my motivations and actions in the Watergate affair were intentionally self-serving and illegal. I now understand how my own mistakes and misjudgments have contributed to that belief and seemed to support it."

3. Letter from Richard Nixon to

Arthur Sampson, administrator of the General Services Administration, September 8, 1974, Nixon Pardon—Press Releases, 9/8/74, Box 34, Philip Buchen Files, Gerald R. Ford Library. In addition to the clemency issue, the questions of ownership and possession of Richard Nixon's presidential materials were crucial challenges confronted by Gerald Ford. Following Nixon's resignation, Nixon requested that his presidential materials—some 46 million pieces of paper, plus tape reels—be shipped to the Nixon home in San Clemente, California. Tradition to that point held that presidents owned their presidential materials; however, Nixon was involved in an ongoing criminal investigation. Ford did not want to keep Nixon's materials around, but he was understandably uncomfortable about simply shipping them to Nixon under these circumstances. Nixon signed on to the "Nixon-Sampson Agreement," which gave Nixon nearly complete control over his presidential materials. This agreement was later superseded by the Presidential Recordings and Materials Preservation Act of 1974, which turned Nixon's records and the responsibility for their use over to the National Archives. Further discussion of ownership of Nixon's presidential materials is beyond the scope of this chapter, although some suspect that the price of Nixon's agreement to the records agreement may have been a pardon. These suspicions have never been proven.

4. Gerald R. Ford, "The President's News Conference of September 16, 1974," *Public Papers of the Presidents, 80:* September 16, 1974, 146, 151–152.

5. Memorandum from Leon Jaworski to Philip Buchen, September 4, 1974, Folder: Nixon Pardon—General (2), Box 32, Philip Buchen Files, Gerald R. Ford Library.

6. Gerald R. Ford, "The President's News Conference of September 16, 1974," *Public Papers of the Presidents, 80:* September 16, 1974, 147, 148; Memorandum from John Marsh to Robert Goldwin, September 12, 1974, Folder: Richard Nixon—Pardon: General 9/74–6/76, Box 25, John Marsh Files, Gerald R. Ford Library.

7. Hugh Macgill, "The Nixon Pardon: Limits on the Benign Prerogative," *Connecticut Law Review 7* (1974): 62.

8. See Mark Rozell, "President Ford's Pardon of Richard M. Nixon: Constitutional and Political Considerations," *Presidential Studies Quarterly 24* (1994): 121; *Ex parte Garland,* 71 U.S. 333 (1866); *Ex parte Grossman,* 267 U.S. 87 (1925); *Brown v. Walker,* 161 U.S. 591 (1896).

9. Leon Jaworski, *The Right and the Power* (New York: Reader's Digest Press, 1976), 247–248.

10. Mark Rozell, "In Defense of President Ford's Pardon of Richard M. Nixon" in *Gerald Ford and the Politics of Post-Watergate America,* Bernard Firestone and Alexej Ugrinsky, eds. (Westport, CT: Greenwood Press, 1993), 45.

11. Macgill, "The Nixon Pardon," 84.

12. Orr Kelly, "Ford Bypassed Routine in Giving Nixon Pardon," *Washington Star-News,* September 11, 1974, Folder: Nixon Pardon—Correspondence (2), Box 32, Philip Buchen Files 1974–1977, Gerald R. Ford Library. Ford's successors George H. W. Bush, Bill Clinton, and George W. Bush also did not rely upon the Pardon Attorney's Office for their most controversial clemency decisions.

13. Rozell, "In Defense of President Ford's Pardon of Richard M. Nixon," 46; see also Rozell, "President Ford's Pardon of Richard M. Nixon," 129.

14. P. S. Ruckman Jr., "It Appears There Might Be a Possibility of Developing Plan!," blog entry for July 24, 2008, Pardonpower.com (accessed 7/25/08).

15. Timothy Ingram, "Could Nixon Pardon Nixon?" *Washington Post*, June 30, 1974.

16. Robert Nida and Rebecca L. Spiro, "The President as His Own Judge and Jury: A Legal Analysis of the Presidential Self-Pardon Power," *Oklahoma Law Journal* 52 (1999): 205, 216–217, 218, 220. See also *Ex parte Garland*, 71 U.S. 333 (1866); *Ex parte Grossman*, 267 U.S. 87 (1925); and *Schick v. Reed*, 419 U.S. 256 (1974).

17. Timothy Ingram, "Could Nixon Pardon Nixon?" *Washington Post*, June 30, 1974.

18. Leonard Boudin, "The Presidential Pardons of James R. Hoffa and Richard M. Nixon: Have the Limitations on the Pardon Power Been Exceeded?" *University of Colorado Law Review* 48 (1976): 36.

19. Alexander Hamilton, James Madison, and John Jay, *The Federalist Papers*, Clinton Rossiter, ed. (New York: Mentor, 1999), 47.

20. Brian Kalt, "Pardon Me? The Constitutional Case against Presidential Self-Pardons," *Yale Law Journal* 106 (1996): 780–781, 797, 808–809; *Schick v. Reed*, 419 U.S. 256 (1974).

21. Timothy Ingram, "Could Nixon Pardon Nixon?" *Washington Post*, June 30, 1974.

22. William Greider, "Presidential Words and Deeds," *Washington Post*, September 13, 1974, Folder: Nixon Pardon and Papers—Press Conference 1974/09/16 (Ford) (03), Box 35, Philip Buchen Files 1974–1977, Gerald R. Ford Library.

23. Gerald R. Ford, *A Time to Heal* (New York: Harper & Row, 1979), 158, 179.

24. Carroll Kilpatrick, "Pardons Position Softened," *Washington Post*, September 12, 1974.

25. Rowland Evans and Robert Novak, "Did Somebody Get to Ford?" *Houston Post*, September 13, 1974, Folder: Nixon Pardon—Correspondence (2), Box 32, Philip Buchen Files 1974–1977, Gerald R. Ford Library. Richard Nixon lived until the age of eighty-one. He died on April 22, 1994, shortly after suffering a stroke.

26. "Nixon Pal Credits Haig for Pardon," *Detroit Free Press*, September 17, 1974, Folder: Pardon, Richard Milhous Nixon, 1913–, Nixon Vertical File, Gerald R. Ford Library.

27. Everett Holles, "Haig Denies That He Urged Ford to Pardon Nixon," *New York Times*, September 18, 1974.

28. Robert Hartmann, *Palace Politics* (New York: McGraw-Hill, 1980), 266.

29. Daniel Ostrander, "The Pardoning of Richard Nixon," 1989, 4. Uncataloged papers, Box 11 Nu-Pi, Gerald R. Ford Library.

30. George Lardner Jr. and Lou Cannon, "'Anxiety' Report Prompted Ford," *Washington Post*, September 10, 1974.

31. Lou Cannon, "An Act of Mercy," *Washington Post*, September 11, 1974.

32. Jaworski, *The Right and the Power*, 237–238; Karen Elliott, "The Pardon of Nixon Was Timely, Legal, Jaworski Believes," *Wall Street Journal*, October 16, 1974, Folder: Nixon Pardon—Hungate Subcommittee: General, Box 34, Philip Buchen Files, Gerald R. Ford Library.

33. Ford, *A Time to Heal*, 161.

34. Carroll Kilpatrick, "Nixon Pardon Stirs Outcry against Ford," *Washington Post*, September 10, 1974.

35. News Summary, September 9, 1974, Folder: 9/9/74, President's Daily News Summaries 9/2/74, Box 2, Staff Secretary's Office, Gerald R. Ford Library.

36. Letter to Mr. and Mrs. Philip Baldwin from Philip Buchen, February 28, 1975, Folder: Nixon Pardon—Correspondence (5), Box 32, Philip Buchen Files, Gerald R. Ford Library.

37. Mark Rozell, *The Press and the Ford Presidency* (Ann Arbor: University of Michigan Press, 1992), 52; United Press International, "terHorst Felt Aides Used Him," *Washington Post*, September 10, 1974; Ford, *A Time to Heal*, 175–176.

38. Weekend News Review, September 9, 1974, Folder: 9/9/74, President's Daily News Summaries, 9/2/74, Box 2, Staff Secretary's Office, Gerald R. Ford Library.

39. Bob Woodward, discussant, in *Gerald R. Ford and the Politics of Post-Watergate America*, Bernard Firestone and Alexej Ugrinsky, eds. (Westport, CT: Greenwood Press, 1993), 74.

40. Weekend News Review, September 9, 1974, Folder: 9/9/74, President's Daily News Summaries 9/2/74, Box 2, Staff Secretary's Office, Gerald R. Ford Library.

41. News Summary, September 9, 1974, Folder: 9/9/74, President's Daily News Summaries 9/2/74, Box 2, Staff Secretary's Office, Gerald R. Ford Library.

42. Weekend News Review, September 9, 1974, Folder: 9/9/74, President's Daily News Summaries 9/2/74, Box 2, Staff Secretary's Office, Gerald R. Ford Library.

43. Richard Cheney, "The 1976 Presidential Debates: A Republican Perspective," October 1977, 13. Folder: Post Election Analysis—Speeches and Reports (6), 1976 Presidential Campaign: PFC Priority States, Box 62, Robert Teeter Papers, Gerald R. Ford Library.

44. News Summary, September 9, 1974, Folder: 9/9/74, President's Daily News Summaries 9/2/74, Box 2, Staff Secretary's Office, Gerald R. Ford Library.

45. Letters to the Editor, *Washington Post*, September 12, 1974.

46. "Nixon's Crisis—and Ford's," *Newsweek*, September 23, 1974, 32.

47. "Grand Rapids Paper Blasts Ford Decision," *Ann Arbor News*, September 10, 1974, Folder: Pardon, Richard Milhous Nixon 1913–, Nixon Vertical File, Gerald R. Ford Library.

48. Richard Lyons and Bob Kuttner, "Mood in Congress: Great Sigh of Relief," *Washington Post*, August 10, 1974.

49. Clark Mollenhoff, *The Man Who Pardoned Nixon* (New York: St. Martin's Press, 1976), 87.

50. Richard Lyons and Bob Kuttner, "Mood in Congress: Great Sigh of Relief," *Washington Post*, August 10, 1974.

51. William Hungate, discussant, in *Gerald R. Ford and the Politics of Post-Watergate America*, Bernard Firestone and Alexej Ugrinsky, eds. (Westport, CT: Greenwood Press, 1993), 65.

52. Walter Mondale, "Harnessing the President's Pardon Power," *American Bar Association Journal* 61 (1975): 108.

53. Mark Rozell, "In Defense of President Ford's Pardon of Richard M. Nixon," in *Gerald R. Ford and the Politics of Post-Watergate America*, Bernard Firestone and Alexej Ugrinsky, eds. (Westport, CT: Greenwood Press, 1993), 48.

54. Cannon, *Time and Chance*, 385.

55. Weekend News Review, September 9, 1974, Folder: 9/9/74, President's Daily News Summaries 9/2/74, Box 2, Staff Secretary's Office, Gerald R. Ford Library.

56. "Support for Ford Declines Sharply," *New York Times*, September 12, 1974.

57. Louis Harris, "Majority Disagree with Pardon of Nixon," *Detroit Free Press*, October 7, 1974, Folder: Pardon, Richard Milhous Nixon 1913–, Nixon Vertical File, Gerald R. Ford Library.

58. Louis Harris, "49 Per Cent Rate Ford Negatively," *Washington Post*, October 14, 1974.

59. Louis Harris, "66% Give Ford Benefit of Doubt on Pardon," *Washington Post*, October 21, 1974.

60. George Gallup, "Approval of Ford Rises to 55%," *Washington Post*, October 31, 1974.

61. President Ford had met with Philip Buchen, Robert Hartmann, John Marsh, and Alexander Haig in the Oval Office on August 30 to discuss his inclination to pardon Nixon. See Barry Werth, *31 Days* (New York: Nan A. Talese, 2006), 243–246. Henry Kissinger was also in the loop. See Ford, *A Time to Heal*, 161; Rozell, *The Press and the Ford Presidency*, 53.

62. Nomination of Gerald R. Ford of Michigan to Be Vice President of the United States, Hearings before the Committee on Rules and Administration, U.S. Senate, 93rd Cong., 1st sess. (Washington, DC: U.S. Government Printing Office, 1973), November 5, 1973, 124.

63. Richard Reeves, *A Ford, Not a Lincoln* (New York: Harcourt Brace Jovanovich, 1975), 65.

64. Gerald Ford, "The President's News Conference of August 28, 1974," *Public Papers of the Presidents*, 39: August 28, 1974, 57 (emphasis added).

65. Ibid., 58.

66. Clifton Daniel, "Presidential Clemency," *New York Times*, August 29, 1974, Folder: Nixon Pardon—General (2), Box 32, Philip Buchen Files, Gerald R. Ford Library.

67. Carroll Kilpatrick, "Decision Deferred," *Washington Post*, August 29, 1974 (emphasis added).

68. Werth, *31 Days*, 221.

69. Peter Milius, "Ford Grants Nixon a Pardon," *Washington Post*, September 9, 1974.

70. Rozell, *The Press and the Ford Presidency*, 62, 58, 84, 167.

71. Stephen Stathis, "On Pardons and Testimony," *New York Times*, October 9, 1974. Because the National Archives was unable to confirm Lincoln's appearance, Ford was "officially" the first president to submit to questions from a congressional committee.

72. "Ford Pardon Testimony Set in Historic Room," October 16, 1974, Folder: Nixon Pardon—Hungate Subcommittee: General, Box 34, Philip Buchen Files, Gerald R. Ford Library.

73. Special News Summary, October 17, 1974, Folder: Nixon Pardon—Hungate Subcommittee: Ford Testimony (3), Box 34, Philip Buchen Files, Gerald R. Ford Library.

74. Haynes Johnson, "Ford's Historic Visit: Questions Remain," *Washington Post*, October 18, 1974.

75. Special News Summary, October 17, 1974, Folder: Nixon Pardon—Hungate Subcommittee: Ford Testimony (3), Box 34, Philip Buchen Files, Gerald R. Ford Library.

76. Gerald R. Ford, "Statement and

Responses to Questions from Members of the House Judiciary Committee concerning the Pardon of Richard Nixon," Public Papers of the Presidents, 155: October 17, 1974, 346.

77. Ibid., 368.

78. John Herbers, "The Man from Grand Rapids Is Still the Man from Gr . . . ," New York Times, October 20, 1974.

79. Question Number 063, Accession Number 0130893, Yankelovich, Skelly, and White telephone poll of 1,023 adults conducted in September 1974, Public Opinion Online, Roper Center, University of Connecticut.

80. Office of the Clerk, U.S. House of Representatives, Statistics of the Congressional Election of November 4, 1974, compiled by Benjamin Guthrie, 46, http://clerk.house.gov/member_info/elec tionInfo/1974election.pdf (accessed 8/9/07); U.S. Senate, Party Division in the Senate, 1789–present, http://www.senate .gov/pagelayout/history/one_item_and_ teasers/partydiv.htm (accessed 8/9/07).

81. "Democrats: Now the Morning After," Time, November 18, 1974, 8, 10–11.

82. Memorandum from Leonard Garment to Philip Buchen, August 28, 1974, Folder: Nixon Pardon—General (2), Box 32, Philip Buchen Files, Gerald R. Ford Library. Garment ominously refers to Nixon's dire situation twice in the two-page "Garment memo": He warns that without a pardon, "the whole miserable tragedy will be played out to God knows what ugly and wounding conclusion." Also, he suggests that "at this point most of the country does not want Richard Nixon hounded, perhaps literally, to death."

83. Bob Woodward and Carl Bernstein, "Ford Disputed on Events Preceding Nixon Pardon," Washington Post, December 18, 1975.

84. Gerald R. Ford, "Statement and Responses to Questions from Members of the House Judiciary Committee concerning the Pardon of Richard Nixon," Public Papers of the Presidents, 155: October 17, 1974, 346.

85. Ibid., 368.

86. Bob Woodward and Carl Bernstein, "Ford Disputed on Events Preceding Nixon Pardon," Washington Post, December 18, 1975.

87. Memorandum from Philip Buchen to William Greener, December 19, 1975, Folder: Nixon Pardon—General (3), Box 32, Philip Buchen Files, Gerald R. Ford Library.

88. "Ford Denies Story on Pardon," Washington Post, December 19, 1975, Folder: Nixon Pardon-Correspondence, Box 2, Benton Becker Papers, Gerald R. Ford Library.

89. "House Panel Drops Probe of Ford Pardon of Nixon," Detroit Free Press, February 20, 1976, Folder: Pardon, Richard Milhous Nixon, 1913–, Nixon Vertical Files, Gerald R. Ford Library; Richard Lyons, "Judiciary Panel Rejects Move to Reopen Nixon Pardon Inquiry," Washington Post, February 20, 1976.

90. According to Seymour Hersh, former Nixon aides Charles Colson and Alexander Butterfield suggested that Ford "knew how to play the game" and "was the tool of the Nixon Administration," respectively. See Seymour Hersh, "The Pardon," The Atlantic Monthly, August 1983, 56. Folder: Pardon, Richard Milhous Nixon, 1913–, Nixon Vertical File, Gerald R. Ford Library; "How Haig Paved the Way for Nixon's Pardon," New York Post, April 3,

1979, Folder: Nixon Pardon—Legal Precedent, Box 2, Benton Becker Papers, Gerald R. Ford Library.

91. Melvin Small, *The Presidency of Richard Nixon* (Lawrence: University Press of Kansas, 1999), 297.

92. Cannon, *Time and Chance*, 293.

93. Daniel Schorr, "Will Bush Pardon Himself?" *New York Times*, December 29, 1992 (identifying St. Clair as the author of the papers); but see Daniel Schorr, "New Gerald Ford Biography Reveals Nixon Pardon Process," *All Things Considered*, National Public Radio, May 8, 1994 (identifying Buzhardt as the author).

94. Small, *Presidency of Richard Nixon*, 294–295; Cannon, *Time and Chance*, 289–300. The June 23, 1972, tape transcripts of conversations between Richard Nixon and H. R. Haldeman contemplate ordering the Central Intelligence Agency (CIA) to interfere with the Federal Bureau of Investigation (FBI) inquiry into Watergate. The release of these transcripts prompted all of Nixon's Republican backers on the House Judiciary Committee to switch their positions from "against" to "for" Nixon's impeachment. As Nixon remarked to Alexander Haig and Ronald Ziegler, "Well, I screwed up real good, didn't I?"; "How Haig Paved the Way for Nixon's Pardon," *New York Post*, April 3, 1979, Folder: Nixon Pardon—Legal Precedent, Box 2, Benton Becker Papers, Gerald R. Ford Library.

95. Scott Armstrong, Robert Kaiser, and Walter Pincus, "Raising the Option of a Nixon Pardon," *Washington Post*, December 21, 1980.

96. Cannon, *Time and Chance*, 294.

97. "How Haig Paved the Way for Nixon's Pardon," *New York Post*, April 3, 1979, Folder: Nixon Pardon—Legal Precedent, Box 2, Benton Becker Papers, Gerald R. Ford Library.

98. Ford, *A Time to Heal*, 9–10.

99. Werth, *31 Days*, 204–205.

100. Ibid., 205.

101. Cannon, *Time and Chance*, 307.

102. "Haig Confronts His Critics Head-On," *U.S. News and World Report*, January 19, 1981, 6.

103. Scott Armstrong, Robert Kaiser, and Walter Pincus, "Raising the Option of a Nixon Pardon," *Washington Post*, December 21, 1980.

104. Bob Woodward, *Shadow* (New York: Simon & Schuster, 1999), 35; Cannon, *Time and Chance*, 391.

105. Hersh, "The Pardon," 56.

106. Ibid.

107. Mollenhoff, *Man Who Pardoned Nixon*, 84.

108. Bob Woodward, discussant, *Gerald R. Ford and the Politics of Post-Watergate America*, Bernard Firestone and Alexej Ugrinsky, eds. (Westport, CT: Greenwood Press, 1993), 74.

109. Stephen Ambrose, "The Nixon-Ford Relationship," in *Gerald R. Ford and the Politics of Post-Watergate America*, Bernard Firestone and Alexej Ugrinsky, eds. (Westport, CT: Greenwood Press, 1993), 20–22.

110. Lou Cannon, "A Political Comeback That Just Missed," *Washington Post*, November 4, 1976.

111. Louis Harris, "Pardon of Nixon an Issue in Presidential Campaign," *Detroit Free Press*, August 30, 1976, Folder: Pardon, Richard Milhous Nixon, 1913–, Nixon Vertical File, Gerald R. Ford Library.

112. Melvin Small, *The Presidency of Richard Nixon* (Lawrence: University Press

of Kansas, 1999), 301; "1976 Presidential Election Summary Report," 22, National Surveys—Post-Election-MOR Summary Report Analyses November 1976, Box 62, Robert Teeter Papers, 1976 Presidential Campaign: PFC Priority States, Gerald R. Ford Library.

113. "1976 Presidential Election Summary Report," 28; "1976 Congressional Quarterly's Guide to 1976 Elections," *Congressional Quarterly*, July 1977, "Introduction," Box 70, Robert Teeter Papers, Election Results and Analyses: 1976, Gerald R. Ford Library.

Chapter 5. Special Counsel Investigations, Pre- and Post-Watergate

1. Terry Eastland, *Ethics, Politics and the Independent Counsel* (Washington, DC: National Legal Center for the Public Interest, 1989), 24–25.

2. Much of this chapter is derived from my article "Presidential Misuse of the Pardon Power," *Presidential Studies Quarterly* 38 (2008): 722–734.

3. Charles Johnson and Danette Brickman, *Independent Counsel* (Washington, DC: CQ Press, 2001), 8–10.

4. Ibid.

5. Eastland, *Ethics*, 8.

6. Ibid.

7. Johnson and Brickman, *Independent Counsel*, 8–10.

8. Gerald S. Greenberg, ed., *Historical Encyclopedia of U.S. Independent Counsel Investigations* (Westport, CT: Greenwood Press, 2000), 147.

9. C. Vann Woodward, ed. *Responses of the Presidents to Charges of Misconduct* (New York: Dell, 1974), 136.

10. Greenberg, *Historical Encyclopedia*, 146–147.

11. Timothy Rives, "Grant, Babcock, and the Whiskey Ring," *Prologue*, vol. 32, 2000: 143–153 (accessed online via the National Archives Web site, www.archives.gov, on 6/27/08).

12. Ibid., 146.

13. Greenberg, *Historical Encyclopedia*, 163.

14. Rives, "Grant, Babcock, and the Whiskey Ring," 147–148, 152.

15. Ibid.; Ulysses S. Grant, Pardon warrant for William O. Avery and William McKee, 1876, Document 0011F878.TIF, Compact disc set of Microfilm Set T967, Office of the Pardon Attorney, Department of Justice; Ulysses S. Grant, Pardon warrant for John McDonald, 1877, Document 0011F896.TIF, Compact disc set of Microfilm Set T967, Office of the Pardon Attorney, Department of Justice.

16. Rutherford B. Hayes, Pardon warrant for John A. Joyce, 1877, Document 001114A1.TIF, Compact disc set of Microfilm Set T967, Office of the Pardon Attorney, Department of Justice.

17. See Thomas Jefferson, *The Writings of Thomas Jefferson*, vol. 10, Paul Leicester Ford, ed. (New York: G. P. Putnam's Sons, 1905), 394–405; Nancy Isenberg, *Fallen Founder* (New York: Viking Penguin, 2007), 346–347; and Peter Charles Hoffer, *The Treason Trials of Aaron Burr* (Lawrence: University Press of Kansas, 2008), 142–144.

18. Greenberg, *Historical Encyclopedia*, 164, 290.

19. Jerry A. O'Callaghan, "Senator Mitchell and the Oregon Land Frauds," *Pacific Historical Review* 21 (1952): 259.

20. Greenberg, *Historical Encyclopedia*, 86–87, 288, 275.

21. David H. Stratton, *Tempest over Teapot Dome* (Norman: University of Oklahoma Press, 1998), 342.

22. Greenberg, *Historical Encyclopedia*, 95–97, 99–100, 335.

23. Stratton, *Tempest*, 327.

24. "All the members of the New Mexico State Legislature signed a petition to President Hoover for a pardon for Fall. Governor Arthur Seligman, the Democratic head of New Mexico, and both United States Senators from that state, Bronson Cutting and Sam Bratton, who had been members of the second Teapot Dome Senate investigating committee, forwarded the petition to the President without recommendations except for earnest consideration. The petition was not granted." (See M. R. Werner and John Starr, *Teapot Dome* [New York: Viking Press, 1959], 290.)

25. Stratton, *Tempest*, 336. Interestingly, Fall's "right hand man and advisor" in Mexico was Henry O. Flipper, the first recipient of a posthumous pardon in American history, thanks to President Bill Clinton.

26. Greenberg, *Historical Encyclopedia*, 221–222, 232–233, 334–335.

27. Ibid., 335.

28. John F. Kennedy, Pardon warrant for Matthew Connelly, 1962, Documents 00174D41.TIF, 00174D42.TIF, Compact disc set of Microfilm Set T967, Office of the Pardon Attorney, Department of Justice.

29. Woodward, *Responses of the Presidents*, 286–287, 292.

30. Ibid., 292; Lyndon B. Johnson, Pardon warrant for T. Lamar Caudle, 1965, Documents 00172368.TIF, 00172369.TIF, Compact disc set of Microfilm Set T967, Office of the Pardon Attorney, Department of Justice.

31. Woodward, *Responses of the Presidents*, 285–286; Lyndon B. Johnson, Pardon warrant for James P. Finnegan,

1967, Documents 001723A1.TIF, 001723A2.TIF, Compact disc set of Microfilm Set T967, Office of the Pardon Attorney, Department of Justice.

32. Johnson and Brickman, *Independent Counsel*, 43.

33. Katy Harriger, *The Special Prosecutor in American Politics*, 2d ed. (Lawrence: University Press of Kansas, 2000), 43.

34. Eastland, *Ethics*, 20.

35. Johnson and Brickman, *Independent Counsel*, 43.

36. Eastland, *Ethics*, xii, 35, 46; Johnson and Brickman, *Independent Counsel*, 79.

37. Title VI of the Ethics in Government Act of 1978, Pub. L. No. 95-521, 92 Stat. 1824; Ken Gormley, "An Original Model of the Independent Counsel Statute," *Michigan Law Review* 97 (1998–1999): 604.

38. Niles Godes and Ty Howard, "Independent Counsel Investigations," *American Criminal Law Review* 35 (1997–1998): 878.

39. Harriger, *Special Prosecutor*, 70.

40. Katy Harriger, "Damned If She Does, Damned If She Doesn't," *Georgetown Law Journal* 86 (1997–1998): 2104–2105.

41. Greenberg, *Historical Encyclopedia*, 279, 280.

42. Lawrence Walsh, "Political Oversight, the Rule of Law, and Iran-Contra," *Cleveland State Law Review* 42 (1994): 591.

43. George H. W. Bush, Pardon warrant for Caspar Weinberger, Elliott Abrams, Duane Clarridge, Alan Fiers, Clair George, and Robert McFarlane, 1992, Documents 03010112.TIF, 03010113.TIF, 03010114.TIF, 03010115.TIF, 03010116.TIF, Compact disc set of Microfilm Set T967, Office of the Pardon Attorney, Department of Justice.

44. George Lardner Jr. and Walter Pincus, "Walsh Wants to Question President; Iran-Contra Prosecutor to Study Bush's Notes, Seek January Session," *Washington Post*, December 27, 1992.

45. Jonathan Alter, "Life Is Fleeting, Man," *Newsweek*, April 8, 2002; William J. Clinton, 2001, Pardon warrant for Henry Cisneros, Documents 0227013.TIF, 001CC68B.TIF, Compact disc set of Microfilm Set T967, Office of the Pardon Attorney, Department of Justice; William J. Clinton, 2001, Pardon warrant for John Deutch, Document 02280119.TIF, Compact disc set of Microfilm Set T967, Office of the Pardon Attorney, Department of Justice.

46. William J. Clinton, 2001, Pardon warrant for Marc Rich, Document 0227018.TIF, Compact disc set of Microfilm Set T967, Office of the Pardon Attorney, Department of Justice.

47. *Morrison v. Olson*, 487 U.S. 654, 670–672, 673, 675–676 (1988).

48. Ibid., 678–679, 682–683, 692, 693, 695.

49. Ibid., 701–702; 28 U.S.C. Section 592(b)(1).

50. Gormley, "An Original Model," 644.

51. *Morrison v. Olson*, 487 U.S. 654, 705, 706 (1988).

52. Ibid., 711, 713.

53. Ibid., 731.

54. Stephen Wolf, "In the Pursuit of Power without Accountability," *South Dakota Law Review* 35 (1990): 3, 21.

55. Louis Fisher, "The Independent Counsel Statute," in *The Clinton Scandal and the Future of American Government*, Mark J. Rozell and Clyde Wilcox, eds. (Washington, DC: Georgetown University Press, 2000), 76.

56. Harriger, *Special Prosecutor*, 40.

Chapter 6. Three Recent Presidents and Abuse of the Pardon Power

1. Joel Brinkley, "Birth of a Scandal and Mysteries of Its Parentage," *New York Times*, December 25, 1992.

2. Ibid.

3. Ibid.

4. Ibid.

5. Caspar Weinberger, *In the Arena* (Washington, DC: Regnery, 2001), 347; Lawrence Walsh, *Iran-Contra: The Final Report* (New York: Times Books, 1994), back cover, 414.

6. Walsh, *Iran-Contra*, 415; Weinberger, *In the Arena*, 366.

7. Irvin Molotsky, "Bush Aides Urging Weinberger Pardon in Iran-Arms Affair," *New York Times*, November 7, 1992.

8. Lawrence Walsh, *Firewall* (New York: W. W. Norton, 1997), 448.

9. Dan Morgan and David Broder, "President to Disclose 'Everything'; White House Disputes Walsh's Charges of Iran-Contra Coverup," *Washington Post*, December 26, 1992.

10. Bob Woodward, *Shadow* (New York: Simon & Schuster, 1999), 201.

11. Walsh, *Firewall*, 449.

12. Ibid., 459.

13. Walter Pincus, "Weinberger May Receive Bush Pardon; Walsh Says He Has Not Been Consulted," *Washington Post*, December 24, 1992.

14. Dan Morgan and David Broder, "President to Disclose 'Everything'; White House Disputes Walsh's Charges of Iran-Contra Coverup," *Washington Post*, December 26, 1992.

15. Woodward, *Shadow*, 203.

16. Walsh, *Firewall*, 464.

17. Irvin Molotsky, "Bush Aides Urging Weinberger Pardon in Iran-Arms Affair," *New York Times*, November 7, 1992.

18. Walsh, *Iran-Contra*, 415.

19. Walter Pincus, "Weinberger May Receive Bush Pardon; Walsh Says He Has Not Been Consulted," *Washington Post*, December 24, 1992.

20. Bob Cohn, "Anatomy of a Pardon: Why Weinberger Walked," *Newsweek*, January 11, 1993, 22.

21. Woodward, *Shadow*, 213.

22. Ibid., 213–214.

23. Caspar Weinberger passed away on March 28, 2006, of complications from pneumonia.

24. George H. W. Bush, "Proclamation 6518, Grant of Executive Clemency," *Federal Register* 57: 62145.

25. Walter Pincus, "Bush Pardons Weinberger in Iran-Contra Affair; 5 Others Also Cleared; Angry Walsh Indicates a Focus on President," *Washington Post*, December 25, 1992.

26. George H. W. Bush, "Proclamation 6518, Grant of Executive Clemency," *Federal Register* 57: 62145.

27. Bill McAllister, "The Pardon: An Absolute and Controversial Presidential Power," *Washington Post*, December 25, 1992.

28. Lawrence Walsh, "Independent Counsel's Statement on the Pardons," *New York Times*, December 25, 1992.

29. Ibid.

30. Ibid.

31. Ibid.

32. David Johnston, "Prosecutor Shifts Attention to Bush on Iran Arms Deal," *New York Times*, December 26, 1992.

33. Bob Cohn, "Walsh on the President: 'The Horror of It,'" *Newsweek*, January 4, 1993, 16.

34. Walter Pincus and George Lardner Jr., "Walsh Report Details Evidence against Weinberger," *Washington Post*, February 9, 1993.

35. Katy Harriger, *The Special Prosecutor in American Politics*, 2d ed. (Lawrence: University Press of Kansas, 2000), 221.

36. Question Number 002, Accession Number 0190059, National telephone poll of 608 adults conducted December 28, 1992, Public Opinion Online, Roper Center, University of Connecticut.

37. Question Number 053, Accession Number 0190946, National telephone poll of 1,510 adults conducted January 14–17, 1993, Public Opinion Online, Roper Center, University of Connecticut.

38. Question Number 032, Accession Number 0190374, National telephone poll of 1,179 adults conducted January 12–14, 1993, Public Opinion Online, Roper Center, University of Connecticut.

39. Fred Barnes, "Pardon Me," *New Republic*, December 21, 1992.

40. Question Number 003, Accession Number 0190060, National telephone poll of 608 adults conducted December 28, 1992, Public Opinion Online, Roper Center, University of Connecticut.

41. Question Number 054, Accession Number 0190947, National telephone poll of 1,510 adults conducted January 14–17, 1993, Public Opinion Online, Roper Center, University of Connecticut.

42. Katharine Seelye, "Clinton to Commute Radicals' Sentences," *New York Times*, August 12, 1999.

43. Ibid.

44. Amy Waldman, "New York's Puerto Ricans Show Little Solidarity on Clemency Issue," *New York Times*, September 9, 1999.

45. David Johnston, "Federal Agencies Opposed Leniency for 16 Militants," *New York Times*, August 27, 1999.

46. George Lardner Jr., "Lawmakers Weigh in on FALN Clemency," *Washington Post*, September 6, 1999.

47. James Dao, "House Panel Subpoenas Records on Clinton's Clemency Offer," *New York Times*, September 2, 1999; Dirk Johnson, "Puerto Ricans Clinton Freed Leave Prisons," *New York Times*, September 11, 1999.

48. James Dao, "House Panel Subpoenas Records on Clinton's Clemency Offer," *New York Times*, September 2, 1999.

49. Katharine Seelye, "Clinton Refuses Subpoena for Material on Clemency," *New York Times*, September 17, 1999.

50. Sumana Chatterjee, "Clinton Won't Fully Comply with Clemency Subpoena," *CQ Weekly*, September 18, 1999, 2176.

51. Tom Squitieri, "House Rebukes Clinton on Clemency for FALN Members; Senate Is Scheduled to Vote on Its Own Resolution Monday," *USA Today*, September 10, 1999.

52. Katharine Seelye, "Clinton Says Clemency Plan Was Unrelated to First Lady," *New York Times*, September 10, 1999.

53. Tom Squitieri, "Senate Rebukes Clinton on Clemency; Joins House in Criticizing Deal for FALN Members," *USA Today*, September 15, 1999.

54. Katharine Seelye, "Director of F.B.I. Opposed Clemency for Puerto Ricans," *New York Times*, September 22, 1999.

55. David Johnston, "Justice Dept. Opposed Clemency for Puerto Rican Militants in '96," *New York Times*, October 20, 1999.

56. David Visa and Lorraine Adams, "FALN a Threat, Reno Says; Hatch Faults Justice Dept. as Clemency Report Is Released," *Washington Post*, October 21, 1999.

57. Katharine Seelye, "Clinton Refuses Subpoena for Material on Clemency," *New York Times*, September 17, 1999.

58. Katharine Seelye, "Clinton Says Clemency Plan Was Unrelated to First Lady," *New York Times*, September 10, 1999.

59. Mary Dalrymple, "GOP Concludes Politics Affected Clemency Offer," *CQ Weekly*, November 13, 1999, 2713.

60. Neil Lewis, "Report by House Republicans Says Clemency for Puerto Ricans Was Campaign Move," *New York Times*, November 9, 1999.

61. Tom Squitieri and Kathy Kiely, "Clemency Issue Shadows Clintons," *USA Today*, September 16, 1999.

62. Debra Rosenberg, "Letter from Air Force One: Clinton's Farewell Trip," January 18, 2001, *Newsweek* Web Exclusive on MSNBC.com, Archives Article ID 005510E9DB0989158EC9F (accessed 7/24/07).

63. Weston Kosova, "Backstage at the Finale," *Newsweek*, February 26, 2001, 30.

64. Peter Slevin and George Lardner Jr., "Rush of Pardons Unusual in Scope, Lack of Scrutiny; Back-Door Lobbying Had Large Role in Clinton's Decisions, Observers Say," *Washington Post*, March 10, 2001.

65. Debra Rosenberg, Michael Isikoff, and Mark Hosenball, "Thinkin' about Tomorrow," *Newsweek*, January 29, 2001.

66. Amanda Bower et al., "We Beg Your Pardon," *Time*, January 29, 2001, 18.

67. Jonathan Peterson and Lisa Getter, "Clinton Pardons Raise Questions of Timing, Motive," *Los Angeles Times*, January 29, 2001.

68. Bower et al., "We Beg Your Pardon," 18.

69. Amy Goldstein and Susan Schmidt, "Clinton's Last-Day Clemency Benefits 176; List Includes Pardons for Cisneros, McDougal, Deutch, and Roger Clinton," *Washington Post*, January 21, 2001.

70. Marc Lacey, "Clinton Pardons Deutch but Not Milken or Hubbell," *New York Times*, January 21, 2001.

71. Amy Goldstein and Susan Schmidt, "Clinton's Last-Day Clemency Benefits 176; List Includes Pardons for Cisneros, McDougal, Deutch, and Roger Clinton," *Washington Post*, January 21, 2001.

72. Don Van Natta Jr. and Marc Lacey, "Access Proved Vital in Last-Minute Race for Clinton Pardons," *New York Times*, February 25, 2001.

73. Margaret Love, "The Pardon Paradox: Lessons of Clinton's Last Pardons," *Capital University Law Review* 31 (2003): 198–199.

74. David Johnston, "U.S. Is Beginning Criminal Inquiry in Pardon of Rich," *New York Times*, February 15, 2001.

75. Peter Slevin and George Lardner Jr., "Key to Presidential Pardon Is Access; Many Forgiven by Clinton Had Political or Personal Ties," *Washington Post*, January 22, 2001.

76. Robert O'Harrow Jr. and James Grimaldi, "Pardon Bypassed Procedures; Lawyers Close to Clinton Lobbied for Fugitive Trader," *Washington Post*, January 24, 2001.

77. David Johnston, "U.S. Is Beginning Criminal Inquiry in Pardon of Rich," *New York Times*, February 15, 2001.

78. James Grimaldi and Robert O'Harrow Jr., "Fugitive's Pardon Ended 17-Year Effort; Stubborn Refusal to Serve Jail Time Kept Marc Rich Abroad," *Washington Post*, January 28, 2001.

79. Robert O'Harrow Jr. and James Grimaldi, "Pardon Bypassed Procedures; Lawyers Close to Clinton Lobbied for Fugitive Trader," *Washington Post*, January 24, 2001.

80. Sheila Kaplan, Douglas Pasternak, and Gary Cohen, "Exit Bill Clinton with One Last Mess," *U.S. News & World Report*, February 5, 2001, 20.

81. Associated Press, "Rich's Ex-Wife Says Pardon Not Tied to Donations," *Washington Post*, January 25, 2001.

82. James Grimaldi, "Denise Rich Gave Clinton Library $450,000," *Washington Post*, February 10, 2001.

83. Michael Isikoff, "A Million-Dollar Pledge Raises More Questions for Clinton," *Newsweek* Web Exclusive, February 22, 2001.

84. Michael Isikoff, "Pardon Mess Thickens," *Newsweek* Web Exclusive, March 1, 2001.

85. Patrick McGeehan and Alison Cowan, "Influential Backers Helped Commodities Trader Win Pardon," *New York Times*, January 24, 2001.

86. Michael Dobbs, "Pardon Smoothed by Ties to Israel; Barak, Others Aided Rich's Campaign," *Washington Post*, February 25, 2001.

87. Michael Dobbs, "Rich Was Political Donor in Israel; Jerusalem Mayor, Who Backed Pardon, Says He Had Forgotten '93 Contribution," *Washington Post*, February 22, 2001.

88. Alison Cowan, "Some Used in Pardon Effort Were Unaware of Purpose," *New York Times*, January 26, 2001.

89. James Grimaldi and Robert O'Harrow Jr., "Fugitive's Pardon Ended 17-Year Effort; Stubborn Refusal to Serve Jail Time Kept Marc Rich Abroad," *Washington Post*, January 28, 2001.

90. Milt Freudenheim, "The Fugitive

Commodities Trader Who Can Go Home Again," *New York Times*, January 22, 2001.

91. "Rich Says His Pardon Corrected Injustice," *New York Times*, February 25, 2001.

92. Peter Slevin and James Grimaldi, "Ex-Aides Say They Fought Rich Pardon," *Washington Post*, March 2, 2001.

93. Richard Berke, "This Time, Clintons Find Their Support Buckling from Weight of New Woes," *New York Times*, February 23, 2001.

94. Associated Press, "Carter Calls Pardon of Rich 'Disgraceful,'" *Washington Post*, February 21, 2001.

95. Peter Slevin and George Lardner Jr., "Rush of Pardons Unusual in Scope, Lack of Scrutiny; Back-Door Lobbying Had Large Role in Clinton's Decisions, Observers Say," *Washington Post*, March 10, 2001.

96. Mike Allen, "Pardon of Rich to Stand, Bush Says," *Washington Post*, January 30, 2001.

97. Alison Mitchell with Raymond Hernandez, "Lott Criticizes Clintons for Gifts and Pardon of Exiled Trader," *New York Times*, January 30, 2001.

98. John Harris, "Controversy Casts Shadow on Clinton's Party Role; Democrats Squirm at Damage Done in White House Exit," *Washington Post*, February 14, 2001.

99. Jane Mayer, "Marc Rich's Friend in the Bush White House," *New Yorker*, February 5, 2001, 31.

100. David Johnston, "U.S. Is Beginning Criminal Inquiry in Pardon of Rich," *New York Times*, February 15, 2001.

101. Robert O'Harrow Jr., "Secrecy Stressed in Bid to Win Rich's Pardon; Hearing Told of Lawyers' Strategizing," *Washington Post*, February 9, 2001.

102. David Johnston and Don Van

Natta Jr., "Prospect of Pardon Inquiry Sets Off Sparks, but Little Zeal," *New York Times*, February 14, 2001.

103. James Grimaldi and Dan Eggen, "Criminal Probe of Pardon Begins; Gifts from Ex-Wife of Rich Are Focus," *Washington Post*, February 15, 2001.

104. James Grimaldi and Dan Eggen, "House Panel Expands Probe of Rich Pardon; 3 Former Clinton Aides Subpoenaed," *Washington Post*, February 16, 2001.

105. Matt Bai, "Clinton's Popularity Takes a Dive," *Newsweek* Web Exclusive, February 17, 2001.

106. Bill Clinton, "My Reasons for the Pardons," *New York Times*, February 18, 2001.

107. Ibid.

108. John Harris and James Grimaldi, "Clinton: Pardons Served 'Justice,'" *Washington Post*, February 18, 2001.

109. Bill Clinton, "My Reasons for the Pardons," *New York Times*, February 18, 2001.

110. John Harris and James Grimaldi, "Clinton: Pardons Served 'Justice,'" *Washington Post*, February 18, 2001.

111. James Grimaldi and Peter Slevin, "Hillary Clinton's Brother Was Paid for Role in 2 Pardons," *Washington Post*, February 22, 2001.

112. "Bar Clears Hugh Rodham in Clemency Case," *New York Times*, July 22, 2001.

113. Peter Slevin and James Grimaldi, "Hillary Clinton Criticizes Brother; Husband's Brother Also Lobbied for Pardons but Failed," *Washington Post*, February 23, 2001.

114. Dan Eggen, "All of Last-Day Pardons Subject to Probe; Justice Department Clears U.S. Prosecutor in N.Y. to Widen Scrutiny of Clinton," *Washington Post*, March 13, 2001.

115. Susan Schmidt and Dan Eggen, "Pardons Probe Course a Mystery; Case Could Be Huge If N.Y. Prosecutor Pursues Aggressively," *Washington Post*, March 14, 2001.

116. Charles Johnson and Danette Brickman, *Independent Counsel* (Washington, DC: CQ Press, 2001), 222, 241.

117. Eric Lichtblau, "Special Counsel Is Named to Head Inquiry on Leak," *New York Times*, December 31, 2003.

118. George W. Bush, State of the Union Address, January 28, 2003, http://www.whitehouse.gov/releases/2003/01/20030128-19.html (accessed 8/1/07).

119. Joseph Wilson, "What I Didn't Find in Africa," *New York Times*, July 6, 2003.

120. Robert Novak, "Mission to Niger," *Washington Post*, July 14, 2003.

121. Jacques Steinberg, "Threat of Jailing Is Lifted with Reporter's Testimony," *New York Times*, August 25, 2004.

122. David Johnston and Richard Stevenson, "Former Envoy Talks in Book about Source of C.I.A. Leak," *New York Times*, April 30, 2004.

123. Ibid.

124. David Johnston et al., "For Two Aides in Leak Case, 2nd Issue Rises," *New York Times*, July 22, 2005.

125. Eric Schmitt, "An Influential Bush Insider Who Is Used to Challenges," *New York Times*, October 29, 2005.

126. Mark Leibovich, "In the Spotlight and on the Spot: Scooter Libby, Backstage No More," *Washington Post*, October 23, 2005.

127. Adam Liptak, "Reporter Jailed after Refusing to Name Source," *New York Times*, July 7, 2005.

128. David Johnson and Douglas Jehl, "*Times* Reporter Free from Jail; She Will Testify," *New York Times*, September 30, 2005.

129. Michael Duffy et al., "Let's Make a Deal," *Time*, October 10, 2005, 24.

130. Judith Miller, "My Four Hours Testifying in the Federal Grand Jury Room," *New York Times*, October 16, 2005.

131. Ibid.

132. E. J. Dionne Jr., "What the 'Shield' Covered Up," *Washington Post*, November 1, 2005.

133. David Johnston and Richard Stevenson, "Cheney Aide Charged with Lying in Leak Case," *New York Times*, October 29, 2005; Office of the Special Counsel, "Press Release Describing the Indictment of I. Lewis Libby," *Washington Post*, October 28, 2005.

134. David Johnston and Richard Stevenson, "Cheney Aide Charged with Lying in Leak Case," *New York Times*, October 29, 2005.

135. Eric Lichtblau, "Ex-Aide Enters Not Guilty Plea in Leak Charges," *New York Times*, November 4, 2005.

136. Richard Stevenson, "White House Tries to Keep Distance from Leak Case," *New York Times*, November 6, 2005.

137. Eric Lichtblau, "Journalists Said to Figure in Strategy in Leak Case," *New York Times*, November 16, 2005.

138. Neil Lewis, "First Source of C.I.A. Leak Admits Role, Lawyer Says," *New York Times*, August 30, 2006.

139. Editorial, "End of an Affair," *Washington Post*, September 1, 2006.

140. David Johnston, "New Questions about Inquiry in C.I.A. Leak," *New York Times*, September 2, 2006.

141. Carol Leonnig, "Cheney Willing to Testify at Libby Trial; Defense Says It Will Call Vice President," *Washington Post*, December 20, 2006.

142. Vaughn Ververs, "A Pardon for Libby?" CBS News, March 7, 2007, http://www.cbsnews.com/stories/2007/03/07/politics/main2542158.shtml (accessed 8/13/07).

143. Carol Leonnig and Amy Goldstein, "Libby Guilty on 4 of 5 Counts," Washington Post, March 7, 2007.

144. The Editors, "Pardon Libby," National Review, March 6, 2007.

145. Jeffrey Toobin, "Toobin: Presidential Pardon May Be on Libby Agenda," CNN, March 6, 2007, http://www.cnn.com/2007/POLITICS/03/06/toobin.libby/index.html (accessed 8/13/07).

146. Dana Perino, Press Briefing, March 6, 2007, http://www.whitehouse/gov/news/releases/2007/03/20070306-5.html (accessed 8/13/07); Tony Snow, Press Briefing, March 7, 2007, http://www.whitehouse.gov/news/releases/2007/03/20070307-4.html (accessed 8/13/07).

147. Charles Krauthammer, "Fitzgerald's Folly," Washington Post, March 9, 2007.

148. Jeffrey Jones, "Americans 3-to-1 against a Libby Pardon," Gallup Poll News Service, March 16, 2007.

149. Peter Baker and Carol Leonnig, "Bush Deflects Pressure to Give Libby a Pardon," Washington Post, March 8, 2007.

150. Frank Newport and Joseph Carroll, "Americans Generally Negative on Recent Presidential Pardons," Gallup Poll News Service, March 9, 2007.

151. Scott Shane, "Pardon Libby? Left and Right Erupt in a Fight," New York Times, March 7, 2007.

152. Carol Leonnig and Amy Goldstein, "Libby Given 2-1/2 Year Prison Term," Washington Post, June 6, 2007.

153. Ibid.

154. Scott Shane and Neil Lewis, "Bush Commutes Libby Sentence, Saying 30 Months 'Is Excessive,'" New York Times, July 3, 2007; William Otis, "Neither Prison nor Pardon," Washington Post, June 7, 2007.

155. William Otis, "Neither Prison nor Pardon," Washington Post, June 7, 2007.

156. Margaret Love, "Begging Bush's Pardon," Los Angeles Times, June 7, 2007.

157. Carol Leonnig and Amy Goldstein, "Libby Loses Bid to Stay Out of Jail for Appeal," Washington Post, June 15, 2007.

158. Associated Press, "Libby Is Assigned an Inmate Number," Los Angeles Times, June 29, 2007.

159. Sheryl Gay Stolberg, "For President, Libby Case Was a Test of Will," New York Times, July 3, 2007; Peter Baker, "Post Politics Hour," Washington Post, July 3, 2007; "President Bush Meets with President Putin of Russian Federation," July 2, 2007, http://www.whitehouse.gov/news/ releases/2007/07/20070702-2.html (accessed 8/13/07).

160. George W. Bush, Grant of Executive Clemency, July 2, 2007, http://www.whitehouse.gov/news/releases/2007/07/20070702-4.html (accessed 8/13/07).

161. Michael Abramowitz, "A Decision Made Largely Alone," Washington Post, July 3, 2007; Sheryl Gay Stolberg and Jim Rutenberg, "Bush Is Said to Have Held Long Debate on Decision," New York Times, July 4, 2007.

162. Michael Abramowitz, "A Decision Made Largely Alone," Washington Post, July 3, 2007.

163. George W. Bush, "Statement by the President on Executive Clemency for Lewis Libby," July 2, 2007, http://www.whitehouse.gov/news/releases/2007/07/20070702-3.html (accessed 8/13/07).

164. Associated Press, "Bush Spares Libby from Prison Term," MSNBC, July 2, 2007, http://www.msnbc.msn.com/id/19570081/ (accessed 7/27/07).

165. Statement of Special Counsel, Office of Special Counsel, Department of Justice, July 2, 2007, http://www.usdoj.gov/usao/iln/osc/documents/2007_07_02_stmt_of_special_counsel.pdf (accessed 8/13/07).

166. Jeffrey Toobin, "Bush Commutes Libby's Sentence," CNN, July 2, 2007, http://transcripts.cnn.com/TRANSCRIPTS/0707/02/sitroom.03.html (accessed 8/13/07).

167. Associated Press, "Attorneys See Irony in Libby Case," New York Times, July 3, 2007.

168. Associated Press, "Bush Spares Libby from Prison Term," MSNBC, July 2, 2007, http://www.msnbc.msn.com/id/19570081/ (accessed 7/27/07).

169. Amy Goldstein, "Bush Commutes Libby's Prison Sentence," Washington Post, July 3, 2007.

170. Mary Lu Carnevale, "More to Come on Libby?" Wall Street Journal, July 3, 2007, http://blogs.wsj.com/washwire/2007/07/03/more-to-come-on-libby/ (accessed 8/13/07).

171. Editors, "Bush and Libby," Wall Street Journal, July 3, 2007, http://online.wsj.com/article/SB118342314501456066.html (accessed 7/10/07).

172. Amy Goldstein, "Bush Commutes Libby's Prison Sentence," Washington Post, July 3, 2007.

173. Adam Liptak, "Commuting Prison Term Is Implicit Critique of Sentencing Standards," New York Times, July 4, 2007.

174. Amy Goldstein, "Bush Commutes Libby's Prison Sentence," Washington Post, July 3, 2007.

175. Associated Press, "Bush Won't Rule Out Full Libby Pardon," New York Times, July 4, 2007.

176. Reggie Walton, Order filed July 3, 2007, in United States v. I. Lewis Libby, U.S. District Court for the District of Columbia, SCOTUS blog, http://www.scotusblog.com/movabletype/archives/Walton%20order%207-3-07.pdf (accessed 8/13/07).

177. Fred Fielding, Letter to Patrick Fitzgerald, July 6, 2007, How Appealing blog, July 9, 2007, http://howappealing.law.com/LibbyWhiteHouseLetter.pdf (accessed 8/13/07).

178. Lyle Denniston, "All Sides Agree: Libby Must Remain Supervised," SCOTUS blog, July 9, 2007, http://www.scotusblog.com/movabletype/archives/2007/07/08-week/ (accessed 8/13/07).

179. John Conyers, Letter to President George W. Bush, July 6, 2007, House Judiciary Committee Web site, http://judiciary.house.gov/Media/PDFS/Conyers070709.pdf (accessed 8/13/07).

180. Fred Fielding, Letter to John Conyers, July 11, 2007, House Judiciary Committee Web site, http://judiciary.house.gov/Media/PDFS/Fielding070711.pdf (accessed 8/13/07).

181. Jeffrey Jones, "Two in Three Say Bush Should Not Have Intervened in Libby Case," Gallup Poll News Service, July 10, 2007. Telephone poll of 1,014 adults conducted July 6–8, 2007.

182. Ibid.

183. E. J. Dionne Jr., "An Unpardonable Act," Washington Post, July 6, 2007.

Conclusion

1. Richard Stevenson, "A Presidential Power This President Uses Rarely," New York Times, December 25, 2002.

2. Bob Woodward, *Shadow* (New York: Simon & Schuster, 1999), 37.

3. John Robert Greene, *The Presidency of Gerald R. Ford* (Lawrence: University Press of Kansas, 1995), 66.

4. Craig Smith and Kathy Smith, "The Coalitional Crisis of the Ford Presidency: The Pardons Reconsidered," American Political Science Association, 1992, 2, 4. Uncataloged papers, Box 15 (Sm-Sy), Gerald R. Ford Library.

5. Smith and Smith, "Coalitional Crisis," 16–17.

6. Craig Smith and Kathy Smith, *The White House Speaks* (Westport, CT: Praeger, 1994), 72.

7. Ibid.

8. Question 002, Accession Number 0061880, Harris poll of 1,544 adults conducted September 23–27, 1974, Public Opinion Online, Roper Center, University of Connecticut.

9. Karlyn Kohrs Campbell and Kathleen Hall Jamieson, *Deeds Done in Words* (Chicago: University of Chicago Press, 1990), 168–169, 170.

10. Ibid., 177–181.

11. Alexander Hamilton, James Madison, and John Jay, *The Federalist Papers*, Clinton Rossiter, ed. (New York: Mentor, 1999), 417.

12. *Murphy v. Ford*, 390 F. Supp. 1372 (D.C. Mich. 1975).

13. *Burdick v. United States*, 236 U.S. 79 (1915); Smith and Smith, "Coalitional Crisis," 20.

14. Question Number 003, Accession Number 0099300, Opinion Research Corporation telephone survey of 629 adults conducted on September 9, 1974, Public Opinion Online, Roper Center, University of Connecticut.

15. Lou Cannon, "An Act of Mercy," *Washington Post*, September 11, 1974.

16. Smith and Smith, *The White House Speaks*, 70–71.

17. Gerald Ford, "The President's News Conference of September 16, 1974," *Public Papers of the Presidents*, 80: September 16, 1974, 147.

18. Special News Summary, October 17, 1974, Folder: Nixon Pardon— Hungate Subcommittee: Ford Testimony (3), Box 34, Philip Buchen Files 1974– 1977, Gerald R. Ford Library.

19. "Nixon Pardon Still Haunts Ford," *Ann Arbor News*, April 22, 1979, Folder: Pardon, Richard Milhous Nixon, 1913–, Nixon Vertical File, Gerald R. Ford Library.

20. James Cannon, *Time and Chance* (New York: HarperCollins, 1994), 386.

21. Stanley Kutler, "Clearing the Rubble: The Nixon Pardon," in *Gerald R. Ford and the Politics of Post-Watergate America*, Bernard Firestone and Alexej Ugrinsky, eds. (Westport, CT: Greenwood Press, 1993), 33–34.

22. Rowland Evans and Robert Novak, ". . . With an 'Expected' Pardon," *Washington Post*, September 12, 1974.

23. Barry Werth, *31 Days* (New York: Nan A. Talese, 2006), 309.

24. Ibid., 246.

25. Cannon, *Time and Chance*, 377.

26. Werth, *31 Days*, 313.

27. Mark J. Rozell, *The Press and the Ford Presidency* (Ann Arbor: University of Michigan Press, 1992), 82, 231.

28. David Broder, "Government: More Than the Presidency," *Washington Post*, September 18, 1974.

29. William Raspberry, "The Pardon and the Tapes," *Washington Post*, September 20, 1974.

30. Question 030, Accession Number 0046869, Gallup poll of 1,524 adults conducted June 11–14, 1976; Question

003, Accession Number 0407170, ABC News telephone poll of 1,004 adults conducted June 7–9, 2002, Public Opinion Online, Roper Center, University of Connecticut.

31. Adam Clymer, "Ford Wins Kennedy Award for 'Courage' of Nixon Pardon," New York Times, May 21, 2001.

32. Remarks of Senator Edward Kennedy, John F. Kennedy Library and Museum, Boston, Massachusetts, May 21, 2001, http://www.jfklibrary.org/pica_2001_emk_remarks.html (accessed 11/15/05).

33. Woodward, Shadow, 37.

34. Carl Bernstein, "Remembering E. Howard Hunt and Watergate," online forum hosted by Washingtonpost.com on January 24, 2007 (transcript currently unavailable) (accessed 1/24/07).

35. Hamilton et al., Federalist Papers, 417.

36. Biddle v. Perovich, 274 U.S. 480 (1927).

37. United States v. Wilson, 32 U.S. 150 (1833).

38. Hamilton et al., Federalist Papers, 415.

39. David Johnston, "Bush Diary at Issue," New York Times, December 25, 1992.

40. David Johnston, "Prosecutor Shifts Attention to Bush on Iran Arms Deal," New York Times, December 26, 1992.

41. David Johnston, "Aides Say Top Democrats Backed Weinberger Pardon," New York Times, December 27, 1992.

42. David Johnston, "Bush Diary at Issue," New York Times, December 25, 1992.

43. R. W. Apple, "The President as Pardoner: A Calculated Gamble," New York Times, December 25, 1992.

44. Hamilton et al., Federalist Papers, 417.

45. United States v. Wilson, 32 U.S. 150, 160–161 (1833); Biddle v. Perovich, 274 U.S. 480, 486 (1927).

46. Hamilton et al., Federalist Papers, 415–416.

47. Lawrence E. Walsh, Firewall (New York: W. W. Norton, 1997), 507.

48. Samuel Dash, "Independent Counsel: No More, No Less a Federal Prosecutor," Georgetown Law Journal 86 (1997–1998): 2094.

49. Margaret Love, "The Pardon Paradox: Lessons of Clinton's Last Pardons," Capital University Law Review 31 (2003): 186–187, 188.

50. Hamilton et al., Federalist Papers, 417.

51. Editorial, "An Indefensible Pardon," New York Times, January 24, 2001.

52. United States v. Wilson, 32 U.S. 150 (1833); Biddle v. Perovich, 274 U.S. 480 (1927).

53. Hamilton et al., Federalist Papers, 415.

54. Carrie Johnson, "Round of Bush Pardons Includes No Big Names," Washington Post, November 25, 2008.

55. "Presidential Clemency Actions by Administration: 1945 to Present," updated August 1, 2007, Office of the Pardon Attorney, U.S. Department of Justice, on file with author.

56. John McKinnon, Evan Perez, and Gary Fields, "Libby's Backers Push for Pardon," Wall Street Journal, March 7, 2007.

57. Hamilton et al., Federalist Papers, 415–416.

58. Bill Clinton's volatile clemency actions were not as closely tied to executive branch investigations as those

of his predecessor and successor, but they were just as inappropriate.

59. Samuel Kernell, *Going Public*, 4th ed. (Washington, DC: CQ Press, 2007); Jeffrey Tulis, *The Rhetorical Presidency* (Princeton, NJ: Princeton University Press, 1987).

60. Jerry Carannante, "What to Do about the Executive Clemency Power in the Wake of the Clinton Presidency?" *New York Law School Law Review* 47 (2003): 349.

61. See, for example, Stephen A. Wolf, "In the Pursuit of Power without Accountability: How the Independent Counsel Statute Is Designed and Used to Undermine the Energy and Independence of the Presidency," *South Dakota Law Review* 35 (1990): 1.

62. See, for example, Charles Tiefer, "The Specially Investigated President," *University of Chicago Law School Roundtable* 5 (1998): 143.

63. Walter F. Mondale, "Harnessing the President's Pardon Power, "*A.B.A. Journal* 61 (1975): 108.

64. Gregory Sisk, "Suspending the Pardon Power during the Twilight of a Presidential Term," *Missouri Law Review* 67 (2002): fn a1.

65. Carannante, "Executive Clemency Power," 349.

66. Hamilton et al., *Federalist Papers*, 415–416.

67. Ibid., 417.

Appendix. Notes on Scholarship

1. See Chapter 2: *United States v. Wilson*, 32 U.S. 150 (1833); *Ex parte Wells*, 59 U.S. 307 (1855); *Ex parte Garland*, 71 U.S. 333 (1866); *United States v. Padelford*, 76 U.S. 531 (1869); *United States v. Klein*, 80 U.S. 128 (1871); *Knote v. United States*, 95 U.S. 149 (1877); *Carlesi v. New York*, 233 U.S. 51 (1914); *Burdick v. United States*, 236 U.S. 79 (1915); *Ex parte Grossman*, 267 U.S. 87 (1925); *Biddle v. Perovich*, 274 U.S. 480 (1927); *Schick v. Reed*, 419 U.S. 256 (1974); and *Hoffa v. Saxbe*, 378 F. Supp. 1221 (D.D.C. 1974).

2. A representative sample includes James Barnett, "Grounds of Pardon in the Courts," *Yale Law Journal* 20 (1910): 131; Charles Bonaparte, "The Pardoning Power," *Yale Law Journal* 19 (1910): 603; Samuel Williston, "Does a Pardon Blot Out Guilt?" *Harvard Law Review* 28 (1915): 647; Hugh Fisher, "The Pardoning Power of the President," *Georgetown Law Journal* 12 (1923–1924): 89; Ernest Morris, "Some Phases of the Pardoning Power," *American Bar Association Journal* 12 (1926): 183; Henry Weihofen, "The Effect of a Pardon," *University of Pennsylvania Law Review* 88 (1939): 177; Henry Weihofen, "Legislative Pardons," *California Law Review* 27 (1939): 371; Henry Weihofen, "Pardon: An Extraordinary Remedy," *Rocky Mountain Law Review* 12 (1939–1940): 112.

3. Two key clemency works were published in 1939 and 1941: Wayne Morse et al., *The Attorney General's Survey of Release Procedures*, vol. 3 (Washington, DC: Government Printing Office, 1939); Willard Humbert, *The Pardoning Power of the President* (Washington, DC: American Council on Public Affairs, 1941).

4. See, for example, S. Elizabeth Gibson, "Presidential Pardons and the Common Law," *North Carolina Law Review* 53 (1975): 785; Patrick Cowlishaw, "The Conditional Presidential Pardon," *Stanford Law Review* 28 (1975): 149; Leonard Boudin, "The Presidential Pardons of James R. Hoffa and Richard M. Nixon: Have the Limitations on the Pardon Power Been Exceeded?" *University*

of Colorado Law Review 48 (1976): 1; William Duker, "The President's Power to Pardon: A Constitutional History," *William & Mary Law Review* 18 (1977): 475; John Stanish, "The Effect of a Presidential Pardon," *Federal Probation* 42 (1978): 3; Christopher Joyner, "Rethinking the President's Power of Executive Pardon," *Federal Probation* 43 (1979): 16.

5. See Daniel Kobil, "The Quality of Mercy Strained: Wresting the Pardoning Power from the King," *Texas Law Review* 69 (1991): 569; Stephen Carter, "The Iran-Contra Pardon Mess," *Houston Law Review* 29 (1992): 883; James Jorgensen, "Federal Executive Clemency Power: The President's Prerogative to Escape Accountability," *University of Richmond Law Review* 27 (1993): 345; Kathleen Moore, "Pardon for Good and Sufficient Reasons," *University of Richmond Law Review* 27 (1993): 281.

6. Charles Berger, "The Effect of Presidential Pardons on Disclosure of Information: Is Our Cynicism Justified?" *Oklahoma Law Review* 52 (1999): 163; Margaret Love, "Of Pardons, Politics and Collar Buttons: Reflections on the President's Duty to Be Merciful," *Fordham Urban Law Journal* 27 (2000): 1483; Carl Cannon and David Byrd, "The Power of the Pardon," *National Law Journal* 32 (2000): 774; Brian Hoffstadt, "Normalizing the Federal Clemency Power," *Texas Law Review* 79 (2001): 561; Harold Krent, "Conditioning the President's Conditional Pardon Power," *California Law Review* 89 (2001): 1665; Mark Strasser, "The Limits of the Clemency Power on Pardons, Retributivists, and the United States Constitution," *Brandeis Law Journal* 41 (2002): 85; Jerry Carannante, "What to

Do about the Executive Clemency Power in the Wake of the Clinton Presidency?" *New York Law School Law Review* 47 (2003): 325; Todd Peterson, "Congressional Power over Pardon and Amnesty: Legislative Authority in the Shadow of Presidential Prerogative," *Wake Forest Law Review* 38 (2003): 1225; Mark Strasser, "Some Reflections on the President's Pardon Power," *Capital University Law Review* 31 (2003): 143; Margaret Love, "The Pardon Paradox: Lessons of Clinton's Last Pardons," *Capital University Law Review* 31 (2003): 185.

7. Sentencing Law and Policy blog, http://sentencing.typepad.com/ (accessed 8/23/07).

8. See Jurist blog, http://jurist.law.pitt .edu/pardons.htm (accessed 8/23/07).

9. Max Farrand, *Records of the Federal Convention of 1787*, available online via the Library of Congress's American Memory Collection, http://memory.loc.gov/ ammem/amlaw/lwfr.html (accessed 8/26/07); Alexander Hamilton, James Madison, and John Jay, *The Federalist Papers*, Clinton Rossiter, ed. (New York: Mentor, 1999).

10. Representative works include Everett Brown, "The Restoration of Civil and Political Rights by Presidential Pardon," *American Political Science Review* 34 (1940): 295; William Pederson, "Amnesty and Presidential Behavior: A 'Barberian' Test," *Presidential Studies Quarterly* 7 (1977): 175; John Orman and Dorothy Rudoni, "Exercise of the President's Discretionary Power in Criminal Justice Policy," *Presidential Studies Quarterly* 9 (1979): 415; David Shichor and Donald Ranish, "President Carter's Vietnam Amnesty: An Analysis of a Public Policy Decision," *Presidential Studies Quarterly* 10 (1980): 443; Louis

Fisher, "When Presidential Power Backfires: Clinton's Use of Clemency," *Presidential Studies Quarterly* 32 (2002): 586; Jeffrey Crouch, "Presidential Misuse of the Pardon Power," *Presidential Studies Quarterly* 38 (2008): 722–734.

11. David Adler, "The President's Pardon Power," in *Inventing the American Presidency*, Thomas Cronin, ed. (Lawrence: University Press of Kansas, 1989), 209.

12. Mark Rozell, "President Ford's Pardon of Richard M. Nixon: Constitutional and Political Considerations," *Presidential Studies Quarterly* 24 (1994): 121; Mark Rozell, "The Presidential Pardon Power: A Bibliographic Essay," *Journal of Law and Politics* 5 (1989): 459.

13. P. S. Ruckman Jr. maintains a clemency blog (http://pardonpower .com). He used to host a Web site containing clemency information available to the public at http://www.rvc .cc.il.us/faclink/pruckman/ pardoncharts/ juristcharts.htm. (Both accessed 9/12/07.) He posted three published papers on the site: P. S. Ruckman Jr., "Presidential Character and Executive Clemency: A Reexamination," *Social Science Quarterly* 76 (1995): 213; P. S. Ruckman Jr., "Executive Clemency in the United States: Origins, Development, and Analysis (1900–1993)," *Presidential Studies Quarterly* 27 (1997): 251; and P. S. Ruckman Jr., with David Kincaid, "Inside Lincoln's Clemency Decision Making," *Presidential Studies Quarterly* 29 (1999): 84. He also made several unpublished papers available on the site: P. S. Ruckman Jr., "Federal Executive Clemency in the United States, 1934–1994: An Empirical Analysis," unpublished paper; P. S. Ruckman Jr., "Federal Executive Clemency in the United States, 1789–

1995: A Preliminary Report," unpublished paper; P. S. Ruckman Jr., "'Last-Minute' Pardon Scandals: Fact and Fiction," unpublished paper; P. S. Ruckman Jr., "The Pardoning Power: The Other 'Civics Lesson,' or 'Clinton's Clemency Caper in Context,'" unpublished paper; P. S. Ruckman Jr., "Policy as an Indicator of 'Original Understanding': Executive Clemency in the Early Republic (1789–1817)," unpublished paper; P. S. Ruckman Jr., "President-Centered and Presidency-Centered Explanations of Federal Clemency Policy," unpublished paper. As of November 2008, this Web site is no longer active. His most recent work is "Seasonal Clemency Revisited: An Empirical Analysis," an unpublished paper on file with the author. Ruckman is also working on a book-length manuscript about the pardon power.

14. Ted Jones et al., "A Multifactorial Analysis of Presidential Clemency: 1900–2002," presented at the Annual Midwest Meeting of the American Political Science Association, Chicago, Illinois, April 14–18, 2004, obtained via e-mail from coauthor Jack McGuire; Anthony Eksterowicz and Robert Roberts, "The Specter of Presidential Pardons," *White House Studies* 6 (2006): 377; Andrew Whitford and Holona Ochs, "The Political Roots of Executive Clemency," 2006, available at Social Science Research Network, http://ssrn.com/ abstract=888579 (accessed 8/23/07); H. Abbie Erler, "Executive Clemency or Bureaucratic Discretion? Two Models of the Pardons Process," *Presidential Studies Quarterly* 37 (2007): 427. Journalist George Lardner is writing a book on the history of federal executive clemency.

BIBLIOGRAPHY

Books

Abrams, Elliott. *Undue Process*. New York: Free Press, 1993.

Adler, David Gray. "The President's Pardon Power," in *Inventing the American Presidency*. Thomas Cronin, ed., 209–235. Lawrence: University Press of Kansas, 1989.

Blackstone, William. *Commentaries on the Laws of England*, adapted by Robert Malcolm Kerr. Boston: Beacon Press, 1962.

Bush, George W. *A Charge to Keep*. New York: William Morrow, 1999.

Campbell, Karlyn Kohrs, and Kathleen Hall Jamieson. *Deeds Done in Words*. Chicago: University of Chicago Press, 1990.

Cannon, James. *Time and Chance*. New York: HarperCollins, 1994.

Corwin, Edward S. *The President: Office and Powers, 1787–1984*, 5th ed. New York: New York University Press, 1984.

Dorris, Jonathan Truman. *Pardon and Amnesty under Lincoln and Johnson*. Chapel Hill: University of North Carolina Press, 1953.

Eastland, Terry. *Ethics, Politics and the Independent Counsel*. Washington, DC: National Legal Center for the Public Interest, 1989.

Edwards, George C., III, and Alec M. Gallup. *Presidential Approval*. Baltimore: Johns Hopkins University Press, 1990.

Farrand, Max. *Records of the Federal Convention of 1787*. New Haven, CT: Yale University Press, 1966.

Firestone, Bernard J., and Alexej Ugrinsky, eds. *Gerald R. Ford and the Politics of Post-Watergate America*. Westport, CT: Greenwood Press, 1993.

Fisher, Louis. *Congressional Abdication on War and Spending*. College Station, TX: A&M University Press, 2000.

———. "The Independent Counsel Statute," in *The Clinton Scandal and the Future of American Government*. Mark J. Rozell and Clyde Wilcox, eds. Washington, DC: Georgetown University Press, 2000.

———. *The Politics of Executive Privilege*. Durham, NC: Carolina Academic Press, 2004.

Ford, Gerald R. *A Time to Heal*. New York: Harper & Row, 1979.

Greene, John Robert. *The Presidency of Gerald R. Ford*. Lawrence: University Press of Kansas, 1995.

Hamilton, Alexander, James Madison, and John Jay. *The Federalist Papers*. Clinton Rossiter, ed. New York: Mentor, 1961.

Harriger, Katy J. *The Special Prosecutor in American Politics*, 2d ed. Lawrence: University Press of Kansas, 2000.

Hartmann, Robert T. *Palace Politics*. New York: McGraw-Hill, 1980.

Hoffer, Peter Charles. *The Treason Trials of Aaron Burr*. Lawrence: University Press of Kansas, 2008.

Humbert, W. H. *The Pardoning Power of the President*. Washington, DC: American Council on Public Affairs, 1941.

Isenberg, Nancy. *Fallen Founder*. New York: Viking Penguin, 2007.

Jaworski, Leon. *The Right and the Power*. New York: Reader's Digest Press, 1976.

Jefferson, Thomas. *The Writings of Thomas Jefferson*, vol. 10. Paul Leicester Ford, ed. New York: G.P. Putnam's Sons, 1905.

Johnson, Charles A., and Danette Brickman. *Independent Counsel*. Washington, DC: CQ Press, 2001.

Kurland, Philip B., and Ralph Lerner, eds. *The Founders' Constitution*. Chicago: University of Chicago Press, 1987.

Kutler, Stanley I. *The Wars of Watergate*. New York: Alfred A. Knopf, 1990.

Locke, John. *Second Treatise of Government*. C. B. Macpherson, ed. Indianapolis: Hackett, 1980.

Mollenhoff, Clark R. *The Man Who Pardoned Nixon*. New York: St. Martin's Press, 1976.

Montesquieu. *The Spirit of the Laws*, vol. 1. Thomas Nugent, trans. New York: Hafner Press, 1949.

Moore, Kathleen Dean. *Pardons*. New York: Oxford University Press, 1989.

Morse, Wayne L., Henry Weihofen, and Hans Von Hentig, eds. *The Attorney General's Survey of Release Procedures*, vol. 3. Washington, DC: Government Printing Office, 1939.

O'Neill, Tip. *Man of the House*. New York: Random House, 1987.

Reeves, Richard. *A Ford, Not a Lincoln*. New York: Harcourt Brace Jovanovich, 1975.

Rozell, Mark J. "In Defense of President Ford's Pardon of Richard M. Nixon," in *Gerald R. Ford and the Politics of Post-Watergate America*. Bernard Firestone and Alexej Ugrinsky, eds. Westport, CT: Greenwood Press, 1993.

———. "President Ford's Pardon of Richard M. Nixon," in *Triumphs and Tragedies of the Modern Presidency*. David Abshire, ed. Westport, CT: Praeger, 2001.

———. *The Press and the Ford Presidency*. Ann Arbor: University of Michigan Press, 1992.

Small, Melvin. *The Presidency of Richard Nixon*. Lawrence: University Press of Kansas, 1999.

Smith, Craig Allen, and Kathy B. Smith. *The White House Speaks*. Westport, CT: Praeger, 1994.

Taft, William Howard. *Our Chief Magistrate and His Powers*. New York: Columbia University Press, 1925.

terHorst, Jerald F. *Gerald R. Ford and the Future of the Presidency*. New York: Third Press, 1974.

Tiefer, Charles. *The Semi-Sovereign Presidency*. Boulder: Westview Press, 1994.

Walsh, Lawrence E. *Firewall*. New York: W. W. Norton, 1997.

———. *Iran-Contra: The Final Report*. Times Books, 1994.

Weinberger, Caspar W., with Gretchen Roberts. *In the Arena*. Washington, DC: Regnery, 2001.

Werth, Barry. *31 Days*. New York: Nan A. Talese, 2006.

Woodward, Bob. *Shadow*. New York: Simon & Schuster, 1999.

Case Law

United States v. Wilson, 32 U.S. 150 (1833)

Ex parte Wells, 59 U.S. 307 (1855)

Ex parte Garland, 71 U.S. 333 (1866)

Armstrong's Foundry, 73 U.S. 766 (1868)

United States v. Padelford, 76 U.S. 531 (1869)

United States v. Klein, 80 U.S. 128 (1871)

Armstrong v. United States, 80 U.S. 154 (1872)

Carlisle v. United States, 83 U.S. 147 (1872)

Osborn v. United States, 91 U.S. 474 (1876)

Knote v. United States, 95 U.S. 149 (1877)

The Laura, 114 U.S. 411 (1885)

Hart v. United States, 118 U.S. 62 (1886)

Boyd v. United States, 142 U.S. 450 (1892)

Brown v. Walker, 161 U.S. 591 (1896)

Carlesi v. New York, 233 U.S. 51 (1914)

Burdick v. United States, 236 U.S. 79 (1915)

Ex parte Grossman, 267 U.S. 87 (1925)

Biddle v. Perovich, 274 U.S. 480 (1927)

Hoffa v. Saxbe, 378 F. Supp. 1221 (D.D.C. 1974)

Schick v. Reed, 419 U.S. 256 (1974)

Murphy v. Ford, 390 F. Supp. 1372 (D.C. Mich. 1975)

Bjerkan v. United States, 529 F.2d 125 (C.A. Ill. 1975)

Morrison v. Olson, 487 U.S. 654, 671 (1988).

Public Citizen v. U.S. Dept. of Justice, 491 U.S. 440 (1989)

United States v. Noonan, 906 F.2d 952 (C.A. 3 1990)

In re North, 62 F.3d 1434 (C.A. D.C. 1994)

In re Abrams, 689 A.2d 6 (D.C. 1997)

Ohio Adult Parole Authority v. Woodard, 523 U.S. 272 (1998)

Law Review Articles

Barnett, James D. "Grounds of Pardon in the Courts," *Yale Law Journal* 20 (1910): 131.

Bennett, Robert S. "Press Advocacy and the High-Profile Client," *Loyola of Los Angeles Law Review* 30 (1996–1997): 13.

Berger, Charles D. "The Effect of Presidential Pardons on Disclosure of Information: Is Our Cynicism Justified?" *Oklahoma Law Review* 52 (1999): 163.

Bonaparte, Charles J. "The Pardoning Power," *Yale Law Journal* 19 (1910): 603.

Boudin, Leonard B. "The Presidential Pardons of James R. Hoffa and Richard M. Nixon: Have the Limitations on the Pardon Power Been Exceeded?" *University of Colorado Law Review* 48 (1976): 1.

Buchanan, G. Sidney. "The Nature of a Pardon under the United States Constitution," *Ohio State Law Journal* 39 (1978): 36.

Cannon, Carl M., and David Byrd. "The Power of the Pardon," *National Law Journal* 32 (2000): 774.

Carannante, Jerry. "What to Do about the Executive Clemency Power in the Wake of the Clinton Presidency?" *New York Law School Law Review* 47 (2003): 325.

Carter, Stephen L. "The Iran-Contra Pardon Mess," *Houston Law Review* 29 (1992): 883.

Comments. "The Pardoning Power of the Chief Executive," *Fordham Law Review* 6 (1937): 255.

Cowlishaw, Patrick R. "The Conditional Presidential Pardon," *Stanford Law Review* 28 (1975): 149.

Cozart, Reed. "The Benefits of Executive Clemency," *Federal Probation* 32 (1968): 33.

———. "Clemency under the Federal System," *Federal Probation* 23 (1959): 3.

Dash, Samuel. "Independent Counsel: No More, No Less a Federal Prosecutor," *Georgetown Law Journal* 86 (1997–1998): 2077.

Duker, William F. "The President's Power to Pardon: A Constitutional History," *William & Mary Law Review* 18 (1977): 475.

Ellis, T. S., III. "The Independent Counsel Process: Is It Broken and How Should It Be Fixed?" 54 *Washington & Lee Law Review* 54 (1997): 1515.

Feerick, John D. "The Pardoning Power of Article II of the Constitution," *New York State Bar Journal* 47 (1975): 7.

Fisher, Hugh A. "The Pardoning Power of the President," *Georgetown Law Journal* 12 (1923–1924): 89.

Freeman, Harrop A. "A Historical Justification and Legal Basis for Amnesty Today," *Law and Social Order* (1971): 515.

Garland, David S., ed. "The President's Power of Commutation," *New York Law Review* 5 (1927): 399.

Gibson, S. Elizabeth. "Presidential Pardons and the Common Law," *North Carolina Law Review* 53 (1975): 785.

Godes, Niles L., and Ty E. Howard. "Independent Counsel Investigations," *American Criminal Law Review* 35 (1997–1998): 875.

Gormley, Ken. "An Original Model of the Independent Counsel Statute," *Michigan Law Review* 97 (1998–1999): 601.

Hall, Joseph S., Nicholas Pullen, and Kandace Rayos. "Independent Counsel Investigations," *American Criminal Law Review* 36 (1999): 809.

Harriger, Katy J. "Can the Independent Counsel Statute Be Saved?" *Law and Contemporary Problems* 62 (1999): 131.

———. "Damned If She Does and Damned If She Doesn't: The Attorney General and the Independent Counsel Statute," *Georgetown Law Journal* 86 (1997–1998): 2097.

———. "The History of the Independent Counsel Provisions: How the Past Informs the Current Debate," *Mercer Law Review* 49 (1997–1998): 489.

Hoffstadt, Brian M. "Normalizing the Federal Clemency Power," *Texas Law Review* 79 (2001): 561.

Johnson, Scott P., and Christopher E. Smith. "White House Scandals and the Presidential Pardon Power: Persistent Risks and Prospects for Reform," *New England Law Review* 33 (1999): 907.

Jorgensen, James. "Federal Executive Clemency Power: The President's Prerogative to Escape Accountability," *University of Richmond Law Review* 27 (1993): 345.

Joyner, Christopher C. "Rethinking the President's Power of Executive Pardon," *Federal Probation* 43 (1979): 16.

Kalt, Brian. "Pardon Me?: The Constitutional Case against Presidential Self-Pardons," *Yale Law Journal* 106 (1996): 779.

Kobil, Daniel T. "The Quality of Mercy Strained: Wresting the Pardoning Power from the King," *Texas Law Review* 69 (1991): 569.

Koh, Harold H. "Begging Bush's Pardon," *Houston Law Review* 29 (1992): 889.

Krajick, Kevin. "The Quality of Mercy," *Corrections,* June 1979, 46–53.

Krent, Harold J. "Conditioning the President's Conditional Pardon Power," *California Law Review* 89 (2001): 1665.

Lardner, George. "The Role of the Press in the Clemency Process," *Capital University Law Review* 31 (2003): 179.

Levin, Carl, and Elise J. Bean. "The Independent Counsel Statute: A Matter of Public Confidence and Constitutional Balance," *Hofstra Law Review* 16 (1978–1988): 11.

Love, Margaret Colgate. "Of Pardons, Politics, and Collar Buttons: Reflections on the President's Duty to Be Merciful," *Fordham Urban Law Journal* 27 (2000): 1483.

———. "The Pardon Paradox: Lessons of Clinton's Last Pardons," *Capital University Law Review* 31 (2003): 185.

Macgill, Hugh C. "The Nixon Pardon: Limits on the Benign Prerogative," *Connecticut Law Review* 7 (1974): 56.

Mondale, Walter. "Harnessing the President's Pardon Power," *American Bar Association Journal* 61 (1975): 107.

Moore, Kathleen Dean. "Pardon for Good and Sufficient Reasons," *University of Richmond Law Review* 27 (1993): 281.

Morris, Ernest. "Some Phases of the Pardoning Power," *American Bar Association Journal* 12 (1926): 183.

Nida, Robert, and Rebecca L. Spiro. "The President as His Own Judge and Jury: A Legal Analysis of the Presidential Self-Pardon Power," *Oklahoma Law Journal* 52 (1999): 197.

Peterson, Todd David. "Congressional Power over Pardon and Amnesty: Legislative Authority in the Shadow of Presidential Prerogative," *Wake Forest Law Review* 38 (2003): 1225.

Sisk, Gregory. "Suspending the Pardon Power during the Twilight of a Presidential Term," *Missouri Law Review* 67 (2002): 13.

Stanish, John R. "The Effect of a Presidential Pardon," *Federal Probation* 42 (1978): 3.

Steiner, Ashley M. "Remission of Guilt or Removal of Punishment: The Effects of a Presidential Pardon," *Emory Law Journal* 46 (1997): 959.

Strasser, Mark. "The Limits of the Clemency Power on Pardons, Retributivists, and the United States Constitution," *Brandeis Law Journal* 41 (2002): 85.

———. "Some Reflections on the President's Pardon Power," *Capital University Law Review* 31 (2003): 143.

Tiefer, Charles. "The Specially Investigated President," *University of Chicago Law School Roundtable* 5 (1998): 143.

Turley, Jonathan. "Presidential Papers and Popular Government: The Convergence of Constitutional and Property Theory in Claims of Ownership and Control of Presidential Records," *Cornell Law Review* 88 (2003): 651, 671–677.

Walsh, Lawrence. "Political Oversight, the Rule of Law, and Iran Contra," *Cleveland State Law Review* 42 (1994): 587.

Weihofen, Henry. "The Effect of a Pardon," *University of Pennsylvania Law Review* 88 (1939): 177.

———. "Legislative Pardons," *California Law Review* 27 (1939): 371.

———. "Pardon: An Extraordinary Remedy," *Rocky Mountain Law Review* 12 (1940): 112.

Williston, Samuel. "Does a Pardon Blot Out Guilt?" *Harvard Law Review* 28 (1915): 647.

Wolf, Stephen A. "In the Pursuit of Power without Accountability: How the Independent Counsel Statute Is Designed and Used to Undermine the Energy and Independence of the Presidency," *South Dakota Law Review* 35 (1990): 1.

———. "The Independent Counsel Process: Is It Broken and How Should It Be Fixed?" *Washington and Lee Law Review* 54 (1997): 1515.

Political Science Articles

Crouch, Jeffrey. "Presidential Misuse of the Pardon Power," *Presidential Studies Quarterly* 38 (2008): 722–734.

Dorris, J. T. "Pardon Seekers and Brokers: A Sequel of Appomattox," *Journal of Southern History* 1 (1935): 286–287.

Eksterowicz, Anthony, and Robert Roberts. "The Specter of Presidential Pardons," *White House Studies* 6 (2006): 377.

Fisher, Louis. "When Presidential Power Backfires: Clinton's Use of Clemency," *Presidential Studies Quarterly* 32 (2002): 586–599.

Jones, Ted, Jack McGuire, and David Nice. "A Multifactorial Analysis of Presidential Clemency: 1900–2002," presented at the Annual Midwest Meeting of the American Political Science Association, Chicago, Illinois, April 14–18, 2004.

Rozell, Mark J. "President Ford's Pardon of Richard M. Nixon: Constitutional and Political Considerations," *Presidential Studies Quarterly* 24 (1994): 121.

———. "The Presidential Pardon Power: A Bibligraphic Essay." *Journal of Law and Politics* 5 (1989): 459.

Ruckman, P. S., Jr. "Executive Clemency in the United States: Origins, Development, and Analysis (1900–1993)," *Presidential Studies Quarterly* 27 (1997): 251.

———. "'Last-Minute' Pardon Scandals: Fact and Fiction," unpublished paper, available at http://www.rvc.cc.il.us/faclink/pruckman/pardoncharts/Paper2.pdf (accessed 11/15/05).

———. "Policy as an Indicator of 'Original Understanding': Executive Clemency in the Early Republic (1789–1817)," unpublished paper, available at http://www.rvc.cc.il.us/faclink/pruckman/pardoncharts/Paper7.pdf (accessed 11/15/05).

———. "President-Centered and Presidency-Centered Explanations of Federal

Clemency Policy," unpublished paper, available at http://www.rvc.cc.il.us/faclink/
pruckman/pardoncharts/Paper1.pdf (accessed 11/15/05).
———. "Seasonal Clemency Revisited: An Empirical Analysis," unpublished paper on
file with author.
Whitford, Andrew B., and Holona L. Ochs. "The Political Roots of Executive
Clemency," available at http://ssrn.com/abstract=888579.

INDEX

Abrams, Elliott, 36–37, 95, 104
Accountability, presidential
  congressional responses to pardons,
    25–26, 52
  framers' intent, 98, 142, 144–145, 146
  for Nixon pardon, 136
  timing of pardons and, 125, 139
"Act of grace" pardons
  case law, 29–30, 31, 136
  framers' intent, 146
  of Nixon, 73, 136
  pre-Watergate, 56, 60, 147
  by Washington, 56
  of Weinberger, 139
Act of Settlement (1700), 12, 15
Adams, John, pardons, 56
Adams, Roger, 22, 31, 112, 113
Alien and Sedition Acts, 56
Allen, George, 61
Ambrose, Stephen, 83
Amnesties
  after Civil War, 40, 41–43, 45, 47,
    162n99
  congressional power, 50–51
  definition, 20
  for draft evaders, 35
  following wars, 56
  general, 40, 50–51
  presidential powers, 44, 47
  Whiskey Rebellion, 55–56
Ancient societies, 10–11
Armed Forces of National Liberation. See
  FALN pardons
Armitage, Richard, 120, 122
Armstrong, John, 42
Armstrong's Foundry, 42
Armstrong v. United States, 44, 162n99
Articles of Confederation, 14

Ashcroft, John, 117
Attorneys general
  annual reports, 22–23
  role in pardon process, 21, 23, 24, 62
  See also Justice Department
Avery, William O., 89

Babbitt, Bruce, 95
Babcock, Orville, 88, 89, 91
Babylon, Code of Hammurabi, 10
Barabbas, 11
Barak, Ehud, 116
Barrett, Bob, 72–73
Bennett, Robert, 137
Berger, Raoul, 70
Berman, Douglas, 125
Bernstein, Carl, 74, 80, 135
Biddle v. Perovich, 30–31, 135, 136, 142
Bjerkan v. United States, 34
Blackstone, William, 13
Bollman, Erick, 89
Bonaparte, Charles, 87, 90
Bork, Robert, 70, 93
Boyd v. United States, 34
Bracton, Henry de, 33
Braswell, Glenn, 116–117
Bristow, Benjamin, 88
Broder, David, 134
Brown, Ron, 95
Brown, Theodore, 50
Brown v. Walker, 49–50, 68
Buchen, Philip, 67, 72–73, 80, 81, 132
Burdick v. United States, 132
Burr, Aaron, 89
Bush, George H. W.
  diaries, 95, 105–106
  knowledge of Iran-Contra affair, 95,
    102, 103–104, 105–106, 137

Nixon pardon, *continued*
  discussions with Congress, 133
  Haig's role, 72, 80–84
  historical context, 135–136
  Hungate subcommittee hearings, 26,
      78–79, 80, 81, 82–83, 132
  legacy, 146
  legal challenge, 132
  legal validity, 67–70
  mistakes, 129, 130, 131, 132–133
  normal process bypassed, 22
  political consequences, 79–80, 84, 92,
      129, 136
  public relations problem, 73, 76–79
  questions about, 66–73
  reactions, 73–79, 131, 134, 135
  reasons for decision, 67, 72, 80, 83, 91–
      92, 130–132, 136
  timing, 66, 68–69, 71–73, 131, 138
  uniqueness, 1–2
  Watergate investigation ended by, 84–
      85
Nolan, Beth, 114, 116
Noonan, United States v., 35–36
North, Oliver, 94, 102, 129
Novak, Robert
  on Nixon pardon, 72
  revelation of Plame identity, 118, 120
Nunn, Sam, 138

O'Connor, Sandra Day, 35, 51–52
Office of the Pardon Attorney. *See* Pardon
    Attorney, Office of
Ohio Adult Parole Authority v. Woodard, 35, 51–
    52
Olmert, Ehud, 113
Olson, Theodore, 96
Oregon land frauds, 89–90
Osborn v. United States, 45–46, 163n107
Osbourne, Thomas, 12
Otis, William, 122

Padelford, Edward, 42–43
Padelford, United States v., 42–43
Pardon Attorney, Office of, 21–23
  backlog, 64, 64(fig.), 112

  bypassed by presidents, 21–22, 112
  recommendations, 22, 55, 62, 63
  role, 21, 22, 27
  screening process, 21, 27, 54–55, 63,
      112
  workload, 64, 64(fig.), 112
  See also Pardon process
Pardon power, 29–39
  abuses, 4, 5, 31, 101, 128–129, 142, 146,
      147, 149
  amnesties included in, 44, 47
  as check and balance, 14, 148
  constitutional clause, 9
  duty, 24–25, 27, 29
  exclusivity, 18, 51, 145
  extent, 29, 31–32, 34–35
  forms, 20
  goals, 26–27
  historical roots, 10–13
  impeachment exception, 9, 15, 68, 71
  limits, 9, 15–16, 35
  paradoxes, 2–4, 127–128
  pre-indictment, 41
  public understanding, 9, 24
  rationales, 28–31
  "safety valve" function, 63
  scope, 19, 41–42
  self-pardons, 70–71
  timing, 32
  See also "Act of grace" pardons; Framers'
      intent; Legislative clemency power;
      Public interest rationale
Pardon process
  applications, 21, 22–23, 64
  attorney general's role, 21, 23, 24, 62
  bypassed by presidents, 21–22, 69, 112
  evolution, 62–64
  fairness, 24
  federal regulations, 21, 23–24, 63,
      157n79
  investigations, 23
  Justice Department reports, 22–23
  recommendations, 22, 24
  secrecy, 22–23
  typical applicants, 54
  victims' roles, 23–24